The Hanging of Thomas Jeremiah

THE HANGING OF THOMAS JEREMIAH

*A Free Black Man's
Encounter with Liberty*

J. WILLIAM HARRIS

Yale University Press
New Haven & London

Published with assistance from the Annie Burr Lewis Fund.

Set in Adobe Caslon type by Keystone Typesetting, Inc.
Printed in the United States of America by Sheridan Books, Ann Arbor, Michigan.

Library of Congress Cataloging-in-Publication Data
Harris, J. William, 1946–
    The hanging of Thomas Jeremiah : a free black man's encounter with liberty / J. William Harris.
        p.   cm.
    Includes bibliographical references and index.
    ISBN 978-0-300-15214-2 (clothbound : alk. paper)
1. Jeremiah, Thomas, d. 1775–Trials, litigation, etc. 2. Free African Americans—South Carolina—Charleston—Social conditions. 3. Free African Americans—Legal status, laws, etc.—South Carolina—Charleston. 4. Liberty—Political aspects—United States—History—18th century. 5. Liberty—Social aspects—United States—History—18th century. 6. Slavery—United States—History—18th century. 7. Charleston (S.C.)—Race relations—18th century. 8. Charleston (S.C.)—Social conditions—18th century. 9. Laurens, Henry, 1724–1792.
10. Campbell, William, 1745–1781. I. Title.
F279.C453J474 2009
975.7'91502092—dc22
[B]   2009015233

A catalogue record for this book is available from the British Library.

This paper meets the requirements of ANSI/NISO Z39.48-1992 (Permanence of Paper).

10   9   8   7   6   5   4   3   2   1

To the Memory of Laura Rockefeller
1959–2001

Contents

Illustrations

Map 1. South Carolina and Georgia Low Country.

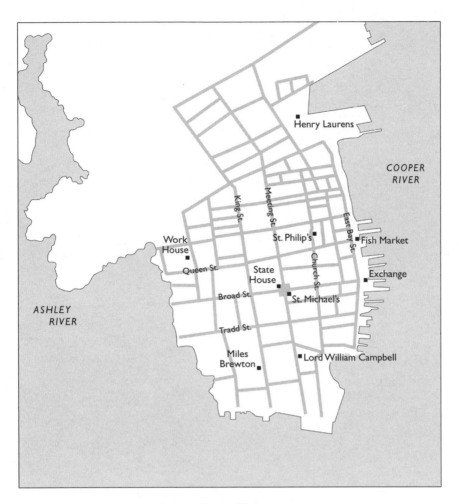

COOPER
RIVER

Henry Laurens

King St.

Meeting St.

East Bay St.

Work
House

St. Philip's

Fish Market

Queen St.

State
House

Church St.

Exchange

Broad St.

St. Michael's

ASHLEY
RIVER

Tradd St.

Miles
Brewton

Lord William Campbell

Map 2. Charles Town in 1775.

Prologue
Trials

ON THE MORNING OF August 18, 1775, a cart was hauled from the Charles Town, South Carolina, Work House on Magazine Street to the execution place on the workhouse green. On the cart was a black man, Thomas Jeremiah, known around the city as "Jerry the pilot." He had been convicted just a week earlier of conspiring to foment a slave insurrection. The green was a good place for hangings, with room for the crowds that came to witness them. On this day the witnesses undoubtedly included many slaves, from the city and from nearby plantations, since a principal point of the grisly ritual was to "deter others from offending in the like manner."[1] On the green was no elaborate standing gallows, with raised platform and trapdoor; local authorities had erected a simple crossbar with legs strong enough to support a man's body. If those authorities were hoping for a last-minute confession or a sign of repentance, they would be disappointed. Jeremiah, a contemporary wrote, "met death like a man and a Christian, avowing his innocence to the last moment of his life."[2]

The cart was drawn under the gallows, the rope tightened around Jeremiah's neck, and the cart pulled away. There was no attempt in this era to gauge the height of a gallows so as to snap a victim's neck. Death would come, instead, by strangulation. As one historian has written, "Nobody doubted that hanging was a slow and painful way of killing people"; the hanged "urinated, defecated, screamed, kicked, and choked as they died." The crowd probably watched Jeremiah thrash for a minute or two or, if the noose was poorly set, even five minutes or more. The executioners waited until he was surely dead, then took his body down and laid it on a dry woodpile. A fire was lit, and the ashes of Thomas Jeremiah's body were carried off into the August sky.[3]

It was a cruel end to an extraordinary life. Thomas Jeremiah was, despite conviction as an instigator of a slave insurrection, no slave, but an owner of slaves himself. He was an accomplished mariner, harbor pilot, and fisherman. A contemporary estimated his worth at £1,000 sterling, the equivalent of about $200,000 today, which made him one of the wealthiest men of African descent in British North America. The rise to such heights by a free black man in eighteenth-century South Carolina, where slaves outnumbered whites almost two to one and the number of free African Americans was under five hundred, was remarkable.

Not in the crowd that day, but deeply interested in the execution, were two of the wealthiest and most influential men in the city of Charles Town. Henry Laurens was, that summer of 1775, South Carolina's most important leader, president of the Provincial Congress, of the Council of Safety, and of the Charles Town General Committee, three extralegal bodies that had seized effective power from the colony's royal government. Laurens had earned his wealth—wealth on a far greater scale than Jeremiah's—as a seller of slaves and wholesale merchant; he had invested his profits in a half-dozen slave plantations that made him one of the richest men in the American colonies. He was convinced, or so he said, that executing Thomas Jeremiah was fully justified as part of Americans' defense of their liberties. Though a reluctant rebel, by the summer of 1775 he was prepared "to Stake his Estate, his Life, upon the prospect of Securing freedom & happiness for future Generations" of Americans. But what kind of freedom, and for which Americans?

The second man, interested to the point of obsession, was the royal governor of the colony, Lord William Campbell. Campbell had arrived in the colony just a few weeks earlier to take up his post, although, from past visits and from his marriage in 1763 to a beautiful Charles Town heiress, Sarah Izard, he knew the city well. Learning of Thomas Jeremiah's trial and sentence, he investigated and, convinced of Jeremiah's innocence, tried to save his life. For many hours before the execution, Campbell had been exchanging hand-delivered letters with Henry Laurens, trying to persuade him that a great injustice was about to be perpetrated. It was all in vain. Indeed, he had been warned that, if he issued a pardon, a Charles Town crowd would lynch Jeremiah in front of his own house on Meeting Street. In an anguished letter to his superior in London, the day after the execution, Campbell cried, "I could not save him My Lord!"[4]

The execution of August 18 was, in some ways, the culmination of events of the past three months. In the first week of May, Charles Town's citizens learned that the British army had, on April 19, marched into the Massachusetts countryside and been met by colonial militiamen at Lexington and Concord, where "embattled farmers" fired "the shot heard round the world" and launched a war that would end in America's independence. That news had arrived four days after alarming news of a different sort, a "secret communication" sent to Henry Laurens from London, claiming that the British government had made plans for "instigating the slaves to insurrection." These dual threats mingled in the minds of white Carolinians to create the belief that the British ministry (they would not yet blame the king himself) would stop at nothing to crush Americans' determination to protect their sacred liberties. Thomas Jeremiah, they concluded, was the man chosen by a "rash wrongheaded cruel administration" to lead a slave rebellion, and his execution was intended to thwart that administration's "devilish machinations."[5]

The execution was also the culmination of much longer and deeper developments. South Carolina was part of a worldwide empire that reached from the edges of the Arctic to the river valleys of India, knit together by the exchange of slaves, agricultural products, and manufactured goods, carried by the world's dominant merchant fleet and protected by the world's greatest navy. Charles Town, where rice and indigo were shipped out in return for slaves and manufactures, was one of the most prosperous of the empire's outposts. Its rich planters and merchants had built British North America's most striking cityscape, with wide streets, imposing mansions, and public buildings that impressed even visitors from other wealthy ports. The rice and indigo were grown by slaves who made up a majority of the colony's population, and the city was home to the largest urban slave population in the American colonies.

Thomas Jeremiah, Henry Laurens, and William Campbell, one a free black, one a Charles Town merchant-planter, and one a son of a Scottish nobleman, had risen along with the vast empire; all had succeeded by merit, industry, and acceptance of risk. Jeremiah had begun as a harbor pilot, navigating men-of-war and merchant ships over the dangerous bar that nearly blocked Charles Town's harbor from the sea. Laurens had built one of the great American fortunes as a merchant, by shipping and selling African slaves, English manufactures, and Carolina rice and indigo. Campbell, the younger son of a duke, had fought, as an adolescent, on the lower decks of Royal Navy ships in battles that expanded the British Empire in India; he had served as a captain in the navy, a member of Parliament, and a colonial administrator. All three were slave owners—Laurens, a planter with hundreds of slaves on several plantations; Campbell, owner of a Savannah River plantation with scores of slaves; even Jeremiah, owner of a sophisticated fishing craft manned by his own slaves. In the summer of 1775, the lives of all three, and their understandings of the meaning of British liberty, came into collision as they were swept up in the turmoil of the American rebellion against British rule.

Henry Laurens loved the "Mother Country," England, and was devoted to what he saw as its deep-rooted tradition of liberty. By 1774, though, he had become convinced that the British ministry was trying to "enslave" Americans like him. If the king was determined, he wrote to one correspondent, "that none but Slaves & his Officers their Task Masters Shall reside in America," he was ready to "risque all my Estate & my Life" to prevent it.[6] He could foresee "that our firmness in Patriotism & Love of Country will be put to trial & possibly by a Severe test." In the summer of 1775, Laurens indeed was put to a "severe test," as were William Campbell and Thomas Jeremiah. None would finally escaped unscathed.

PART I

Liberty and Slavery

Figure 1. This 1774 view of Charles Town from the harbor, by Thomas Leitch, promised purchasers "so exact a Portrait of the Town, as it appears from the Water, that every House in View will be distinctly known." The Exchange Building is framed by the steeples of St. Michael's, on the left, and St. Philip's, on the right. (OLD SALEM, INC.: COLLECTION OF THE MUSEUM OF EARLY SOUTHERN DECORATIVE ARTS)

CHAPTER ONE

"Slavery may truly be said to be the peculiar curse of this land"

"The liveliest, pleasantest, and politest place"

CHARLES TOWN WAS NOT a big place in 1775, but it was the fourth largest in Britain's North American colonies, and its whites, a little fewer than half of its twelve thousand or so residents, were the richest on the continent. Renowned for its wealth and refinement, the city impressed many a visitor. For those who arrived by ship, their first sight was the tip of the steeple on St. Michael's, soaring 186 feet, the landmark captains looked for when they arrived off the bar that protected the harbor. There they anchored, staying well away from the outermost shoals, and fired off a cannon to alert the pilots who waited on Sullivan's Island. Once on board, a pilot—often, a slave or free black man such as Thomas Jeremiah—steered carefully between the underwater shoals at North and South Breakers, keeping the lighthouse on James Island straight ahead on a west by north heading. After four miles, he swung the ship to north by northwest, keeping No Man's Land shoal well to starboard and avoiding the shallow water off to port. It was eight more miles until the ship was past Cummins Point and into Rebellion Road, with its comfortable depth of five or six fathoms. Now all Charles Town's steeples came into view, five miles to the west. To one arriving Englishman, the prospect from the harbor was "strikingly beautiful." The steeples of St. Michael's and St. Philip's framed the new Exchange Building on the waterfront, the most notable of "several large capital good looking buildings" (fig. 1). With arcaded entrances to the open first story and Ionic columns and pilasters decorating the second story, all topped by a domed, octagonal cupola with Venetian windows, the Exchange was one of the finest public buildings in all the colonies, the symbol of the city's prospering transatlantic trading economy.[1]

One 1773 visitor, Josiah Quincy, Jr., a young lawyer and radical patriot from Massachusetts, was astonished to see, on his arrival, hundreds of ships in the harbor. The scene "far surpassed all I had ever seen in Boston." When he stepped on shore, "the number of inhabitants and appearance of the buildings far exceeded my expectation." Among the most imposing was St. Michael's. It was built on the "Four Corners," where Broad Street crossed Meeting Street, the most prominent public space in Charles Town and the fulfillment of a vision of founding proprietor Anthony, Lord Ashley-Cooper, whose "Grand Modell" for "a great port town" had called for a two-acre square at the city's center. On the northwest corner was the State House, planned and built in the 1750s, its arched entrances opening onto a courtroom at street-level, its second story decorated with projecting columns and capitals. In the "handsome rooms" of the second story, the colony's appointed council and elected Commons House of Assembly met. Across Broad Street was the "Watch House," erected in the 1760s, with an "imposing pediment, supported by four massy pillars of the Tuscan order."[2]

Making possible the building boom, public and private, was the highly profitable Atlantic trade. Directly and indirectly it supported dozens of skilled craftsmen and craftswomen—riggers and rope makers, clock makers and jewelers, seamstresses and milliners, coopers and tanners, tailors and cabinet makers. Some sold their products from their own shops: wig maker Peter Butler offered lip salves, scented water, and toothbrushes along with his wigs in his Broad Street place; milliner Sarah Damon sold hosiery and haberdashery, as well as hats, on Union Street. Many more men, and some women, sold dry goods, wine and spirits, sugar and tea in more than two hundred retail shops. But most directly responsible for the boom and profiting from the trade were the small number of families who dominated Charles Town's economy and made up as close to an aristocracy as existed in any of the American colonies.[3]

The source of this elite group was not the famous Fundamental Constitutions of South Carolina, drawn up by an original proprietor of the colony with the help of John Locke. This document had called for religious tolerance and a representative assembly, as well as for a titled nobility, with "seigniories" and "baronies," "landgraves" and "caciques." Conditions in the New World did not support such pretensions. Most in Charles Town's elite were descendants of early arrivals who had come with connections and capital. Second or lesser sons of the English gentry and merchants were well represented among the early immigrants, as were the children of rich Barbadian planters. Many won large grants of lands from the colony's founders, and others built fortunes from modest beginnings. Stephen Bull, an early settler, was the eldest son of a deeply indebted English gentleman; his son and grandson rose to serve South Carolina as lieutenant governors. Thomas Pinckney, fourth son of "substantial and respectable citizens" in the north of England, arrived in Charles Town in 1692 with £120 in his pocket, probably from earnings as a privateer. Among his grandchildren and great-grandchildren were signers of the Constitution and a candidate for president of the United States. Several other leading families traced their origins to Huguenots who fled France in the 1680s. One was Pierre Manigault, a cooper and distiller turned merchant. His wife, Judith Giton Manigault, described her early days in Carolina as plagued with "every kind of affliction—disease—famine—pestilence—poverty—hard labor. I have been for six months together without tasting bread, working the ground like a slave." By 1775, their son, Gabriel Manigault, may have been the richest man in North America. Another was Andre Laurens, whose son John became a successful saddler, and whose grandson Henry was a leading merchant and planter. These successful, and lucky, early families bought up the best land, carved out prosperous plantations, and founded the large merchant firms that eventually controlled Carolina's wholesale trade.[4]

South Carolina, like the rest of the British world, was a patriarchal society. Men exercised all public political power and, at least in theory, nearly all domestic power. Girls should strive, in the words of Henry Laurens to his young daughter Martha, "to be virtuous, dutiful, affable, courteous, modest," so that she be assured of becoming "a fine lady." Yet gentry women managed complex households, including slaves, took an important role in their children's education, and served at times as "deputy husbands," managing family property when their husbands were away or otherwise occupied. While none was prepared for a paying occupation, many received good educations from the same tutors who taught their brothers. Martha Laurens not only learned to play the harpsichord and execute fine needle work but also studied French, botany, mathematics, and geography. She convinced her father to ship to her from London two globes, terrestrial and celestial, together with the instruments to measure distances on them. Laurens complied, though he also admonished her that "when you are measuring the surface of this world, remember you are to act a part on it, and think of a plumb pudding and other domestic duties."[5]

The most celebrated example in the colony of such female learning was Eliza Lucas Pinckney. When Eliza Lucas's father, a British officer, was posted to the West Indies in 1739, she was left behind in South Carolina, at the age of sixteen, to manage his three plantations. Her experiments with indigo helped to establish the plant as a major commercial crop in South Carolina. In 1744 she married Charles Pinckney, a widower, and reverted to domestic duties, "making it the business of my life to please a man of Mr. Pinckney's merrit even in trifles." She gave birth to a daughter, Harriott, and two sons, Thomas and Charles Cotesworth, both of whom played leading roles in the Revolution. After her husband died in 1758, she again became an active manager of the family's extensive plantation properties.[6]

The leading families consolidated and protected their fortunes with marriages among them, not uncommonly marriages of cousins or exchange marriages (in which sets of siblings from one family married siblings from another). Eliza Lucas Pinckney's sons' marriages allied her family with the Middletons, Mottes, and Brewtons. Miles Brewton, one of the city's richest merchants, was also connected by marriage to the Izard family. Other Izard descendants married into the Manigault family. Henry Laurens and his business partner, George Austin, married half-sisters from a leading planter family, Eleanor and Ann Ball. One historian cites an example of a leading planter whose marriage made him "the brother-in-law of his two nieces," and concludes, "The family trees of the wealthiest planter-merchant families were, by the late eighteenth century, so interconnected that it is difficult to determine where one ends and the other begins."[7]

These families were responsible for Charles Town's grand public buildings. Many, such as St. Michael's Church, followed popular British style without copying any single source (figs. 2, 3). Successful men purchased pews for their families; in the rear, "a number of Poor White People" sat on benches, and the few black church members sat in the gallery and under the belfry. Nearby, other new buildings added in the years just before the American Revolution included a new "assembly room" for dances and musical performances and an elegant theater. Still, most of the social life of the gentry took place in private spaces. After his first dinner at a busy coffeehouse, Josiah Quincy, the Massachusetts visitor of 1773, usually dined at the home of a leading merchant, lawyer, or planter. He ate turtle at the home of Thomas Lynch, a "plain, sensible, honest man" who had represented South Carolina at the Stamp Act Congress in 1765. He enjoyed a "prodigious fine pudding made of what they call rice flour" at the home of merchant Thomas Lough-

Figure 2. The steeple of St. Michael's was the landmark for ship captains approaching Charles Town. (Library of Congress)

ton Smith and examined a "richly embroidered lady's work-bag" made by Mrs. Smith, one "far surpassing anything of the kind I ever saw." At the home of Roger Smith, he met Thomas Bee, "a planter of considerable opulence," "a gentleman of sense, improvement, and politeness." At a fine tavern, he spent an evening at the Friday-Night Club with "substantial gentlemen" who con-

Figure 3. Interior of St. Michael's. Many of the detailed furnishings, as well as the organ, were imported from England.
(Library of Congress)

versed on Negroes, rice, and British policy. He watched Flimnap defeat Little
David at the racetrack outside of town, where £2,000 in wagers changed
hands, and visited the "handsome, square, spacious room" of the private
Charles Town Library Society, with its "large collection of very valuable
books, cuts, globes, etc." At a concert sponsored by the St. Cecelia Society
(where a personal invitation was required) the "two bass-viols and French
horns were grand," and "a Frenchman just arrived, played a first fiddle and
solo incomparably, better than any I ever had heard."[8]

Quincy was familiar with the parlors of the great New England merchants—he had married the daughter of one of them, William Phillips—but

for him none matched the hall in Miles Brewton's mansion: the "grandest . . . I ever beheld, azure blue satin window curtains, rich blue paper with gilt, mashee borders, most elegant pictures, excessive grand and costly looking glasses etc." Brewton, a Charles Town merchant "of a very large fortune" amassed in the slave trade, had only recently built his "superb house said to have cost him £8,000" (equivalent to about $1.5 million in 2008). Quincy and a large company sat at "a most elegant table, three courses, nick-nacks, jellies, preserves, sweetmeats, etc.," followed by "two sorts of nuts, almonds, raisins, three sorts of olives, apples, oranges, etc.," and accompanied by "the richest wine I ever tasted: Exceeds Mr. Hancock's, Vassall's, Phillip's and other much in flavour, softness, and strength." The sideboard displayed "a very large exquisitely wrought Goblet, most excellent workmanship and singularly beautiful." The scene of wealth and gentility was completed by a painted bunting that flitted around the room, "under our chairs and the table, picking up crumbs, etc., and perching on the window, side board and chairs: vastly pretty!"[9]

It was precisely the effect Miles Brewton intended. His house embodied the ideals of order and refinement so prized by genteel British society on both sides of the Atlantic. The double house with its symmetrical design, imposing two-storied portico, formal entry flanked by elegant, half-turned stairways, and ironwork fence setting it off from the hurly-burly of the street, embraced the Palladian Renaissance style that dominated taste in Georgian England. (The facade may have been inspired by an illustration in an English transla-tion of Andrea Palladio's *Four Books of Architecture*, in the collection of the Library Society.) Much of its detailed carving was executed by Ezra Waite, "Civil Architect, House-Builder in general, and Carver, from London," who claimed credit for the "Ionick entablature" at the top of the front balcony and around the eaves and for most of the carved door frames and fireplace over-mantels (figs. 4–6). Guests could step from the hall out onto the second-story balcony, or descend the stairs and pass out the back door under a large Venetian window and into the garden behind the house, to continue their polite conversations.[10]

Even among the gentry, few could afford a house as large and elegant as Brewton's; others built "single" houses, one room deep, three rooms wide, and at least two stories tall, based, in part, on the London townhouse. Their large balconies caught cooling breezes from the sea. Creating the unique Charles Town style, builders turned single houses sideways to the street on narrow lots. The room facing the street might serve as an office, while a different

Figure 4. Miles Brewton's magnificent mansion on King Street, built with profits earned in the slave trade, was "said to have cost him £8,000." (LIBRARY OF CONGRESS)

Figure 5. Detail of carvings for the balcony of the Miles Brewton House. (LIBRARY OF CONGRESS)

Figure 6. Josiah Quincy, Jr., was a guest at a "most elegant table" in the
hall of Brewton's mansion. (LIBRARY OF CONGRESS)

entrance, through a fence or a carriageway, separated the family's private
space and enforced, discreetly, the ideals of order and hierarchy (fig. 7).[11]

Other gentry preferred estates on the city's outskirts where they could
cultivate extensive gardens. In 1764, the merchant Henry Laurens moved into
a new brick house, of sixty feet by thirty-eight feet, on an estate he named
Rattray Green in the new suburb of Ansonborough. It had room for a large
library with books shelved behind glass doors, a second-floor ballroom, a
mirrored dining room, and a drawing room with a harpsichord for his daughter Martha. On the grounds were a countinghouse, a kitchen, a smokehouse,
and a stable. Piazzas overlooked the harbor and the marshes. A walled garden, 200 yards long by 150 yards wide, was "enriched with everything useful
and ornamental that Carolina produced" and with plants Laurens had procured from his merchant friends, among them trees bearing olives, limes,
ginger, and French varieties of apples, pears, and plums.[12]

London was the measure of all things for style. Years later, John Drayton
would write that "the citizens of Carolina were too much prejudiced in favour
of British manners, customs and knowledge, to imagine that elsewhere, than
in England, anything of advantage could be obtained." English craftsmen

Figure 7. This shows a re-creation, with period furniture, of the bedroom of Humphrey Sommers, an English brick mason who became a contractor and built a "single house" in Charles Town. The chest shown belonged to Daniel Cannon, another artisan turned contractor and a major figure in the city's politics in the Revolutionary era.
(OLD SALEM, INC.: COLLECTION OF THE MUSEUM OF EARLY SOUTHERN DECORATIVE ARTS)

carved the exterior and interior details of St. Michael's, English wrought iron lined its altar, and baptisms took place at its English-made font. Local artisans such as cabinetmaker Richard McGrath advertised themselves as "lately from London," and Henry Laurens's garden was under the direction of John Watson, "a complete English gardener." Those who could afford it imported their furniture, their silver plate, and their carriages directly from England. Peter Manigault, whose wealth rivaled that of Miles Brewton, sent to England for "a light Coach, without a Boot, the Bottom part of the Body not rounded as was lately the Fashion, lined with blue English Leather, the Cloth on the Coach Box blue trimmed with Yellow. . . . painted fashionably but not gaudy." In 1771, perhaps inspired by, or jealous of, Brewton's new house and furnishings, Manigault sent to London a list of items for purchase, "to have them out as soon as possible & the plainer the better so that they are fashionable." He half apologized for the list: "I suppose you will think either my Wife or myself very extravagant." But he had seen Brewton's "Bills for Furniture & Plate which I assure you, are twice as large." An inventory of Peter Manigault's possessions in 1774, after his death in England from tuberculosis, lists in nine pages of small type the fruits of his shopping: more than a dozen mahogany tables and beds; three mahogany tea tables; twenty-one pairs of sheets; a large Indian carpet; thirty-eight paintings and prints; two sets of blue-and-white china, each with service for at least twenty-four; silver plate worth £277 sterling; a telescope; a barometer; and lots of Madeira wine—two pipes (each holding more than 120 gallons), ninety dozen bottles, and five casks worth together over £200 sterling.[13]

The character and possessions of the gentry had given Charles Town its reputation as "the liveliest, the pleasantest, and the politest place, as it is one of the richest too, in all America." That "politeness"—a word then connoting not just good table manners but a high level of culture—was measured and displayed not only in the ownership of fine houses and furniture but also in entertainment, in clothing, in conversation, in penmanship, in ease of carriage while sitting and walking. In these, too, English style ruled. From time to time, Charles Town hosted visits of theater companies, almost always with light fare from the London stage: *The Recruiting Officer,* a romantic comedy and satire and the first known play performed there, and others whose titles explain the genre—*Bold Stroke for a Wife; The Provoked Husband; A Wonder! A Woman Keeps a Secret.* Thomas Griffith, a "Riding-Master, from London," taught "Young Gentlemen and Ladies to ride, with the same Safety, Ease and Gentility, as is now practiced in the best Riding-Schools in London." Even cookbooks, while incorporating such low country specialties as stewed crabs or pickled shrimp, were full of recipes for such typical English dishes as potted beef and marmalade.[14]

As sign and record of their status and character, the Charles Town gentry commissioned portraits to adorn their parlors. Many sat for Jeremiah Theus, a popular local "limner" from Germany. Others took advantage of opportunities to sit for more accomplished artists, in northern cities or abroad. Miles Brewton's was painted by Sir Joshua Reynolds in London. Ralph and Alice Delancey Izard sat for a monumental dual portrait by John Singleton Copley, whom they met in Italy in 1775. Copley portrayed the Izards as sophisticated connoisseurs on the Grand Tour, seated at ease at a high-style table, examining a drawing of a group of sculptures, with Rome's Colosseum in the background (fig. 8).[15]

Figure 8. *Mr. and Mrs. Ralph Izard (Alice DeLancey).* The Izards met John Singleton Copley while on the grand tour, in Rome. Copley painted this monumental double portrait with the couple apparently discussing classical sculpture, with the Colosseum in the background. Museum of Fine Arts, Boston, Edward Ingersoll Brown Fund.
(Photograph © 2009 Museum of Fine Arts, Boston)

To prepare their children for both the world of work and the world of refinement, gentry families sent them to private schools that offered instruction in history, moral philosophy, and geometry, in Latin and Greek for those with social or academic ambitions, in practical areas such as accounting and navigation, and, for girls, in French, music, needlework, and writing. Those who could afford it then sent their sons to England, to study at Oxford or Cambridge or at the Inns of Court. Instructors, among them Thomas Pike, offered lessons in dancing, fencing, and music, and by the 1770s, Pike's annual ball for "young Ladies and Gentlemen" was a major social event. A disapproving visitor huffed in 1772: "The Annual Ball for Children was this Evening at Pikes Rooms, where I understood were great Numbers of young and old—It has been a Custom for some Years on this Occasion to spare no Expence in adorning the Children from 6 to 12 or 14 years old for their

Appearance at the Ball where young old and Middle also appear in their best to see the poor little Things dance, act in dumb Shew &c—I could pity them all—which I did sincerely."[16]

Charles Town was at its best in early spring, when the weather was pleasant and the flowering trees blossomed. In other seasons, to step outside the homes of the gentry was to move from the world of refinement into the grittier sensations of a rough, working city. Charles Town's sidewalks were paved, but not its sandy streets; tolerable in mild conditions, they were "disagreeable . . . in hot or windy weather." There was always the chance of being run down by "servants of Gentlemen" driving their carriages "at the most unwarrantable Rates, by which Means the Lives of many are daily endangered." Despite regulations to the contrary, "all Kinds of Filth" were tossed into the streets, and grand juries regularly complained about the leavings of "Cows and Horses . . . fed on the Pavements of the said Streets (particularly after Dark) to the great Annoyance of the Inhabitants thereof." Garbage piled up in the yards behind the big houses added its smells to those from the manure of milk cows and horses and human waste from the privies. Wealthy property owners, Miles Brewton for one, installed underground drains to carry away at least some of the garbage. Less scrupulous owners sometimes put up "necessary houses" for their slaves "without making a vault, or putting in a tub, but left open behind," or left stagnant pools of water "by which Means numberless Insects are produced, rendering at the same Time the Inhabitants on the adjoining Lots very sickly." Everywhere, after the last frost of the spring, mosquitoes swarmed "in such numbers, that, during the day, it requires no small trouble for the inhabitants to defend themselves in every quarter against them; and, during the night, to exclude them from their beds" with gauze curtains. They did not know that mosquitoes also carried malaria, endemic along the coast of South Carolina, giving rise to the pithy description of the colony as "in the spring a paradise, in the summer a hell, and in the autumn a hospital."[17]

Along the Cooper River, from the fish market near the Exchange and the Lower Market below, unsold food was tossed into the river; at that "very offensive" market, slave butchers ignored regulations and slaughtered calves, sheep, and other animals, throwing the remains in the harbor water. The tanyards had been pushed outside the city, but when the wind came from their direction, their even more obnoxious odors were added to the mix. During one May week, a particularly "noisesome smell" wafted across to the city from the uninhabited swamps across the Ashley River. A "Gentleman" investigated and discovered the cause: the putrefying bodies of dozens of dead slaves, washed ashore after being thrown overboard from a recently arrived slaving ship. It looked like the aftermath of a battle "where they had not had Time to bury their Dead."[18]

"Mad for more Negroes"

The stench of decaying bodies was a visceral reminder of the trade in human beings that linked Charles Town to Africa and made it North America's preeminent port for importing slaves. South Carolina's economy was based on the labor of slaves, above all labor in the fields that produced rice and indigo (a dye made from the leaves of a shrub). One Carolinian, writing in the 1750s, described labor in the rice fields:

> Hoeing, Reaping, Threshing, Pounding have all been done merely by the poor Slaves here. Labour and the Loss of many of their Lives testified the Fatigue they Underwent, in Satiating the Inexpressible Avarice of their Masters. You may easily guess what a Tedious, Laborious, and slow Method it is of Cultivating Lands to Till it all by the Hand, and then to plant 100, 120 Acres of Land by the Hand, but the Worst comes last for after the Rice is threshed, they beat it all in the hand in large Wooden Mortars to clean it from the Husk, which is a very hard and severe operation. . . . [Planters] often pay . . . dear for their Barbarity, by the Loss of many so . . . Valuable Negroes, and how can it well be otherwise, the poor Wretches are Obliged to Labour hard to Compleat their Task.

Indigo workers did not have to work in swamps, but indigo culture offered its own terrible conditions, especially at harvest, when the plants were steeped to extract dye and swarming flies "devour Man & Beast." Planters then were "obliged to have three or four Negroes with boughs to keep them off while they are at meals." It was impossible to induce large numbers of white servants or laborers to do this dangerous and unpleasant work.[19]

Planters may have paid dearly in loss of slaves, but according to one cost estimate, a new planter could make 20 percent on his investment annually, even taking into account the purchase of two more slaves each year, above natural increase, just "to keep up the original stock." Even though South Carolina's slave population had begun to grow naturally, if slowly, by the middle of the eighteenth century, planters and farmers still clamored for more, to plant and harvest their fields. About a hundred thousand African slaves were brought into the colony between 1700 and 1775, nearly all of them into Charles Town. Imports reached an all-time high in 1765; after halts (for political reasons) from 1766 to 1768, and again in 1770, imports surged to a new high in 1773.[20]

Nothing better exemplifies the intimate connection between the slave trade and the rise of Charles Town's gentry than the career of Henry Laurens. Elkanah Watson, a young American merchant who met Laurens in France in 1782, remembered him as a "pleasant and facetious gentleman" of "swarthy complexion . . . medium size, and slender form." Laurens, then fifty-eight, had just sat for a John Singleton Copley portrait, in his role as president of America's Continental Congress from November 1777 to December 1778. Laurens leans back in a soft cushioned chair, his left leg resting on a matching stool (no doubt to relieve one of his periodic attacks of gout). He is attired in the suit of an English gentleman, complete with sword—though in the plain, solid colors of a man at his business, not the gaudy embroidered waistcoat favored by fashionable Englishmen for social occasions. He is framed by massive columns and drapery, but in the background are American pines: a marriage of classical virtues and forest simplicity. On the table before him are documents from his year of service as president of the congress, related to the American alliance with France—a copy of the "Ratification Treaties May 1778," and a letter from Louis XVI (fig. 9). Laurens is scarcely remembered today outside South Carolina, his reputation far overshadowed by the more famous founders from Virginia and Massachusetts, but to the London engraver Valentine Green, who probably commissioned Copley's portrait to serve as the model for his mezzotint, he was the epitome of American civilian leadership. Laurens's image was offered for sale as a suitable companion for Green's print of George Washington, the corresponding symbol of American military leadership.[21]

Born in Charles Town in 1724, Laurens was one of the many Carolina leaders who had risen from "humble and moderate Fortunes to great affluence." His grandfather, a French Huguenot, had fled to England, then North America, as a refugee; his father, a successful saddler and retail merchant, left, at his death in 1747, an estate including four slaves. In 1744, Laurens's father sent him to London to clerk for James Crokatt, a specialist in the Carolina trade. After Laurens returned home, Crokatt offered him a partnership, but because of a mix-up in communications across the Atlantic, Laurens did not respond in time. Laurens accepted instead a partnership with George Austin back in Charles Town, and from that point on his rise was rapid.[22]

By the 1770s, South Carolina's gentry had already earned a reputation

Figure 9. John Singleton Copley painted this portrait of Henry Laurens,
in his role as president of the Continental Congress, in 1782.
(National Portrait Gallery, Smithsonian Institution)

among outsiders as "haughty and insolent" and "remarkably indolent." Josiah Quincy, the visitor from Massachusetts, thought that "cards, dice, the bottle and horses engross prodigious portions of time and attention," the logical consequence, so he believed, of "the number and subjection of their slaves." But this was not Henry Laurens, either in practice or in the judgment of others. Quincy's fellow Massachusetts patriot John Adams, the future U.S. president and a man not easily impressed, met Laurens in Philadelphia in 1777 and pronounced him a "Gentleman of great Fortune, great Abilities, Modesty and Integrity," with "a clear Head and a firm Temper, of extensive Knowledge, and much Travel." Laurens had just taken his seat as a delegate to the Second Continental Congress, and Adams wrote to his devoted wife, Abigail, that if other states would "imitate this Example and send their best Men," it "would be a Pleasure to be here." Just four months later, the delegates chose Laurens to replace John Hancock as president of the Continental Congress.[23]

In character, Laurens might have stepped from the pages of Max Weber's famous analysis of the "Protestant ethic and the spirit of capitalism." He worked hard and expected others to do the same, and "for the dispatch of business he was never exceeded, perhaps never equalled, in Charlestown." He avoided gambling and abhorred drunkenness. According to Philadelphia-trained physician David Ramsay, South Carolina historian and Laurens's son-in-law, his "scrupulous attention to punctuality not only in the discharge of pecuniary engagements, but in being where and in doing what he had promised was almost romantic." He rose early, spent the morning in his countinghouse, and had often finished the day's business while others were just "beginning to deliberate on the expediency of leaving their beds." No wonder that parents of young men who wanted their sons "to be brought up strictly and in habits of doing business with accuracy" tried to place them in Laurens's countinghouse as clerks.[24]

Ramsay wrote that Laurens "soon found out the par of exchange of every man with whom he transacted business." As Laurens himself wrote to one correspondent, "Every Merchant ought to be a Man of strict Honor." His correspondents learned to believe him when he promised, as he did to one, "to render you my best services & as to terms have only to say that I will always do the utmost in my power for you." He told another that "your approbation & good will, will afford me more real satisfaction than merely the prospect of a Commission." Laurens rarely threatened lawsuits, and more rarely instituted them. When he encountered merchants' disagreements, he almost always offered to settle matters by referring them to another, disinterested merchant or to a committee of them, pledging to abide by whatever decision they made. He worked consistently only with merchants—in Europe or North America —whom he trusted in turn. He told one firm that "Upon the whole I am persuaded that you will do the best in your power to make a good Sale," and another that he expected them "to receive & sell . . . at such times as you shall judge best." He could suffer great losses on a transaction with equanimity if they resulted from the accidents of the trade, such as a storm or a sudden fall in prices, but his letters bristled with indignation when he felt deliberately shortchanged even in small matters. When Lachlan Macintosh, a Georgian he knew well enough to call a good friend, tried to pay off a debt in Georgia currency that in Charles Town was accepted only at a steep discount, Laurens wrote to him that "If you persist in doing so, tho' I will not withold my friendship whenever it shall be in my Power to do you an acceptable Service, yet I must forbear merchandizing with you. There is a certain exactness in Commerce which shou'd not be departed from, & for my own part I wou'd rather give a Man a Pound from my own mere motion or at his request, than Submit to the Charge of an extra Shilling in the course of Exchange."[25]

Having risen himself from moderate circumstances, Laurens never looked down on men because they were poorer than he, provided that they were white. He took great pleasure in assisting—with credit, recommendations, and testimonials—young men of ambition and modest means whom he thought of as like himself—honest, hard-working, and honorable. But if a poorer man made no attempts to pay back a loan or, worse, was unable to do so because of drunkenness, Laurens's stern sense of personal morality asserted itself. He rejected one debtor's request for a further loan, telling him that "I am resolved to do nothing more for you until I see by a thorough change of life you are once more a diligent, careful, Sober Tradesman." As David Ramsay noted, "Such diligence, and such knowledge of men and of business, could not fail of success."[26]

Still, whatever his personal qualities, Laurens would never have accumulated his South Carolina fortune without taking full advantage of the greatest of the colony's opportunities: the traffic in human beings and the labor of slaves to raise valuable crops for export. Among his first steps as an independent merchant were visits to established firms in London, Liverpool, and Bristol to seek "Negro Consignments." The partnership of Austin & Laurens operated in standard fashion for Carolina slave traders, accepting consignments of slaves shipped from Africa by British merchants, paying a part of the shipping costs, selling off the slaves, then sending the ships back to Britain loaded with rice, indigo, and other commodities. In return Austin & Laurens pocketed a 5 percent commission on the value of both the incoming and the outgoing cargo. Within a few years, Austin & Laurens had become the city's leading slave merchants. Laurens's meticulous letters to his correspondents in trade, which were "always expressed in strong and precise language, which forcibly conveyed his meaning without a possibility of being misunderstood," are perhaps the most complete and informative documents on the operation of the trade in slaves to British North America.[27]

The records of two 1755 slaving voyages out of Bristol, those of the ships *Pearl* and *Emperor*, exemplify the nature and operation of the trade. Rice was selling well in 1755, and the rise of indigo, easily cultivated on smaller farms in the interior, had created a market for slaves among many "poor industrious People," who "were all mad for more Negroes." Laurens made a special point of marketing slaves to these "poor" farmers, strivers for whom indigo was ticket to a planter's life. When a healthy "parcel" of "well assorted" slaves came to Charles Town's wharves, planters crowded the sale venues, poking and prodding the Africans, "pulling & hauling who should get the good Slaves," collaring one another and coming "very nearly to blows" in their eagerness to get the tallest, strongest, and healthiest.[28]

The slaves on the *Pearl* were consigned to Austin & Laurens, and when they arrived in Charles Town in late June, Laurens anticipated a good sale, though he acknowledged that the *Pearl*'s "mortality has been pretty considerable" (of 275 slaves purchased in Angola, just 243 made it to Carolina). Planters were "full of spirit for buying Slaves," and the *Pearl*'s were "well assorted and in good condition," altogether "a very pretty Cargo." In just two days, Austin & Laurens sold off 241 of the *Pearl*'s slaves at an average price of £33.17 sterling (roughly $7,000 in 2008), which, Laurens wrote to one correspondent, "you must allow a most extraordinary affair for Angola Negroes"—especially since the women, who made up one-third of the "cargo," were "but ordinary."[29]

Laurens and his partner had invested some of their own money in the voyage of the *Emperor*, at two hundred tons twice as big as the *Pearl*. It had set out the previous July under Captain Charles Gwynn, with a cargo worth £7,000, in hopes of trading for 570 slaves. But after many months along the African coast, Gwynn had been unable to buy that many, and before he even left Africa, forty slaves had died on board, probably of smallpox. The *Emperor* sailed west at last with only 350 slaves—"at which rate," Laurens lamented, "she must make but a ragged Voyage." Illness took more Africans before the ship reached the vicinity of Charles Town in April 1755, and before the *Emperor* could cross the bar, Gwynn was "put off the Coast with a violent Gale of Wind." After several days, during which more slaves died, Gwynn headed for Jamaica, arriving in Kingston with just 270 slaves. The bodies of eighty had been tossed into the sea.[30]

The voyage of the *Emperor* was a commercial disaster, made worse because prices in Jamaica were far lower than in the hot market of Charles Town. The first seventy-seven slaves sold for £28 each, "a very poor affair indeed compar'd with our Market," Laurens wrote, "which will greatly agravate the loss upon a destructive Voyage." The difference between Jamaica and Charles Town prices alone, he speculated, would cost investors £2,000. Yet, "'tis fruitless to think of what can't be remedied." The African trade, after all, "is more liable to such Accidents than any other we know of so it highly concerns such as become adventurers in that branch to fortify themselves against every disapointment that the trade is Incident to." On the whole, he concluded, the *Emperor* was "a very unlucky Ship to the concern'd."[31]

Very unlucky to "the concern'd" indeed! The most concerned of all were the 390 Africans who had been torn away from kin and community, marched to the sea, held until traded by their African captors, then shackled to the decks and platforms (specially built for slave cargo) in a ship perhaps seventy-five feet long and twenty-two or twenty-three feet wide at its greatest breadth. Once at sea, though let out on the deck at times, they had lived for months in this close space, amid feces, urine, and vomit, battered by storms and dying by the score, the survivors sold off to labor in the sugar fields of Jamaica. These "parcels" and "cargos," as they are called in Laurens's letters, might as well have been barrels of rice, and to be sure, their value as commodities varied widely according to the state of the markets and characteristics of the "cargo." For South Carolinians, so Laurens told one correspondent, the ideal "assortment" would include "Two thirds at least Men from 18 to 25 Years old, the other young Women from 14 to 18 the cost not to exceed Twenty five Pounds Sterling per head." Although "young Lads from 13 to 15 Years of age" sold for less, they were, if purchased for £20 or so, "very Saleable." "A tall robust people best sute our business," and among the women there should be none, "if Possible," with "fallen breasts." Short or sickly slaves—like the "scabby" and "mangey" slaves who arrived on the *Fortune* in June 1755—sold for very low prices. Slaves from the Gold Coast were preferred above all others, but the region of origin mattered little except for Calabars (from ports in present-day Nigeria), who were "quite out of repute" because so many had committed suicide after being sold in South Carolina.[32]

"For Liberty and Life"

The sheer presence of Africans—a majority of South Carolina's population, and in the rice districts, an overwhelming majority—made the colony different from anything in England or in most of Britain's mainland colonies. Charles Town might be a center of wealth and politeness, but the rice plantations that stretched up and down the coast from Charles Town were often rude, if highly productive, properties. The presence of this suppressed black majority created an all too obvious threat of resistance. One group of "new Negroes," as South Carolinians called recently arrived Africans, had been behind the most frightening slave rebellion in the colony's history, in 1739. Near the Stono River some twenty miles south of Charles Town, a group of enslaved Africans from Kongo (modern Angola), who shared a language, a culture, and the horror of the Middle Passage, had been working on the roads. Inspired by a leader named Jemmy, they had attacked a store, ransacked it for weapons, and left the heads of two clerks, Robert Bathurst and Mr. Gibbs, on the store steps. They moved on from plantation to plantation, acquiring dozens of slave recruits, "burning and destroying all that came in their way," killing white men, women, and children, though sparing a tavern keeper, Mr. Wallace, because "he was a good Man and kind to his slaves." The rebels marched south, beating drums and "calling out Liberty," probably heading for Florida, where the Spanish welcomed runaway slaves. A company of provincial militia caught up with the Stono rebels in an open field and defeated them in a brief battle, driving most of them off and killing those they captured, "some hang'd, and some Gibbeted alive." Altogether some two dozen whites and four dozen slaves were killed. In a grisly bookend to the rebellion, whites "Cutt off their heads and set them up at every Mile Post they came to."[33]

To whites in South Carolina, the insurrection was terrifying—as the legislature put it, "Every one that had a Life to lose were in the most sensible Manner shocked at such Danger daily hanging over their Heads." But they understood perfectly why slaves would want to rebel: they were fighting "for Liberty and Life." The colony responded with a new "Negro Act" to clamp down both on the slaves and on the masters who gave slaves too much leeway or time to themselves, while also adding a few provisions to encourage better treatment, such as limiting work to fifteen hours per day and giving most slaves a day off from labor on Sunday. Writing thirty years after the Stono Rebellion, Lieutenant Governor William Bull (whose own father had narrowly escaped after meeting the rebels on the road), told his superiors in London that "the happy temperament of justice and mercy" in South Carolina law "and the general humanity of the masters" had made the state of slavery "as comfortable in this province as such a state can be," and for that reason there had been no insurrections since 1739. But if there had been no large rebellions, advertisements for runaways filled many columns of the local newspapers, and as one observer noted in 1751, "the instances of Negroes murdering, scorching, and burning their own masters or overseers are not rare." Indeed Bull himself, in a more candid moment, acknowledged the importance of constant vigilance against "insurrection of our domestic enemy."[34]

"The slaves in Charles Town are not under a good regulation"

Roughly six thousand South Carolina slaves worked, not in the country, but in Charles Town itself, where their labor made possible the high polish of civilization that so impressed visitors. At the fancy dinners, for example, "every body must have a vast deal of waiting upon from the oldest to the youngest. One or more servants (in many places) plant themselves in the corners of the room where they stand & upon the slightest occasion they are called. . . . At dinner it wd. seem as if the appetite were to be whetted & the victuals receive it's relish in proportion to the number of attendance." To serve Eliza Lucas Pinckney, while she lived alone as a widow, there was Mary Ann, who "understands roasting poultry in the greatest perfection you ever saw"; Daphne, who "makes me a loaf of very nice bread"; old Ebba, who fattened the poultry; young Ebba, who did "the drudgery part, fetch[ed] wood, and water, and scour[ed]"; Moses, who worked around the house and took care of the yard; and Pegg, who milked the cows and washed. The Pinckney family recipe for biscuits included a full hour of kneading. The fine silks and linens that graced Eliza Pinckney's body, tables, and beds had to be cleaned and ironed by slaves. The instructions for washing silk stockings alone included a first washing, then a soaking, then boiling with lye, then rubbing with a "scalding hot" mixture of soap (also handmade from lye and grease), lye, and blue, then more rubbing. Then they were hung out until half dry and finally put through a clothespress with rollers.[35]

The benefits of slave ownership were not limited to wealthy planters and merchants. In 1774, the possessions of almost two-thirds of the Charles Town men and women whose estates were inventoried at their death included slaves. Shopkeepers, tavern owners, ministers, and schoolmasters owned slaves to stock their shelves, serve their customers, cook their food. In inventories and advertisements, slaves are identified as waiting men, gardeners, barbers, and coachmen; seamstresses and washerwomen; shoemakers, tailors, blacksmiths, saddlers, wheelwrights, cabinet makers, painters, rope makers, silversmiths, and even a gunsmith. Except for those in highly specialized occupations such as bookbinding or watchmaking, white artisans who faced competition from English imports also faced it from slave craftsmen and craftswomen. Some artisans complained about this competition, but many artisans themselves owned skilled slaves. At his death in 1774, for example, Jeremiah Ryan, a tailor, owned three slaves. The next year, Thomas Elfe, a cabinetmaker who sold fine furniture to Eliza Pinckney and other gentry families, died, leaving to his wife three house slaves and to his children other slaves who had been "brought up to my business." An acerbic visitor of the 1780s wrote, with some exaggeration, that "from the highest to the lowest class they must have more or less atten-dance [by slaves]—I have seen tradesmen go through the city followed by a negro carrying their tools—Barbers who are supported in idleness & ease by their negroes who do the business; & in fact many of the mechaniks bear nothing more of their trade than the name."[36]

Slaves were constantly on the move in Charles Town's streets and alleys and on its wharves, lifting and hauling cargo, shopping for their masters, carrying goods and messages, and working at their crafts. Many slave owners in Charles Town—particularly widows with few options for earning an in-come—hired out their slaves by the day, week, month, or year. As a matter of convenience alone, many of these hired slaves lived relatively free of white supervision; owners did not worry too much about where they were or what they were doing, "for their owners care little, how their slaves get the money, so they are paid."[37]

Slaves also dominated the markets for meat, fish, and produce. Slave women bought and sold produce and hawked their wares in the streets. One visitor in 1778 counted more than five dozen "Negro wenches" selling their produce and baked goods in the markets or on the streets. Sunday, in particu-lar, when plantation slaves came into Charles Town and city slaves visited friends and relatives in the country, was a day for slaves to gather, buy, and sell. South Carolina's "Negro Act" expressly permitted slaves to shop for their masters and to sell fish and produce; otherwise, slaves were forbidden to "buy, sell, deal, traffic, barter, exchange, or use commerce"; in particular, no slave in Charles Town "shall be permitted to buy any thing to sell again, or to sell any thing upon their own account." Nevertheless, at the Lower Market, according to one observer, there were constantly "a great number of loose, idle, disorderly negro women, who are seated there from noon 'til night, and buy and sell on their own accounts, what they please, in order to pay their wages, and get as much more for themselves as they can."[38]

The blacks who dominated marketing sold many goods produced by slaves. Most masters allowed their slaves to spend their "own" time—after completing a daily task or on Sundays—working for themselves. Slaves used this time to tend gardens, to trap, fish, and hunt, to weave baskets, and to carve out canoes. Some of what they grew or made they sold in Charles Town, sometimes to aggressive and "insolent" market women who bought up items from "country negroes" and held them for higher prices: "I have seen these very negro women surround fruit-carts, in every street, and purchase amongst them, the whole contents, to the exclusion of every white person." The grand jury in Charles Town regularly complained about the "many idle negro wenches" who were "suffered to cook, bake, sell fruits, dry goods, and other ways traffic, barter, &c. in the public markets and streets of Charles-Town." Such activities crowded out "poor honest white people" who might otherwise support themselves; they were "an Inducement to Theft, it being well known that [slaves] are ready to buy and receive such as are stolen." Slaves' marketing also offered opportunities to runaways like Amey, a "very sensible" slave with "a numerous Acquaintance." According to her owner's advertisement in 1772, she had been sighted "in Charles-Town selling things about the Streets, pretending to be a free Woman." Occasionally, the authorities tried to crack down on these forbidden activities. In March 1773 they seized a quantity of dry goods from slaves selling on the streets and auctioned them off at the Beef Market. Two months later, a "large Quantity of Earthen Ware, &c was seized from NEGRO HAWKERS in Meeting Street." They may have been selling pieces of the unglazed pottery, known as colonoware, sometimes made by slaves themselves (fig. 10).[39]

The market women took advantage of the relative freedom of city slaves in comparison with those on plantations—a freedom that troubled many whites. Not only slaves in the streets but also domestic slaves who cooked, cleaned, and served in the magnificent houses of the rich spent much of their time beyond surveillance in kitchens, stables, and work yards, places whites usually avoided. In the work yard and the stable behind the Heyward mansion on Church Street, slaves tended the horses, cattle, hogs, and chickens that

Figure 10. This colonoware pottery bowl, made by slaves,
was dug by archaeologists from the grounds of Henry
Laurens's Mepkin Plantation, on the Cooper River above
Charles Town. It is marked with the "HL" that Laurens
used to identify his property. (OLD SALEM, INC.: COLLECTION
OF THE MUSEUM OF EARLY SOUTHERN DECORATIVE ARTS)

provided meat and milk for the family; in a separate building they cooked and washed laundry at fireplaces on opposite sides of a large chimney. Whites seldom visited these places, often stiflingly hot, or ventured to the second story, where slaves lived in cramped quarters with low ceilings and windows with wooden shutters that scarcely kept out the drafts in winter or the flies and mosquitoes in summer (figs. 11, 12).[40]

Away from these semiprivate spaces, the city offered many other places where slaves, away from whites' gaze and control, could hide, entertain, and, maybe, plot. Such gatherings prompted regular, but apparently unavailing, protest from the city residents and authorities alike. Charles Town had few lamps to brighten the dark, despite repeated presentments from the grand jury that condemned the "Want of a proper Law for the effectually Lighting the Streets and Alleys." Some wealthy residents put up lamps in front of their homes, but they might find their lamps broken by persons in the streets who preferred not to be seen. Even a bright moon did not keep blacks from meeting in the "little, narrow, dirty and irregular Alleys and Lanes" off the broad main streets, or on the marshy edges of the town, or in rural lanes shaded by live oaks and tall pines.[41]

From the once marshy ground behind the mansion of merchant Miles

Figure 11. This kitchen, in a separate building behind the house built by Daniel Heyward on Church Street in 1772, is laid out in typical fashion for a space dominated by slaves. The stairs lead to slave living quarters on the second story. (LIBRARY OF CONGRESS)

Brewton, archaeologists have uncovered evidence of one such gathering place: charcoal remains, broken bits of African-style pottery, and an unbroken bottle marked with Brewton's own "Mbrewton" monogram—an empty bottle used by slaves to carry away their own drink, or perhaps a full one lifted from Brewton's wine cellar, so they, like Brewton and his guests, could enjoy some of the best wine in America. The city's slaves and free blacks could also meet in still more private spaces. Although the law forbade slaves to rent housing for themselves or to live outside of white supervision, according to an anonymous writer, "The Stranger," "*many rooms, kitchens, &c. are hired to or for the use of slaves in this town;* and, by such slaves, let to others, in *subdivisions,* which serve as places of concealment for run-aways, stolen goods, &c."[42]

So, too, blacks patronized the tipling houses and "dram-shops" that catered to slaves, sailors, and the white poor unable to afford the costly taverns that hosted gentry gatherings. One such survives today: the Pink House on Chalmers Alley, with its three tiny rooms stacked on top of each other, a

Figure 12. The laundry for the Heyward house was on the opposite side of the big fireplace of the kitchen. (LIBRARY OF CONGRESS)

block from the waterfront (fig. 13). This was just one of dozens of choices for
in this city of fewer than thirteen hundred houses, more than a hundred
people held licenses to serve liquor. Slaves could spend their cash on drink,
joining tavern keepers who evaded the Negro Act's ban on selling liquor to
slaves. There, too, or so authorities claimed, they could trade in stolen goods.
Whites complained repeatedly about the large number of "Dram-Shops and
Tipling-Houses in Charles-Town, such as entertain Negroes and other disorderly Persons," and men and women were occasionally indicted for the
crime of "keeping disorderly houses, cooking victuals for, and entertaining
negroes," but this had no effect on the number of licenses issued.[43]

The markets and waterfront also offered space—social as well as physical
—for the small number of black Carolinians who had purchased their freedom, been freed by their masters, or been born to free women. Scipio Handley, for example, had been born to a free black mother who "used to bake
Ginger bread and Cakes and such things." She earned enough to hire a slave
to help her. Like his mother, Handley supported himself in the markets,

Figure 13. In the rooms of this tavern near the harbor, sailors drank and slept with poor whites, slaves, and free blacks in Charles Town. (Library of Congress)

catching and selling fish and buying and selling fruit, earning enough to buy furniture and clothing in Charles Town's shops. Even Handley could not match the success of Thomas Jeremiah, also a fisherman, but far more prosperous. Invoking the Van Neck family of London, merchant-investors who had become famously rich, Henry Laurens wrote that "as a Negro Fisher Man Jerry was comparatively as Rich as a Vannuk, in the Circle of Stock holders."[44]

But the water, especially, provided opportunities for blacks, both slave and free. No slaves pressed against the limits of control more than boatmen and fishermen, unusually mobile and commonly outside the supervision of whites. They were more "apt to be riotous and disorderly," and slave boatmen were also more likely to try to escape. South Carolina's "Negro Act" forbade slaves to "keep any boat, pettiauger, or canoe" for their own "use or benefit" and condemned owners who allowed slaves to do so, since boatmen could not only "traffic and barter in several parts of this Province," and thus take advantage of opportunities to receive and conceal stolen goods, but also "plot and confederate together, and form conspiracies dangerous to the peace and safety of the whole province." In 1772, "The Stranger" complained that the law was clearly failing: "Are there not many slaves permitted to keep boats, canews, &c.? whereby opportunities are afforded them, . . . at their pleasure, to supply the town, with fish, or not; and of course to exact whatever price they think proper, for that easily-procured food, so necessary for the subsistence of, and formerly as great a relief to, the poorer sort of white people?"[45]

The law required slaves who were off the master's premises to carry a ticket that granted them permission to be away and specified an allowed length of time. To enforce the law, and especially to prevent slaves from gathering illegally at night, was the principal assignment of Charles Town's constables, watch, and slave patrol. The watch's hundred-plus men were divided into three companies, each required to take turns mounting guard at night "to prevent disturbances among disorderly negroes, and more disorderly sailors." On Sundays, when whites were expected to be at church services and slaves were excused from labor, a double watch was supposed to be on duty. In addition, a mounted patrol was to ride through rural areas, hunting for runaways and slaves sneaking away for the night. But who would watch the watchmen? The grand jury complained in 1773 that "it is well known that not one Half of the Number of Men required by Law do attend their Duty on Sunday, and at Night; that in the Afternoon on Sundays the Watch House is frequently shut up and not a Man on Duty." When they did show up, constables and watchmen were often as much of a "Nuisance" as rowdy slaves themselves, "beating and abusing" slaves with genuine tickets while letting others off in return for a bribe. Constables were too often "Persons of a mean, low Character," "a disgrace" to the office. Far from enforcing the liquor restrictions, many watchmen, or their wives, held their own liquor licenses, "whereby it becomes their Interest to encourage Negroes, and others, to frequent their Houses, and consequently to protect such disorderly persons."[46]

Grand juries complained that "the slaves in Charles Town are not under a good regulation," and they issued numerous grievances about slave behavior. One took care to capitalize its "ENORMOUS GRIEVANCE, that NO NOTICE WHATEVER IS TAKEN of negroes, and other slaves (and indeed of too many whites) profanely cursing, swearing, and talking obscenely, in the most public manner; to the great annoyance of every person, who has a due sense of decency and virtue, and to the dishonour of our religion." Another recommended that public stocks be erected "in every Cross-Street of this Town, with Power to be lodged in every white Person (as by the Negro Law is given to whip Negroes found without Tickets) to put Offenders therein; as the only Means to stop or check the intolerable Insolence of Negroes, and other Slaves, in blaspheming talking obscenely, and gaming, in the public Streets, as they daily do, but particularly on Sundays." Gatherings of "disorderly" black men and women also attracted other unwelcome characters. One grand jury cited John Sagnussey for "performing, by himself and his Associates, Legerdemain, Tricks, thereby collecting a Number of idle, loose and disorderly Persons, to the Disturbance of the Peace."[47]

South Carolina governor James Glen, writing in 1751, claimed that since most skilled slaves and "civilized" slaves, such as those in Charles Town, were natives of the colony, they "had no notion of liberty" and were "pleased with their masters, contented with their condition, [and] reconciled to servitude." Belying that description was the boisterous and "disorderly" street life of slaves, the nighttime drinking and gambling in dark and crowded taverns. For their Carolina masters, such behavior contradicted the white determination that black men and women, whether slave or free, should quietly and submissively accept their state of radical inequality. The greater concern was that this subtle resistance would provide the space for, would grow into, more open and political forms of resistance. Writing in 1779, Alexander Hewatt, a former Presbyterian minister in Charles Town, thought that the colony had less to fear from "new Negroes" on rice plantations "than from the number of tradesmen and mechanics in towns, and domestic slaves." Enslaved artisans "discover amazing capacities" and use dangerous tools; domestic servants attending white families' tables "hear their conversation, which very often turns upon their own various arts, plots, and assassinations. From such open and imprudent conversation those domestics may no doubt take dangerous hints, which, on a fair opportunity, may be applied to their owners hurt." Slaves had been frequently punished for "killing or poisoning their owners," Hewatt wrote, but there was good reason to think that such crimes "have also frequently happened, when they have passed undiscovered."[48]

That nighttime meetings might be the prelude to dangerous criminal activities or, worse, insurrection was the fear expressed by the "The Stranger," writing in September 1772. He claimed to be English-born but familiar with South Carolina because of an eighteen-month stay in Charles Town. To investigate the true state of slavery in the city, the Stranger said, he had dressed like a sailor and wandered "thro' the Bye-Lanes and Alleys, King-Street, and the Outskirts, and the Interstices between the Stores upon the Wharves." Every weekend, from late Saturday afternoon to Sunday morning, one could encounter on roads just outside of Charles Town hundreds of black Carolinians. He would "rarely meet with more than 40 or 50 tickets or letters in the hands of the *Country Negroes,* and never more than 4 or 5 such licences amongst *those* that *belong to the Town,* who generally make *four-fifths* of these strollers." If challenged, few of those city slaves "will return any answer, and most of those who vouchsafe to do so, will, in a surly and insolent tone, tell him "they belong to *their Master.*" Many carried "heavy hickory sticks or clubs, hanging to which they carry baskets, bags, or jugs, with provisions, liquor, and perhaps plunder."[49]

He claimed to have observed, secretly, such a "Country-Dance, Rout, or Cabal of *Negroes,* within 5 miles distance of this town, on a Saturday night. . . . It consisted of about 60 people, 5-6ths from Town, every one of whom carried something, in the manner just described; as, bottled liquors of all sorts, Rum, Tongues, Hams, Beef, Geese, Turkies and Fowls, both drest and raw, with many luxuries of the table, as sweatmeats, pickles, &c. (which some did not scruple to acknowledge they obtained by means of false keys, procured from a Negro in Town, who could make any Key, whenever the impression of the true one was brought to him in wax) besides other articles." They amused each other with imitations of their masters and mistresses, then "*danced, betted, gamed, swore, quarrelled, fought* and did *every thing* that the *most modern* accomplished gentlemen are not ashamed of.*" More ominously, "They had also their private committees; whose deliberations were carried on in too low a voice, and with so much caution, as not to be overheard by others. . . . Not less than 12 fugitive slaves joined this respectable company before midnight, 8 of whom were mounted on good horses; these . . . went off about an hour before day; being supplied with liquor, &c. and perhaps having also received some instructions." Such meetings were "very common," the Stranger continued; he had been told "that intriguing meetings of this sort *are* frequent even in Town, either at the houses of *free negroes,* apartments *hired to slaves,* or the *kitchens* of such Gentlemen as frequently retire, with their families, into the country, for a few days; and that, at these assemblies, there are seldom fewer than 20 or 30 people, who commit all kinds of excesses. Whenever or wherever such nocturnal rendezvouses are made, may it not be concluded, that their deliberations are never intended for the advantage of the white people?"[50]

By the time he left Charles Town after his 1773 visit, Josiah Quincy, Jr., had become more impressed by the evils of slavery in the colony than the refinement that slavery had made possible. Slavery forced "vast multitudes" to be sunk into "barbarism, ignorance, and the basest and most servile employ!" Its brutality corrupted the "manners of the people," especially young people. The fear of rebellion had led the colony's leaders to enact laws "which savor more of the policy of Pandemonium than the English constitution: . . . laws which would disgrace the tribunal of Scythian, Arab, Hottentot and Barbarian." "Slavery," he concluded, "may truly be said to be the peculiar curse of this land: Strange infatuation! It is generally thought and called by the people its blessing."[51]

CHAPTER TWO

"Those natural and inherent rights that we all feel, and know, as men"

"Worthy of their Mother-Country"

WHEN THE CHARLES TOWN Library Society printed its *Rules and By-Laws* in 1762, an "Advertisement" appeared in its first pages, outlining the society's goals: a "liberal Education, together with the Use of valuable books," to make possible the "Advantages, arising to Mankind, from Learning." Should anyone doubt these advantages, let them compare the state of the Indians of North America, or even the "rude and savage State" of Britain in the days of the Roman Empire, with the "splendid Figure, which *Great Britain*, the Admiration and Envy of the World, at present makes." Unfortunately, such a "splendid Figure" was not necessarily permanent, as could be seen from the current condition of former "Fountains of Learning" like Greece and Egypt, now "oppressed with Slavery, their Learning extinct, their Arts banished." It was the duty of Carolinians to ensure that they not descend to the Indians' state with their "gross Ignorance" and "savage Disposition." The purpose of the Library Society was to hand down "the *European* Arts and Manners to the latest Times" and to prove themselves "worthy of their Mother-Country, by imitating her Humanity, as well as her Industry, and by transporting from her the Improvements in the finer as well as in the inferior Arts."[1]

The "Advertisement" captured both the ambitions and anxieties of the Charles Town elite, proud to be Britons and certain of the superiority of British culture but also fearful of falling short of those high standards. Events like the marriage on April 17, 1763, of Lord William Campbell and Sarah Izard, therefore, must have been reassuring. Campbell, a younger son of the

Duke of Argyll, was a captain in the Royal Navy and commander of HMS *Nightingale*, which had been stationed on the Charles Town watch. Sarah Izard, the daughter of the late Ralph Izard, was "a young lady esteemed one of the most considerable fortunes in the province." The Reverend Robert Smith presided at the wedding, in St. Philip's Anglican Church. Completed in 1723, with a cupola supported by monumental porticos on three sides, huge arched windows, and a soaring vaulted ceiling, St. Philip's was the city's first outstanding building. The marriage strengthened the political and cultural links between Charles Town and the home country. With the recent defeat of France in the worldwide Seven Years' War, the British Empire had reached new heights of power, and Lord William, a handsome scion of British nobility, exemplified that victory and power, winning his captain's commission after serving in a series of naval engagements from the Indian Ocean to the coasts of France. The lovely Sarah, just seventeen, was a member of a family that may have been, collectively, the richest in all North America. The wedding perhaps affirmed to members of the Charles Town gentry that they were indeed "worthy of their Mother-Country." The end of the war, and its attendant disruptions of trade, seemed to promise even greater prosperity ahead. The *Nightingale* sailed on April 28 to Britain, where Lord William would soon become member of Parliament for Argyllshire.[2]

Yet there were reasons to question whether Charles Town's gentry truly were a fully integral part of British society, as they imagined they were. Their ambitions to imitate Britain's "Humanity, as well as her Industry," posed a special problem in a place like South Carolina, with an economy founded on African slavery. Slavery might produce the means to purchase fine furniture and the books on the shelves of the Library Society, but if slave plantations were, in some sense, an expression of true "Industry," were they also compatible with true "Humanity"? Many Britons, and some Americans in colonies to the north, were beginning to express their doubts. And Carolinians, along with other Americans, were soon to learn that they did not count fully as members of the British political system either. The very sessions of Parliament in which Lord William would soon take his seat began to pass legislation that showed both Americans and Britons that their worlds, if indeed they overlapped, were not quite the same after all.

"My Servants are as happy as Slavery will admit of"

Just as Henry Laurens's success as a slave merchant exemplified South Carolina's economic foundation, so his personal experiences as a planter illustrate the ways the colony's elite tried to reconcile African slavery with its professed ideals. Laurens's letters on slave trading provide a chilling, even hellish, record of how people of Africa were reduced in the consciousness of colonial Americans to the status of mere articles of commerce. His letters about his life as planter and slave master document how personal experience and encounters with new ideas challenged white attitudes about, and behavior toward, enslaved Africans.

Among the volumes purchased by the Charles Town Library Society in the years when Laurens—a founding member of the society—was building his fortune were books by writers in France and in Britain who had begun to question slavery's compatibility with Christianity and to assert new ideas about the nature of "humanity." An influential example was the moral philosopher Francis Hutcheson of Scotland. Hutcheson insisted that humans were not motivated purely by self-interest and that all people shared an innate "moral sense" and a "natural impulse to society with their fellows." The moral sense propelled humans toward benevolence and fostered sympathy for those who suffer innocently: "Every Mortal is made uneasy by any grievous Misery he sees another involv'd in, unless the person be imagin'd evil."[3] Whether Laurens knew the work specifically of Frances Hutcheson and similar Enlightenment figures is unknown, but he was certainly influenced by related religious ideas.

According to his son-in-law, Laurens's attention to religious duty was "strict and exemplary." He insisted that his children, both boys and girls, pray and read the Bible daily. He became a faithful member of St. Philip's; "the emergency was great which kept him from church either forenoon or afternoon, and very great indeed which kept him from his regular monthly communion." In the 1750s, he had joined the monthly meetings of a "religious and literary society" founded by the Reverend Richard Clarke, rector of St. Philip's. Laurens knew his Bible well and sprinkled his letters with scriptural quotations. His faith sustained him when his wife died in 1770, a crushing blow that sent him into a months-long depression, but he did his best to "submit to this Stroke of Providence with as much of that dutiful Acquiescence which Christianity requires as my Depraved Heart will admit of."[4]

South Carolina's whites had long been troubled by the relation between slavery and religion. As Christians they were obligated, in theory, to convert African "heathens" whose very heathenism was an oft-cited justification for their enslavement. The bishop of London, in 1727, tried to reassure slave owners that "Christianity, and the embracing of the Gospel, does not make the least Alteration in Civil Property," so slaves' status would not be affected by baptism. Christian freedom had nothing to do with "their outward Condition"; rather, it meant "Freedom from the Bondage of Sin and Satan, and from the Dominion of Mens Lusts and Passions and inordinate Desires." Further, the Gospel required "Diligence and Fidelity, but also Obedience," of slaves and other subordinates, without depriving masters of any "proper Methods of enforcing Obedience," as long as these were not "cruel and barbarous."[5]

The sentiments expressed in the bishop's message had little practical effect in the colony before the arrival, in the late 1730s, of new-style evangelist George Whitefield, a young minister from the "Holy Club" of England's "despised Methodists," led by John and Charles Wesley. In repeated visits to the colonies over the next three decades, Whitefield attracted large and enthusiastic crowds with a charismatic and emotional style of out-of-doors preaching. In South Carolina, many poor whites and slaves flocked to his sermons. Some rich planters also attended. In Charles Town, Whitefield criticized the worldliness of rich men and women who "spent more on their polite entertainments than the amount raised by their rates for the poor." In his "Open Letter to the Inhabitants of Maryland, Virginia, North and South Carolina concerning the treatment of their Negroes" in 1740, Whitefield told slaveowners, "I think that God has a quarrel with you for your abuse and cruelty to the poor Negroes." He had seen plantation owners "faring sumptuously every day," while "many of your slaves had neither convenient food to eat, nor proper raiment to put on, notwithstanding most of the comforts you enjoy, were solely owing to their indefatigable labours." Should God permit an uprising of the slaves, "all good men must acknowledge that the judgement would be just."[6]

Henry Laurens was an adolescent when Whitefield first came over from England, but in later years, he strongly supported Whitefield's work. Laurens also admired the Moravians, a pietist German sect that settled Salem, North Carolina, in the 1760s. Although Laurens served the Moravians as an import-export merchant, his correspondence with them often dwelled on religious topics, and he exchanged religious tracts with one of their ministers, John Ettwein. The Moravians were among the first denominations to take on the task of bringing the Gospel to slaves, and they insisted that all peoples were, in some senses, equal before God and equally deserving to hear the Gospel. One of Ettwein's letters to Laurens, written while Ettwein was traveling through the backcountry settlements of Germans in the Carolinas, raised questions about the effects of slavery on masters and slaves alike. Of masters, he wrote, "I wish their Children may turn out a good Race but am afraid the Negroes have too much Influence upon them and I have observ'd that often where a Man has Slaves his Children become lazy & indolent &c." As for the slaves themselves, he was "very uneasy. If some care was taken of the Souls their Servitude might be a Blessing unto them but I [could] hear nothing of that and even of no Prospect for such a Thing." Laurens replied, "Your observation upon the influence & effect of the Negro Slavery upon the morals & practices of young people are but too justly founded & I have often reflected with much concern on the same subject & wished that our oeconomy & government differ'd from the present system but alass—since our constitution is as it is, what can individuals do?"[7]

By the time of this exchange, Laurens had had several years' experience dealing with Africans, not only as commodities in the trade, but also as people working on his plantations. In 1756, he bought from his brother-in-law, John Coming Ball, a half-share of Wambaw Plantation, on the Santee River about forty miles north of Charles Town. Other purchases followed: Mepkin Plantation, on the West Branch of the Cooper River, about thirty miles above the city; Wright's Plantation along the Savannah River; also plantations called Broughton Island and New Hope in Georgia. By 1766 Laurens owned almost nine thousand acres of plantation land and 227 slaves. Mepkin, nearest to Charles Town, served as Laurens's country seat, with a comfortable residence. It produced provisions, firewood, and lumber, as well as rice and indigo. The distant frontier plantations, which Laurens rarely visited, specialized almost wholly in rice.[8]

From the moment of purchase, slaves necessarily assumed a measure of personhood in the eyes of their owners, no longer mere "parcels." They had to be identified as individuals and given names, the barest beginnings of the recognition of Africans as people. If the classical and literary names frequently given slaves, such as Othello, Valerius, and Lavinia, meant nothing to the new Africans themselves, individual personalities soon asserted themselves. Take Sampson, for example. He was "imported" by Laurens in 1764, but within "very few days" of being sent to Mepkin Plantation, as Laurens later wrote, "the Overseer a very harsh fellow drove him off." The runaway Sampson encountered a "poor worthless" white man who took him in and put him to work for eight months, teaching him the basics of indigo culture and the English language. This white man (unnamed), fearing that his neighbors might report him for harboring a runaway, turned Sampson in to Laurens, but Sampson soon ran off again to the same "Knave who first harbour'd him"—proving, Laurens admitted, "that he had not been unkindly treated there." Laurens decided to sell Sampson "because I will not keep a runaway," but also because he would "be a bad example to the rest of my slaves." Still, Sampson was "as likely a Negro Man . . . as most in the Province." In Sampson, Laurens could have no doubt that he was dealing with a person with a mind and a will of his own, not a mere piece of property.[9]

Laurens developed his plantation properties into a coordinated business enterprise, "governed operationally and politically by commercial strategies." He developed a pragmatic understanding of the slaves who worked his rice and indigo, made his barrels, manned his boats, and served his family at home; he attempted to "find out the par of exchange" they commanded, just as he did with his competitors, creditors, and customers. He let his slaves raise their own crops and earn cash with extra work, and they bartered with him for such items as iron pots, imported pottery, and, on one occasion, "15 very gay Wastcoats which some of the Negro Men may want at 10 Bushels per Wastcoat." On another occasion, he sent "sundry articles" for the overseer to dispose "among the Negroes for their Rice at the prices mark'd to each article which I hope they will take without too much fuss & trouble that I may not be discouraged from being their Factor another Year." Laurens recognized his slaves as people on the other side of a negotiation, one in which he held most of the power but not all of it. He remained the honorable but always prudent merchant, telling his overseer that the slaves' rice should be given "its full value," but, in the case of the waistcoats, suggesting he might get more than ten bushels for each. On another occasion he told an overseer that if provisions fell short, "it will be proper to purchase of your own Negroes all that you know Lawfully belongs to themselves," but only "at the lowest price that they will sell it for."

Some slaves appear in Laurens's letters as favored characters. Cudjoe was a "quiet orderly old Man," who provided good leadership in the quarters. The other slaves "all Respect and Love him." Sam was "a sensible & good fellow"; Laurens trusted him to keep a crew of slaves under his "watchful eye" and to direct new overseers how to set up indigo vats. Hagar was known "for her honesty, care of Negroes, & her great care of Indigo." Although Stepney, a plantation hand who later moved to Charles Town to care for Laurens's garden, got "dead drunk," Laurens trusted him to help Mepkin's overseer with "turning & watching the new Indigo." Stepney was "very honest & if you will speak to him he will not allow anybody within his sight to rob you."[10]

Laurens's principles called for him to treat his slaves with humanity. When May ran away from Wambaw Plantation and showed up in Charles

Town, Laurens sent him back with instructions to the overseer to "take all the care you can" of him. "He is gone without food, without Blanket, & is very weak & infirm. Take care of him & let him rest with very little work until I come. You say you don't like him but remember he is a human Creature whether you like him or not." But slaves were also property, and the property relationship was ultimately more powerful to Laurens than the principle of humanity. When Laurens's brother-in-law and joint owner of Wambaw Plantation, John Coming Ball, died in 1764, his heirs insisted on a clear division of the property. Because the slaves had intermarried without regard to ownership, such a division would mean the division of slave families. To Ball's son, Elias, Laurens wrote that he wanted "to avoid that inconvenience & I will say inhumanity of seperating & tareing assunder my Negroe's several families which I would never do or cause to be done but in case of irresistable necessity." After negotiations failed to resolve the disagreements, Laurens wrote again that "I don't know anything that could have been contrived to distress me & embarrass my plantation again more than this unnecessary division of Fathers, Mothers, Husbands, Wives, & Children who tho Slaves are still human Creatures & I cannot be deaf to their cries least a time should come when I should cry & there shall be none to pity me." In the end the division went forward, as Ball wished.[11]

The principle of humanity was not a principle of equality. In Laurens's hierarchical world, different humans had different places in God's scheme. His slaves were, as he wrote elsewhere, "Men who are doomed to Eat Bread in the Sweat of their Brow." This humanitarian principle was, therefore, fully compatible with the exercise of power by masters over their slaves, and those who did not accommodate, like Stepney or Sam, could expect severe treatment. These recalcitrant slaves' personalities sometimes emerge vividly from Laurens's letters. One overseer was instructed to be "very watchful" of Amos, who had "a great inclination to turn Rum Merchant which I have strictly forbidden." Amy was an "impudent gipsey" who occasioned much "trouble . . . upon the plantation." Laurens hoped to replace her with a compliant Hagar; then Amy could be transferred to fieldwork and made to perform a daily task. George, when Laurens purchased him in 1763, had a reputation as a "Cunning, Quarelsome, Young fellow," and was apparently cunning enough two years later to convince a new overseer to make him a driver—in charge of other slaves. Laurens, alarmed, warned the overseer that George was "an eye Servant, & a great Rogue, & therefore by no means fit to be an overseer of others. You might as well set a Wolf to watch Your Sheep."[12]

Most vivid of all was Abraham (sometimes "Abram" in Laurens's letters), perhaps the most valuable of all Laurens's slaves. The "poltroon," or captain, of the *Baker,* a schooner with a slave crew, he shuttled slaves, family members, rice, indigo, and supplies between Charles Town and Mepkin Plantation. A "very good boatman," Abraham was also a carpenter, cooper, plasterer, and "good hand at the Whip Saw or any other Plantation Business." At the same time, he was a source of constant annoyance, and several of Laurens's letters bristle with warnings to his overseers: "Take care to prevent an intercourse between Boat & Plantation Negroes & let me know how Abra[ha]m the Patroon of the Boat behaves." "Abraham made out only 22 Chords of Wood which he was pleas'd to sell without any orders & therefore I have the greatest reason to suspect him of knavery [for selling additional, stolen wood]. You will be very watchful over all his steps." "Pray be so good as to give a watchful eye to the behaviour of Abraham & his gang. I will have no traffick carried on by them & he is so very sly & artful that you will find all your skill necessary to counteract them." "Dont fail to chastize the first one that transgresses [by stealing potatoes and corn] & particularly Captain Abraham." "You will find Abraham to require a watchful eye & perhaps a streight Arm, if so don't let him trifle with you."[13]

At one point, the exasperated Laurens sent a letter to a dealer in George-town, about sixty miles up the coast, consigning Abraham for sale. In it, he described Abraham as "Carolina born & aged about 34 to 36 Years," adding that he had owned him "these 12 Years," ever since he was "just entring upon Manhood." He then set out, in ledger style, Abraham's "character," good qualities in the left-hand column, bad ones in the right. On the positive side Laurens listed, in first place and capital letters, "SOBER." There were Abraham's many skills; he was also "very active, alert and Strong," "very healthy in general, a good horseman, and very well acquainted all over the Province." And, in the right column: "he will deceive you as often as he can"; "will pilfer trifles" (but "always keeps out of greater scrapes"); "fond of women"; "will feign himself Sick when he is not so." Perhaps worst of all, Abraham was "Ungrateful & disobedient to any Man that uses him well and does not keep him close to work." Laurens thought Abraham had been corrupted by "some pernicious connexions that he has made with Slaves in Charles Town." Not-withstanding his value—three times that of the average slave, according to Laurens—he feared that Abraham's example "will have a very bad effect upon the manners of other of my Negroes." A sale, though, would have the op-posite effect, since "this kind of banishment will alarm" the other slaves.[14]

The word "Ungrateful" captures the sense of himself Laurens had achieved in seeking to reconcile his power over slaves and the immense wealth they produced for him with his own self-understanding as a Christian and a humane man. Slaves were human beings but, like permanent children, subordinate ones, toward whom Laurens owed fatherly concern. Laurens had a duty to provide Abraham and his other slaves good treatment, and they, in turn, had a duty to provide hard work, honesty, and gratitude. Fully convinced of his humanity, Laurens could congratulate himself on his treatment of his slaves. He wrote, rather smugly, to one correspondent that he never really intended to become a planter, "but I have been insensibly drawn into such an extent by means & circumstances quite adventitious. However the reflection is comfortable that my Servants are as happy as Slavery will admit of, none run away, the greatest punishment to a defaulter is to sell him."[15]

Laurens could scarcely know the feelings of his "Servants" on distant rice properties. As one historian has pointed out, such properties might better be described as slave labor camps than as plantations. Despite his claim that "none run away," Laurens did have runaways just like other planters, and if he did not personally whip his slaves, he many times told his overseers to use the whip when they must. Laurens's instructions regarding the troublesome George, for example, were to "take him down early." In 1765 he advised a new overseer to "use gentle means mixed with easy authority first" on his slaves, but if that did not work, to select one or two of "the most stubborn" and "chastise them severely but properly." In the same letter in which he ordered his overseer to "take all the care you can" of the runaway May, he also ordered him to treat another runaway, Castillo, quite differently: "He says you are too hard upon him, tho his back does not shew any thing like it. don't fail to give him his full deserts." Such instructions meant, undoubtedly, the whip. And if selling a slave might not mark the skin, it could be a far worse punishment for any slave with family ties.[16]

"Who . . . can love the Affrican trade?"

Considerations of humanity, according to Laurens's own claims, led him, eventually, to withdraw from the African slave trade. In 1763, after his partner, George Austin, retired and returned to his native England, Laurens began to decline offers to sell big shiploads of African slaves. More than once he cited as his reason personal concerns about the cruelties of the trade. To a Philadelphia merchant in 1768 he explained that he had "quitted the Profits arising from that gainful branch principally because of many acts, from the Masters

& others concerned, toward the wretched Negroes from the time of purchasing to that of selling them again, some of which, altho within my knowledge
were uncontroulable." Four years later, commenting to a correspondent on a
ship captain, William Wallace, with a bad reputation, Laurens wrote that the
"imprudence & wickedness" of captains like Wallace "induced me to relin-
quish the gain upon African Consignments as Soon as my Partnerships were
at an end." In a later letter to the same man he called the trade "So repugnant
to my disposition . . . that it Seems as if nothing but dire necessity could drive
me to it."[17]

Yet Laurens never wholly withdrew from the slave trade, nor did he ever
publicly criticize it. If his letters occasionally cited moral qualms, they far
more often justified his withdrawal based on mundane business concerns. As
Laurens declined offers in 1763 and 1764, he called the trade too risky for a
single merchant without a partner (it was "part of the Negro Contract, for the
Factor to stand to all bad Debts" from the customers). A single man might die
or suffer illness; he wanted to "keep my affairs within such a Compass" as not
to expose any friends and family "to great disappointments & Losses, upon
the precarious Tenure of my Life or health." Thus, to one merchant house in
the West Indies, he explained, in 1764: "I have in general declined the Affrican business, altho I have had the most kind & friendly offers from my
friends . . . but having no partner I do not chuse to embarrass & perhaps
involve myself in concerns too unweildy for a single Man both on his own &
his friends Account."[18]

In the course of a public dispute between Laurens and the local Admiralty
judge, Egerton Leigh, Leigh mocked Laurens for supposedly withdrawing
from the slave trade because of religious scruples. ("He reads the Revelations,
which speak of divers articles of merchandize, and finding that *slaves* and the
souls of men are also in the enumerated list, swears that St. John meant, in his
vision, the pernicious practice of the *African trade;* he therefore withdrew
himself from the horrid and barbarous connection.") Laurens denounced
Leigh's account as "false, calumnious and foolish." He had, in fact, several
reasons for "retiring from that trade": "I was weary of constant Application to
a Counting House"; "not anxious to add Thousands to Thousands, by grasp-
ing at . . . every profitable Branch of Commerce"; "I had no Partner, and was
not disposed to engage one," and so "could not do that Justice to my Constituents which they had a Right to expect." He had simply transferred his
friends' business in slaves "into the Hands of Gentlemen who could transact it
to the greatest Advantage." Thus, a year after writing to his Philadelphia

friend that he had withdrawn from the trade because of its cruelties, he publicly denied that was the reason.[19]

Indeed, Laurens continued to participate in the trade. In one letter declining shipments from Africa, he qualified his refusal: "However a few now & then of a good sort I can Manage well enough for you while the prices keep up." In the very year he wrote his letter to Philadelphia, claiming to have withdrawn from the trade because of the treatment of the "wretched Negroes," he sold several shipments of Africans that had arrived by way of the West Indies. In January 1768 he told one firm in the Caribbean island of St. Christopher, "If you can send me 30 or 40 likely unblemished Negroes soon after this reaches you at a price not exceeding £25 Sterling per head for Angola or £27 for Gambia or Gold Coast consign'd to me on our joint account I will undertake the Sale of them to the Southward & make you satisfactory remittances for the whole." Just three weeks before the Philadelphia letter, he told the same West Indies firm that, for any current balance in Laurens's favor, "please to ship the amount in prime Young Negro Men," since he expected "that healthy young Negroes will sell very high in this Country after the 1st January next." The following year he sold seven slaves for a Bristol trader, explaining that two of the original group of nine had died, including a "poor pining creature [who] hanged herself with a piece of a small Vine." He mentioned the "small" size of the vine as evidence that this woman would not have brought a high price anyway, since it showed that "her carcase was not very weighty." The suicide apparently touched Laurens, since he added a postscript to the letter: "Who that views the above Picture can love the Affrican trade." Yet, a year later he assured a slave buyer on the African coast that if any slaves were sent to Charles Town and "consign'd to me, you may depend upon it that I shall either sell them myself, or put them into such hands as will do you the most Service in the Sale & the most perfect Justice in every Respect. But send none but young ones. I don't mean Children. When a small parcel of old or ordinary Slaves come to hand, it is exceedingly difficult to dispose of them at any Rate."[20]

As a mentor to young, new merchants, Laurens often went out of his way to help them enter the slave trade. For a former clerk, John Hopton, he pledged the enormous amount of £10,000 sterling as surety "in order the more effectually to enable you to make Offers and accept the Sale of African Cargoes." In fact, the same letter in which he called the slave trade "So repugnant to my disposition . . . that it Seems as if nothing but dire necessity could drive me to it," was full of advice to a young protégé, John Lewis

Gervais, on how to proceed as a new man in the trade. He advised Gervais that "you will be better off, if you receive only two African Consignments than you would be if you had more"; he assured him that "I would be your Security for Ten Thousand pounds if Mr. Oswald [Laurens's friend and one of Britain's largest African traders] Shall require it."[21]

When Laurens's Moravian friend John Ettwein wrote to him in 1763 about the bad consequences of slavery, Laurens replied,

> Each can act only in his single & disunited capacity because the sanction of Laws gives the stamp of rectitude to the Actions of the bulk of any community.
>
> If it was to happen that every body or even a considerable majority of people were to change their sentiments with respect to slavery & that they should seriously think the saving of Souls a more profitable event than the ading House to House & laying Field to Field & those laws which now authorize the custom would be instantly abrogated or die of themselves, but while they remain in force & that we see the Negro Trade much promoted of late by our Northern Neighbours who formerly Censur'd & condemn'd it, the difficulties, which a few who would wish to deal with those servants as with brethren in a state of subordination meet with, are almost insurmountable.[22]

Such concern for public opinion explains a great deal about Laurens's troubled, and inconsistent, words and behavior about slavery. It was the foundation of his personal fortune, as it was for every fortune in South Carolina. By the 1770s his property was worth £100,000 sterling—over 80 percent of it in slaves—and was producing returns of 15 percent annually.[23] For Laurens to condemn either slavery itself or the slave trade would, in effect, be to accuse his friends and the entire ruling class of the colony of unchristian conduct and almost certainly also to forfeit his high influence and prestige. He retreated to the ordinary rationales that work for most people in such circumstances: it was too hard to change things, and other people (such as northern merchants or slave-ship captains or overseers) were to blame for the dirty work that came with the institution.

These complicated realities and moral inconsistencies could be easier to bear—indeed to ignore—at moments when favored slaves reassured slave owners of their benevolence. One of those moments came for Laurens when he returned to Charles Town late in 1774 after three years in England. When he arrived at his mansion, he wrote to his son John back in London, "I found nobody here but three of our old Domestics Stepny Exeter and big Hagar, these drew tears from me by their humble & affectionate Salutes & congrat-

ulations my Knees were Clasped, my hands kissed my very feet embraced &
nothing less than a very, I can't say fair, but *full* Buss of my Lips would satisfy
the old Man weeping & Sobbing in my Face—the kindest enquiries over &
over again were made concerning Master Jacky [i.e., John] Master Harry
Master Jemmy—they encircled me held my hands hung upon me I could
scarcely get from them—Ah said the old Man I never thought to see you
again, now I am happy—Ah, I never thought to see you again." John wrote
back that "the sincere Demonstrations of Joy with which you were received by
your ancient Slaves" were proof that life for slaves must be happy under a
good man and, more to the point, "must have afforded you a secret Satisfaction which none but good Men can feel." Stepney might be a drunk, but his
slobbering display confirmed to Laurens his self-image as a kind, paternal
figure. That was worth more than a shipload of rice.[24]

"The broad common ground of those natural and inherent rights "

A few months later, in May 1775, just a few weeks after British troops had
marched into the Massachusetts countryside to be met by American militia in
Lexington and Concord, Henry Laurens was in Charles Town, trying to
prepare for what he feared would be a similar assault by the British in South
Carolina. Writing to a London acquaintance, he insisted that "it requires no
great Sagacity to prove that the terms of Submission required from American
Subjects to Parliamentary Authority are more unjust more intolerable than
the Laws by which I govern my Plantation Negroes." Laurens's justification
of American resistance to British authority shows no sense of irony or aware-
ness of self-contradiction. By that date, however, both American and British
writers had been pointing out the apparent hypocrisy of those whom the
Massachusetts patriot, Josiah Quincy, Jr., sarcastically called "Those Zealots
for Liberty, who are the Enslavers of Negroes."[25]

In South Carolina, the same elite group that made the laws for "Plantation Negroes" also led the colony into rebellion for liberty. Although much of
plantation "law" consisted of whatever the master said it was, masters' power
was enabled and supported by the power of the colonial government. Thus,
Laurens had written to the Reverend John Ettwein that, on slavery, as in
other things, "the sanction of Laws gives the stamp of rectitude to the Actions
of the bulk of any community." He failed to mention that he himself was
among the makers of law in the colony.

In South Carolina the body that gave "the stamp of rectitude" to slavery was the Commons House of Assembly, wholly dominated by wealthy merchants, lawyers, and planters. In the period from 1762 to 1775, about 160 men served in the Commons House (and another 50 or so filled all other important political offices). Only once in these years did voters elect a representative who worked with his hands: printer Peter Timothy, a newspaper owner and slave owner. Members were elected by adult white men who qualified as voters by owning at least fifty acres or paying twenty shillings in taxes, but the property requirements for representatives were far higher than for voters: five hundred acres and ten slaves, or at least £1,000 (local currency) in real estate. Moreover, representation was heavily concentrated in Charles Town itself. The backcountry interior districts, rapidly filling with migrants from colonies to the north, was barely represented, even though it claimed a large majority of the colony's white population. Further, many of the low-country rural plantation districts were represented by residents of Charles Town, since representatives did not have to live in their districts. Altogether, about half of the members of the Commons House lived in Charles Town all or part of the time, and nearly all the leaders of the first rank lived there. In effect, the colony was a kind of city-state run by men like Laurens, first elected to the Commons House in 1757 and immediately one of its most active members.[26]

The government of the colony included a governor, appointed by the king, and a council also appointed by the king. The council advised the governor; the same men sat as an Upper House of the Assembly, giving assent to bills. In outline, this structure of government resembled the king, Lords, and Commons in Britain, and sometimes people imagined it that way, but in practice, the colony's government in the 1770s was mainly in the hands of the Commons House. The governor, always something of an outsider, had but a shadow of the formal power of the king in Britain. His power of appointment was sharply limited, and his salary was a gift of a Commons House more than willing to use it as point of leverage. The members of the council, unlike those in the House of Lords in Britain, were government appointees, with no independent source of legitimacy. Thus, Henry Laurens refused an appointment to the council in 1764 on the grounds that it was mostly filled with placemen with no roots in the colony and that such "injudicious appointments" had reduced its reputation "almost below contempt." Indeed, the Commons House insisted that the council was not part of the legislature at all but a mere advisory body of the governor. The Commons House controlled many areas of government that, in other places, would be under executive authority. Charles Town, for example, had no independent city government.

Major projects such as the building of the Exchange were directed by commissions set up and appointed by the Commons House and dominated by the same merchants, lawyers, and planters who sat in the legislature. Ongoing functions like regulation of markets and the laying out of streets were carried out by commissions whose members were elected annually, while other functions, such as care for the poor, were undertaken by the vestries of the two Anglican parishes, St. Michael's and St. Philip's. These bodies, too, were made up mostly of the same men.[27]

In Charles Town, about half of all adult white men cast votes for the Commons House, a far higher percentage than could vote for Parliament in Britain. Nevertheless, the small social and economic elite of the colony made all the important decisions. Josiah Quincy, Jr., of Massachusetts thought the colony's government profoundly unbalanced. "'Tis true," he wrote, "they have a house of Assembly: but who do they represent? The laborer, the mechanic, the tradesman, the farmer, husbandman or yeoman? No. The representatives are almost if not wholly rich planters. The Planting interest is therefore represented, but I conceive nothing else (*as it ought to be*)." Such men "have in general but little solicitude about the interests or concerns of *the many*" and were "frequently the fittest instruments to enslave and oppress the commonality." But members of the Commons House saw no conflict between their interests and those of the larger community. They professed an ideal of disinterested and virtuous public service, where decisions were based on the public good, not personal advancement. Their wealth, so they thought, guaranteed their independence and made it unlikely that they could be bribed. Their model, they liked to believe, was the incorruptible Cato the Younger, the semilegendary statesman and soldier of the ancient Roman Republic who had committed suicide rather than surrender to the rising tyrant Julius Caesar. One of the rare plays performed in Charles Town before the 1770s that was *not* a comedy was Joseph Addison's *Cato* (1713), portraying the hero as a martyr to liberty. The play's first performance in North America was in Charles Town in 1736, and performances were repeated with some frequency. In 1774 it was put on both by the professional American Company of Comedians and by the pupils of schoolmaster Oliver Dale. The play's conception of government fit comfortably within the hierarchical assumptions of the Carolina elite.[28]

Their collective self-conception as guardians of liberty shaped the conflicts between the South Carolina political elite and the British administration. Long before Parliament's passage of the Stamp Act in 1765 touched off disputes that would ultimately lead to independence, the Commons House had aggrandized powers not intended by either the original proprietors or the British government after South Carolina became a royal colony. None of these powers was more fiercely guarded than the power of the purse—to tax, borrow, and spend—but others were also asserted and jealously protected in a series of protracted battles with the colonial governors over the rights and privileges of the body.

Throughout the 1760s, the colony's leading political radical and the man at the center of their disputes was Christopher Gadsden. The one full extant portrait of Gadsden, by Jeremiah Theus, shows a man somewhat stout, with a receding hairline and a relaxed smile, but with little hint of his contentious, often belligerent, temperament. Gadsden's career paralleled that of Henry Laurens in many ways. They were born the same year, 1724, and elected to the Commons House of Assembly the same year, 1757. Laurens's son-in-law claimed that the two were "attached in their early youth to each other by the strongest ties of ardent friendship," making "common cause to support and encourage each other in every virtuous pursuit, to shun every path of vice and folly." (If true, they must have been prodigies of virtue, since Gadsden was sent off to be educated in England at the age of seven.) In later life, though, they clashed frequently, in part because Laurens was usually cautious and prudent in public affairs, whereas Gadsden was the sort of man who could not leave a boiling pot unstirred nor pass a bonfire without tossing on more sticks of wood.[29]

Gadsden's father was collector of customs in the port; from him Gadsden inherited a plantation and other real estate, a library, and four slaves. He spent years of apprenticeship in England and Philadelphia and two years' service as a purser on a British man-of-war, then returned to Charles Town in 1748 to pursue a career as a merchant. In the 1760s his ambitions turned to an audacious project, building the grandest wharf in Charles Town. Finished in 1774, the wharf included a lock that would keep ships in deep water at low tide and warehouses with space for ten thousand barrels of rice. The *South-Carolina Gazette* hailed it as a "*stupendous Work,*" perhaps "the most extensive of the Kind ever undertaken by any one Man in America." Gadsden was instrumental in organizing a volunteer artillery company in 1757 that was a great popular success; members paraded smartly in uniforms with "Blue Catees turn'd up with Crimson, crimson Jackets & Gold laced Hats." The royal governor, William Henry Lyttleton, refused to allow the Commons House to make the company a fully legal part of the provincial militia, on the grounds that the Commons House had no business with such matters. This was just one of a series of disputes between the governor and the Commons House concerning the conduct and financing of the Cherokee War of 1759–1761, part of the still larger conflict between France and Britain called, in America, the French and Indian War. After the war, Gadsden was the central figure in a dispute between the Commons House and the new governor, Thomas Boone. In 1762, after Gadsden was elected by an overwhelming majority to the Commons House by the voters of St. Paul's Parish, just outside Charles Town, Boone refused to recognize the election on a technicality and called for a new one. The Commons House, which treasured its right to control its own elections, in turn refused to undertake any business or to pay Boone his annual salary unless Boone relented and apologized. The standoff lasted for two years, until London recalled Boone, concluding that he had acted "with more zeal than prudence."[30]

In 1763 Gadsden published a letter "To the Gentleman Electors of The Parish of St. Paul, Stono." In it, he insisted that the Commons House's stand was "absolutely necessary, and the only step that a *free* assembly, *freely* representing a *free people,* that have any regard for the preservation of the happy constitution handed down to them by their ancestors . . . could *freely* take." For without a free assembly, "what security would the people have for their lives, liberty and property? Just as much as there is in Turky, as all depends there on the will of their governor, so should we find all here, too soon depended upon the will of ours! 'Tis a joke to talk of individual liberty of *free* men, unless a collective body, freely chosen from amongst themselves are empowered to watch and guard it; and if this body lose their *collective* freedom, the *individual* must follow of course." It was fortunate, he added, that King George wanted "to reign solely *in* the hearts of *free* people, not over a parcel of *slaves.*"[31]

The Gadsden election controversy was a dress rehearsal for the greater conflicts provoked by passage of new taxes by Parliament—where Lord William Campbell was now sitting as a member from Argyllshire. The American Duties Act of 1764 introduced new trade regulations, lowering duties with the goal of actually raising more money from them; much more alarming to Americans, the Stamp Act in 1765 imposed a tax on all sorts of paper and paper transactions: legal documents, newspaper advertisements, even playing cards. The Commons House, like colonial legislatures throughout America, saw this as a violation of every Englishman's right not to be taxed without his own consent. Gadsden denounced the law in the Commons House, and he was one of three South Carolina delegates to the Stamp Act Congress in New York City, where he often favored the most extreme measures. He wanted to base Americans' protest, not just on the various founding charters issued to the colonies, but "upon the broad common ground of those natural and inherent rights that we all feel, and know, as men, and as descendants of Englishmen we have a right to, and have always thought this bottom suffi-cient for our present, important purpose. . . . There ought to be no New England man, no New Yorker, etc. known on the Continent, but all of us Americans." The Commons House of Assembly endorsed the resolutions of the Stamp Act Congress, instructing its agent in London that "in taxing ourselves and making Laws for our own internal government or police we can by no means allow our Provincial legislatures to be subordinate to any legisla-tive power on earth."[32]

Gadsden did not confine his opposition to the floor of the Commons House or the Stamp Act Congress. He was almost certainly a principal organizer of Charles Town's Sons of Liberty, made up mainly of "mechanics" (skilled craftsmen), who would be hit hard by any tax and who resisted in the city's streets. The tax also provoked the printers whose newspapers were the primary source of news and opinion. In October 1765 the Sons of Liberty met the first shipment of stamps, arriving in Charles Town harbor on the *Planters Adventure,* with an effigy of a stamp collector hanging from a forty-foot scaffold. Then they roamed through Charles Town, stopping to rifle the houses of suspected stamp officials and threatening greater violence. The stamp collector and inspector promised not to enforce the act, and the stamps were stored on a British man-of-war in the harbor. Bowing to pressure from Americans and British merchants, Parliament repealed the Stamp Act in March 1766. Most white South Carolinians celebrated, but Gadsden warned the Sons of Liberty, at a meeting in a pasture on Charles Town Neck, near his own house, that repeal was insufficient because Parliament had also passed the Declaratory Act, insisting on its right to legislate "in all cases what-soever."(Lord William Campbell in all likelihood voted for both repeal and the Declaratory Act.) The broad oak under which he spoke became known as the Liberty Tree.[33]

The eruption of Charles Town's mechanics as a major force in provincial politics was the beginning of a permanent challenge to traditional ideas of hierarchy and deference. Many of these artisans had accumulated significant property, including slaves. Daniel Cannon, a leader of the Sons of Liberty, a carpenter from Scotland and two years older than Henry Laurens, had built up a substantial business as the contractor for many of Charles Town's fine houses and public buildings. By the 1760s, he owned a plantation and interest in a sawmill, and in 1758, he had even imported a cargo of slaves. Before the crisis with Britain erupted in 1763, Cannon had held only one minor office, that of tax assessor and collector in Charles Town, but afterward, he was elected to important commissions and to the vestry of St. Philip's. By 1768, Cannon and other activists in the Sons of Liberty were meeting to nominate candidates to represent St. Philip's Parish in the Commons House, among them Gadsden and Hopkin Price, a former tanner, though now a "man of property." They canvassed for votes with "great diligence."[34]

Cannon and his fellow artisans continued to follow Gadsden's lead in later conflicts with the British administration, including the resistance in all thirteen colonies to the American Revenue Act of 1767. This act taxed imports such as glass, paper, and tea. As did other colonists, South Carolinians passed, at a large public meeting, resolutions to boycott most manufactured imports from Britain and imports of slaves. To enforce the nonimportation agreement, the meeting appointed a committee consisting of thirteen merchants, thirteen planters, and thirteen mechanics, including Daniel Cannon. They then circulated the agreement for signatures and publicly condemned signers who violated it. This was the first time mechanics had won significant positions in an important governing body in the colony, even if that body had no legal standing. Men such as planter William Henry Drayton, who opposed the boycott, complained that South Carolinians should not be governed by "men who were never in a way to study, or to advise upon any points, but rules on how to cut up a beast in the market to the best advantage, to cobble an old shoe in the neatest manner, or to build a necessary house"—all tasks, it should be pointed out, that would most often be done by slaves. "Nature never intended that such men should be profound politicians, or able statesmen; and unless a man makes a proper use of his reading, he is but upon a level with those who never did read." A mechanic acting "in his own sphere" might be useful, "but when he steps out of it, and sets up for a statesman! believe me, he is in a fair way to expose himself to ridicule." Drayton's complaint provoked a sharp response from mechanics in a public letter insisting that mechanics "have exerted themselves nobly, and shewn incontestably, that neither cunning, palaver, abuse, or, in short, any thing else, can divert them from steadily, firmly, and deliberately promoting the common cause at this crisis, by every means in their power." The nonimportation movement, in South Carolina and other colonies, was effective enough to force repeal of most of the new duties in 1770. As with repeal of the Stamp Act, though, Parliament insisted on defending the principle of the matter, as they saw it, by retaining the tax on tea as a symbol of its authority.[35]

Gadsden and the mechanics were also central figures in a bitter political dispute that took place only in South Carolina, again pitting the Commons House against both the royal governor and the British administration. In 1769 Gadsden convinced the Commons House to donate £1,500 to a fund for the support of John Wilkes, a radical politician in London imprisoned for publishing "libels" against King George III. The Commons House ordered the money to be paid in the form of a loan, directly from the treasury, without passing an ordinary bill, which both the council and the governor would have rejected. The secretary of state in London sent back an "Additional Instruction" to the governor, requiring that he reject any future tax bill that omitted certain restrictions on expenditures or that tried to use tax money to pay back the loan. Again, Carolinians protested that this was unconstitutional interference and a denial of their claim that "in taxing ourselves . . . we can by no means allow our Provincial legislatures to be subordinate to any legislative power on earth." For four years the Commons House refused to pass any tax bill at all. Its obstinacy was strongly supported by the Wilkes Club, formed by Daniel Cannon and other veterans of the Sons of Liberty, which backed pro-Wilkes candidates for the Commons House. The visitor Josiah Quincy, Jr., watching the Commons House debate during the continuing stalemate in 1773, found Gadsden "plain, blunt, hot and incorrect—though very sensible. . . . In the course of the debate, he used these very singular expressions for a member of parliament: 'And, Mr. Speaker, if the Governor and Council don't see fit to fall in with us, I say, let the General duty law [authorizing local taxes] and all *go to the Devil*, Sir. And we go about our business.' "[36]

"The Flower of *English* Liberty "

To conservatives like Henry Laurens, the opening of politics to a new class of men was disturbing. Although devoted to the rights of the Commons House and opposed to taxation by Parliament, he nonetheless reacted cautiously to the Stamp Act, and like other Charles Town merchants in 1765, he favored "an humble & dutiful acquiescence to an Act of Parliament however oppressive it may be until by proper representations & remonstrances a repeal of that Act can be obtain'd." His moderation made him so suspect that the Sons of Liberty invaded his house and searched his stable and cellar the night of

October 23, 1765. Only with difficulty did Laurens convince them that he had no stamps. When the mechanics nominated candidates for the Commons House in 1768, one representative they hoped to oust was Laurens himself. He claimed to be above the new practice of openly campaigning for votes, writing that if he lost, it would be because "I walk on in the old road, give no Barbacu nor ask any Man for Votes." In fact, he spent more than £50 sterling hosting election events at a tavern and maneuvered to trade votes to make sure that Hopkin Price, the former tanner, would not win.[37]

Laurens, however, turned prickly and contentious when anyone raised doubts about his conduct, and it was a personal conflict with Charles Town's customs officers that turned him into a hot defender of American rights. The episode began in March 1767 with the appointment of a new collector of customs, Daniel Moore, who seemed to see his office mainly as an opportunity to extort as much as possible from the city's merchants. He and his subordinates raised their fees and began to seize local vessels for trivial violations of the customs regulations. In July, the deputy collector and searcher George Roupell seized two vessels belonging to Laurens, the *Broughton Island Packet* and the *Wambaw*, both small schooners used to carry goods back and forth to his plantations. Since, unlike many merchants in northern ports, Laurens always paid customs duties scrupulously, he was incensed that Moore and Roupell had taken advantage of his failure to follow the exact requirements for certain types of record-keeping (for example, ships leaving port were required to declare their contents before a customs official, but in Georgia, with no such officials near his plantations, Laurens had done so before local magistrates). The judge in Charles Town's Admiralty Court, Egerton Leigh, condemned the *Wambaw* but released the *Broughton Island Packet* on grounds that it had been seized on a frivolous pretext. Laurens, taking advantage of a provision in the law allowing him to countersue for damages in the case of wrongful seizures, won a large verdict against Roupell in May 1768 in the case of the *Broughton Island Packet*. The following month, Roupell seized Laurens's much larger ship, the *Ann*, after a disingenuous manipulation of the procedures for submitting certain customs forms, apparently intending to use the *Ann* as a bargaining chip to get Laurens to drop the suit in the case of the *Broughton Island Packet*.[38]

Laurens was infuriated by the decision of Admiralty judge Leigh in the case of the *Ann*. Leigh ruled in his favor on the grounds that, even though the *Ann* was in technical violation of the law, there was clear evidence of "Design" on the part of the customs officers to libel the ship *"for some private and inexplicable Reason.* " But, attempting to produce a compromise verdict, Leigh also ruled that there had been "probable cause" for the seizure, thus protecting Roupell against another suit for damages. Outraged, Laurens gathered documents related to these cases and published them, with commentary, in a pamphlet in Philadelphia, with a second edition in Charles Town in February 1769. In the Charles Town edition Laurens sharply attacked both Leigh and, more generally, "the Artifices of wicked Officers" in America, and warned that "the Powers of Commissioners and other Officers in *America* are increased to an alarming Height." Leigh responded with *The Man Unmasked, or, the World Undeceived* (May 1769), a mostly personal attack; Laurens retaliated with an *Appendix to the Extracts . . . Together with a Full Refutation of Mr. Leigh's Attempts to Vindicate His Judicial Proceedings* (August 1769). These pamphlets made Laurens well known throughout the colonies as a defender of American rights. His popularity in Charles Town was restored, and by the end of 1770, he, rather than Christopher Gadsden, was chairing popular meetings at the Liberty Tree.[39]

Laurens's denunciation of the Admiralty Courts illustrates a larger theme in Americans' resistance—what mattered was not just taxation without representation but the entire cluster of institutions and customs that protected Britons from arbitrary rule. If the most important of these institutions was a freely elected legislature with sole power to raise taxes, not far behind was an independent judicial system grounded in the common law, with final judgments by a jury of peers, not appointed judges. Trial by jury was, Laurens wrote, using a popular phrase of the day, the "Flower of *English* Liberty . . . the Palladium of their Constitution." Laurens proclaimed, as he continued to do almost until Independence was declared, that he was a "staunch friend to the British constitution and to every honest Man, an Enemy to all innovations and to every oppressor of the People." As late as September 1774 he simply wanted relations with the mother country "re-established upon the Basis on which it Stood in the Year 1764," with the colonies in "a Constitutional Line of Subordination & dependance." But, just as new taxes by Parliament were a dangerous innovation, so the greater powers of the Vice-Admiralty Courts had "extended *beyond their antient Limits,* " with "almost unlimited Power vested in a sole Judge of an American Court of Vice-Admiralty."[40] But what if slaves, too, rebelled against the "almost unlimited Power" of their masters, if they cried out, not just for pity, but for freedom?

"Crying out '*Liberty*'"

In May 1766, Gustavas Vassa, a West Indian slave, landed in Charles Town on the *Prudence,* a Bermuda sloop carrying a cargo of "oppressed natives of Africa" from the island of Montserrat for sale in South Carolina. Vassa (who would later take the name Olaudah Equiano) was not part of the cargo, but a member of the crew. His master, Robert King, had given him leave to buy and sell goods, such as rum and sugar, on his own account and, more extraordinarily, had promised to free him as soon as he had saved his value in the market. The *Prudence* arrived just after word had reached South Carolina of the repeal of the Stamp Act the previous March, and Vassa "saw the town illuminated; the guns were fired and bonfires and other demonstrations of joy shewn."[41]

But the victory for liberty being celebrated in Charles Town that spring meant nothing to slaves like Vassa. White men bought his sugar and rum "with smooth promises and fair words" but "very indifferent payment." Vassa hired a slave crew to row him across the harbor to find a man who had purchased rum and who finally paid him in debased copper dollars: "he took advantage of my being a negro man, and obliged me to put up with those or none, although I objected to them." When Vassa tried to use those copper coins in the Charles Town market, whites threatened to tie him and flog him "without either judge or jury." With difficulty, Vassa escaped to his ship.[42]

Vassa's experience is a reminder that black men and women needed no political theorists to teach them the contradictions between white Americans' claims to liberty, such as control of their own property and the right to fair trial, and their treatment of people of African descent. Nevertheless, the language of liberty, once it issued from the mouths of masters, was available to slaves as well. In fact, Charles Town's slaves had taken up that language for themselves just a few months earlier. In October 1765, crowds of artisans and sailors had rampaged through the streets of Charles Town, threatening violence against the men who had been appointed to collect the new Stamp Tax. Within weeks, the spirit of resistance had spread to slaves, who were heard in the streets at night "crying out '*Liberty*.'" In mid-December, Acting Governor William Bull II shared with his council a report that the wife of a prominent slave owner had overheard two slaves discussing "a design of the Negroes to make a general insurrection & massacre of the White people" on Christmas Eve. Other reports, coming from Johns Island, south of Charles Town's harbor, seemed to corroborate this story and "gave vast trouble throughout the province." Bull, with support from the council, called out the militia; in Charles Town "all were Soldiers in Arms for more than a Week," and extra patrols rode "day & Night for 10 or 14 days in most bitter weather."[43]

Shortly after this insurrection threat had been "discovered," Bull received additional reports that 107 slaves in Colleton County (the location of Johns Island) had left their plantations and joined "a large number of Runaways." Bull hired a party of Catawba Indians, from near the North Carolina border, to track them down, and the Indians eventually brought in seven runaways for a reward. The insurrection, if in fact one was planned, thus was quashed, but fears that one day an insurrection would occur were never far from whites' consciousness. In 1774, Peter Timothy, publisher of the *South-Carolina Ga-zette,* argued for a ban on exports of guns or gunpowder from the colony, noting delicately that "the Inhabitants of this Colony, being always in a more peculiarly critical Situation than those of any other, ought therefore never to be without the most ample Supply of Arms and Ammunition."[44]

White South Carolinians liked to believe that their paternalistic treat-ment of their slaves had inoculated them against rebellion. Acting Governor Bull assured his superiors in England in 1770 that "by the happy temperament of justice and mercy in our Negro Acts, and the general humanity of the master, the state of slavery is as comfortable in this province as such a state can be," though he admitted that "monsters of cruelty sometimes appear." "To the mildness of law and prudent conduct of masters and patrols," he added, "I attribute our not having had any insurrection since the year 1739." Bull's statement was the political version of Henry Laurens's "comfortable" reflec-tion that "my Servants are as happy as Slavery will admit of," that slavery, so planters like Bull and Laurens convinced themselves, was consonant with humanity. To the slaves themselves, humanity was insufficient; they wanted liberty. It remained to be seen how South Carolina's planters could reconcile African slavery with their own resistance to authority and their own determi-nation to defend their liberty, based on "the broad common ground of those natural and inherent rights that we all feel, and know, as men."[45]

CHAPTER THREE

"God will deliver his own People from Slavery"

"Those who every day barter away other mens liberty, will soon care little for their own"

HENRY LAURENS, Christopher Gadsden, and Charles Town's other leading citizens spoke sometimes of "the rights of Englishmen," and sometimes of "natural rights." To them, these were the same thing—the former a special case of the latter. When Gadsden had written, during the Stamp Act crisis, of a "broad common ground of those natural and inherent rights that we all feel, and know, as men," he had added, "and as descendants of Englishmen we have a right to." What made England (and now Britain) special was the complex of customs, laws, and institutions —the constitution—that had grown up there to check the "destructive spirit of Arbitrary Power," that, in the words of historian Jack P. Greene, the British had "retained their identity as a free people by safeguarding their liberty through the laws." People in the unchecked monarchies of Spain or France, or the despotisms of Turkey or Russia or China, had no such protections for their natural rights.[1]

But if the colonists were proud to be freeborn Englishmen, they worried nonetheless that power was always dangerous. A free people could remain free only by constant vigilance; "the encroaching Nature of Power" must "ever be watched and checked." That was the lesson taught by history, and taught, in particular, by a group of British writers from the early decades of the eighteenth century whose work became highly influential in the colonies. The most influential of all were John Trenchard and Thomas Gordon, authors of a series of newspaper essays, under the pen name Cato, reprinted as a book in 1720: *Cato's Letters: or, Essays in Liberty, Civil and Religious, and Other*

Important Subjects. The *South-Carolina Gazette* reprinted several of these essays in 1748, the year of a new London edition of the essays. The volumes sat next to those of Locke and Montesquieu on the bookshelves of many of Carolina's leaders.[2]

The chapter titles of *Cato's Letters* outline the lessons offered: "Liberty proved to be the unalienable Right of all Mankind"; "The Right and Capacity of the People to judge of Government"; "Civil Liberty produces all Civil Blessings"; "Freedom of Speech. . . . is inseparable from publick Liberty"; "The terrible Tendency of publick Corruption to ruin a State, exemplified in that of Rome, and applied to our own"; "Cautions against the Encroachment of Power"; "What Measures are actually taken by wicked and desperate Ministers to ruin and enslave their Country."[3]

"Enslavement" was an essential element of *Cato's* message, and it became an essential element of American arguments against British policies. "As the absolute political evil," writes historian Bernard Bailyn of the pamphleteers of the American Revolutionary era, enslavement "appears in every statement of political principle, in every discussion of constitutionalism or legal rights, in every exhortation to resistance." Thus Christopher Gadsden asked, in June 1769, while defending nonimportation of British goods as a way to protest the Townshend Duties: "What is a slave but one that is at the will of his master, and has no property of his own, but on the most precarious tenure." It was to this "deplorable, this adbject situation" that American colonists had been reduced, "by the oppressive and unconstitutional measures again revived, since the repeal of the Stamp-Act, and particularly by several late acts of P[arliamen]t; one for rasing a revenue in America, the others for extending the jurisdiction of the admiralty."[4]

The "enslavement" referred to so often in American protests was not, however, chattel slavery, the legal ownership of human beings, but what one might today call "tyranny." Christopher Gadsden had no intention of including, in his defense of American rights, any actually enslaved Africans in South Carolina; Africans were, rather, part of the "property" that Carolinians were trying to protect against encroachments of the British government (and commodities being excluded by the boycott, along with paint and paper). Other Americans did, however, see African slavery as an obvious contradiction of Americans' claims to liberty. As early as 1759, Richard Henry Lee of Virginia had denounced the slave trade to his colony's legislature, declaring that slaves were "our fellow creatures, . . . equally entitled to liberty and freedom by the great law of nature."[5] Five years later, in a ringing attack on the expanded powers of the Admiralty Courts as a violation of Americans' natural rights, James Otis of Massachusetts insisted that "the Colonists are by the law of nature free born," including "all men," whether "white or black."

> No better reasons can be given, for enslaving those of any colour, than such as baron Montesquieu has humourously given, as the foundation of that cruel slavery exercised over the poor Ethiopians; which threatens one day to reduce both Europe and America to the ignorance and barbarity of the darkest ages. Does it follow that it is right to enslave a man because he is black? Will short curled hair, like wool, instead of Christian hair, as it is called by those whose hearts are as hard as the nether millstone, help the argument? Can any logical inference in favour of slavery, be drawn from a flat nose, a long or a short face? Nothing better can be said in favour of a trade, that is the most shocking violation of the law of nature. . . . It is a clear truth, that those who every day barter away other mens liberty, will soon care little for their own.[6]

Over the next decade, writers on both sides of the Atlantic made similar arguments, in America, for obvious reasons, more commonly in the northern colonies. In Pennsylvania, Quakers like Anthony Benezet had been attacking African slavery for many years, and in New England, Congregational ministers decried slavery from their pulpits. But no one put the argument better than a former South Carolinian, Alexander Hewatt. Hewatt had come from his native Scotland to Charles Town in 1763 to assume the pulpit of the Scots Presbyterian Church. He left in 1777 because he took Britain's side in the argument with America. Hewatt had, for years, been gathering materials for a history of South Carolina, which he finally published in London in 1779. Hewatt's Tory sympathies are clear, but his *Historical Account of the Rise and Progress of the Colonies of South Carolina and Georgia* was a largely balanced account, widely cited by South Carolina's historians ever since. In ten of its pages, he laid out the Enlightenment view of slavery that had become common in polite British society. He acknowledged that Carolina planters "treat their slaves with as much, and perhaps more tenderness, than those of any British colony where slavery exists"; that slaves were "comparatively speaking . . . well clothed and fed"; that when they fell sick, they were "carefully attended by a physician." Still, this could not make up for the slaves' lack of protection at law or for the many instances of "cruelty and negligence" or for the lack of religious instruction for slaves. Hewatt implored masters to treat their slaves with "tenderness and compassion" and improve their daily lives, but also insisted that for Africans, as for whites, "Freedom, in its meanest circumstances, is infinitely preferable to slavery, though it were in golden fetters." Africans "are by nature equally free and independent, equally susceptible of pain and pleasure, equally averse from bondage and misery, as Europeans themselves." Before he left the province, he freed his two slaves, Diana and her daughter, Susannah. Yet even this defender of natural rights would not give up property freely. Diana had to pay £1,000 in local currency for her freedom, from "the earnings and gains arising from her Labour and Industry from time to time," which Hewatt had allowed her to accumulate. This was about what she and her daughter would have brought in a regular sale.[7]

"The most abject Slavery"

In 1771, Henry Laurens took his three sons to London to be educated, and he remained there himself until November 1774, leaving his merchant business in Charles Town in the charge of his clerk and his plantation affairs in the hands of overseers, friends, and relatives. From afar, Laurens tried to continue to play the role of kindly, but stern, patriarch. He criticized an overseer on one of his Georgia plantations for his "violent Passion & badness of temper," which had caused (he thought) nine slaves to run away. He praised the performance of the overseer on his other Georgia plantation, who "treats my Negroes with Humanity." He claimed to prefer that to an overseer who might "make twice as much Rice" by the exercise "of Cruelty towards those poor Creatures who look up to their Master as their Father, their Guardian, & Protector, & to whom their [sic] is a reciprocal obligation upon the Master." But slaves who did not obey must be punished. Laurens instructed his clerk, Felix Warley, that if Sam got drunk he should send the slave to the Charles Town Work House "under severe threats of Punishment." If other of his slaves misbehaved, either in Charles Town or at Mepkin Plantation, they were to be sent to the Georgia plantations, and when Laurens returned from England there would be "a reckoning of Accounts."[8]

In England, Laurens traveled widely to inspect canals, construction projects, and machinery that might help him and his fellow planters improve their operations. He was disgusted, though, by the "horrible" excesses of luxury and vice he witnessed, for example, in the resort city of Bath, where people of "both Sexes & all Ranks" worked at the card tables for twelve or even eighteen hours a day. It seemed to him that the whole British nation was "full of Wealth & power, wallowing in the Gratifications which Riches are capable of procuring . . . the Fountain Polluted & the foul Streams running through the Hearts & directing the course of Individuals." Corruption had reached such a state, indeed, that Laurens could imagine "that a Couple of Negroes through the Mediation of Money & an active Broker may be one Day" elected to Parliament—the notion of a black member of Parliament representing, perhaps, the ultimate sign of corruption. Finally, he decided to take his oldest son, John, to Geneva, to enroll him in school in that more virtuous environment.[9]

The "corruption" Laurens witnessed strengthened his determination to protect American liberties. "We contend," he wrote in London, "as Englishmen and Freemen, for Nothing less than the very Essence of true Liberty." He defended the South Carolina Commons House in its ongoing dispute over its donation, back in 1769, to the Society for the Bill of Rights in behalf of John Wilkes—even though he considered the decision to donate the money a rash mistake. He wrote to a South Carolina correspondent that he fully supported "the Right of the People to Give and Grant their Money freely and voluntarily, and not in terms, nor under the Restrictions and Limitations of a Royal or Ministerial Mandate." With another South Carolinian, Ralph Izard, he arranged for a Virginia writer, Arthur Lee, to publish a long pamphlet defending South Carolina's stance and arguing that the rights of the colonists were not a gift from Parliament, but, like the liberties of all British subjects, "Coeval with the Constitution." He also met with Lord William Campbell, who had been appointed the next governor of South Carolina, to try to convince him of the right of the South Carolina Commons House to grant money however it wished.[10]

While Laurens was in London, Parliament passed a new law that was destined to spark resistance once again in America, the Tea Act of May 1773. The act was designed to help the struggling British East India Company by granting it a monopoly to sell still-taxed tea in the colonies. Laurens hoped that Americans would resist this new attempt to subject them to taxation, though not with force; they should "make no attempt to lay violent & illegall prohibitions on our fellow Subjects." He was delighted when the first shipments of tea to arrive in Charles Town were rejected without resort to violence. "There is a Constitutional Stubbornness in Such Conduct," Laurens wrote, "which must be approved of by every true English Man & open the understanding of those whose Stubborn attempts to enslave America, are Supported by no better plea then power."[11]

In the famous Boston Tea Party, of December 16, 1773, however, the first tea shipment to Massachusetts was tossed into the harbor. Laurens deplored

Bostonians' use of violent measures, but he deplored even more Britain's response to the Tea Party. In 1774, Parliament passed a series of what the colonists called "Intolerable Acts," closing the port of Boston, dramatically altering the government of Massachusetts, and allowing trials of royal officials accused of capital crimes to be moved to Britain. Laurens warned one correspondent that all who loved constitutional liberty must, during the debates in Parliament, "appear in close Ranks or we must submit to wear the Badge of Slavery." If the king was truly determined that "none but Slaves & his Officers their Task Masters Shall reside in America," then Laurens was "heartily inclined to risque all my Estate & my Life upon this occasion." To his English merchant friends, he defended Americans' protests, and he worked with other Americans in London to promote the American cause. They submitted petitions to the king, Lords, and Commons against the punishment threatened for Boston. In identical petitions to the Lords and Commons in May 1774, thirty signers, more than half of them South Carolinians, declared that "entire Subjection" to Parliamentary authority was no different from "the most abject Slavery." (One signer was John Izard, Jr., a student at Cambridge and the brother of Sarah Izard Campbell.) They begged Parliament "not to attempt reducing them to a State of Slavery, which the English Principles of Liberty, they inherit from their Mother Country, will render worse than death." Laurens, along with most other Carolina leaders, feared that they had become the victims of a "Diabolical Plan" hatched by wicked ministers to destroy Americans' liberties.[12]

While Henry Laurens was defending American rights and criticizing the "Torrent of Bribery & Corruption" he saw in British society, South Carolinians back home were cooperating with other colonies to thwart the new British measures and to respond to a call from Massachusetts to send delegates to a congress (later named the Continental Congress) in Philadelphia. A mass meeting in Charles Town, in June 1774, asked every part of the colony, including the backcountry, to send representatives to Charles Town on July 6. There, 104 representatives were joined by hundreds more Charles Town citizens. This gathering chose Christopher Gadsden, Henry Middleton, Thomas Lynch, and John and Edward Rutledge to attend the upcoming congress in Philadelphia, scheduled for September. The Charles Town meeting, further, created a "General Committee" of ninety-nine (fifteen merchants, fifteen mechanics, and sixty-nine farmers and planters) to enforce the tea embargo and correspond with resistance groups in other colonies.[13]

The Continental Congress at Philadelphia adopted a Declaration of

Rights, denying that Parliament had the right to rule Americans. It proposed that all the colonies adopt an almost total embargo on trade with Great Britain (with an important exception for exports of rice, for which planters had few alternative markets). The Congress adjourned on October 26, calling for a Second Continental Congress to meet, if necessary, on May 10, 1775. When South Carolina's five delegates returned from Philadelphia in November 1774, the General Committee in the colony called for new elections to a "General Provincial Committee" that would meet in January 1775 to discuss the resolves of the Continental Congress. While the Continental Congress was meeting, Laurens was preparing to return to South Carolina from London. He could see no end in sight to the conflict, and he had made his choice for America. "The view is painful," he acknowledged; "nothing less than that confirmed patriotism which is equal to forsaking Father & Mother & House & Land for the Kingdom of Heaven's Sake" could bring the Americans through.[14]

"Let them put away *the accursed thing*"

In London, Laurens had encountered directly the predominant British view of the conflict with America, that Parliament had a reasonable right to exercise full authority over the American colonies, just as it did over all the other Britons who did not get to vote. Britons were appalled at the outbreaks of violence and the destruction of property by American mobs in places like Boston, mobs that ignored the rule of law. Most Britons could not understand the Americans' fear of "enslavement," since the British constitution, with its authority divided among the King, House of Commons, and House of Lords, was perfectly balanced to prevent tyranny. And, they asked, as did Samuel Johnson in a pamphlet, *Taxation No Tyranny,* "How is it that we hear the loudest yelps for liberty from the drivers of negroes?"[15]

Since British merchants were of course the organizers and financiers of the slave trade, it was easy for Americans to turn this charge of hypocrisy back on the supporters of Parliament. It was harder, though, for Americans to dismiss antislavery arguments when they came from British supporters of the American cause. One was Granville Sharp, a government clerk who in 1774 published a pamphlet, *Declaration of the People's Natural Rights to a Share in the Legislature,* that was reprinted multiple times in the colonies. Sharp defended key American claims about legislating for themselves, but he also declared that "the toleration of domestic Slavery in the Colonies greatly weakens the claim of *Natural Right* of our American Brethren to Liberty. Let them put away *the accursed thing* (that horrid *Oppression*) from among them, before they presume to implore the interposition of *divine Justice:* for, whilst they retain their *brethren* . . . in the most shameful involuntary servitude, it is profane in them to look up to the *merciful* Lord of all, and call him *Father!*"[16]

Laurens may not have read Sharp's pamphlet, but he could hardly be unaware of the growth of antislavery sentiments in London. Soon after his arrival in 1771, for example, he attended a performance of *Oroonoko,* a play based on a novel published in 1688; its hero is an African prince, seized and taken into slavery, who then leads a slave revolt in British Surinam. The novel was not intended as an attack on slavery itself (the hero had been a slave trader back in Africa), but by the 1770s, the plot meshed well with growing antislavery sentiment in London. Laurens's only surviving comment called it "that foolish thing Oroonoko."[17]

More ominous for a South Carolinian was the London trial for the freedom of a slave named James Somerset. Somerset had been brought to England by his owner, Charles Steuart, a Scottish merchant who had purchased him in Virginia. After Somerset escaped in 1771, Steuart recaptured him and put him on board the *Ann & Mary,* bound for Jamaica and sale. Somerset had recently been baptized in London, and when his godparents heard about his capture, they applied for, and won, a writ of habeas corpus, requiring that Somerset be brought before a judge. Somerset then appealed for help to Granville Sharp, the pamphleteer, and Sharp recruited lawyers to represent Somerset in court. From February to May 1772, lawyers argued before the judge, Lord Mansfield, over whether Steuart could legally recover James Somerset and sell him in Jamaica. In June Mansfield pronounced his celebrated ruling. Slavery was an "odious" institution, without support in the common law, and "the man"—Somerset—"must be discharged."[18]

Historians of the case have pointed out that Mansfield's ruling was apparently limited to the narrow issue of whether Steuart could compel Somerset to leave Britain. Nonetheless, it was widely interpreted at the time as outlawing all slavery in England, and it was noted in newspapers in South Carolina, as in other colonies. This idea became a point of argument in a pamphlet published in 1774 in Charles Town by "A Back Settler." The anonymous writer was replying to a pamphlet by South Carolina radical William Henry Drayton, *Letter from Freeman of South Carolina, to the Deputies of North America . . . at Philadelphia.* Drayton had insisted that Americans were "undoubtedly possessed of the Birth-rights of Englishmen, Rights evidenced by

Magna Charta," and they must share in every "natural right, liberty, or exemption in any shape, from the Royal influence, power and jurisdiction, which the People of England shall at any time receive." But, replied "A Back Settler," now one of those rights was that slaves were instantly freed "by setting Foot on that happy Territory [England] where Slavery is forbidden to perch." If *Freeman*'s ideas were adopted, the same would be true in America, and "a general Manumission of Negroes" "would complete the Ruin of many *American* Provinces."[19]

Henry Laurens followed the Somerset case closely enough to include a sardonic comment in a letter to a friend back home, that "I was going to tell a long and comical Story, of a Trial between a Mr. Stuart and his Black Man James Somerset, at King's Bench for Liberty." After the verdict was announced, he wrote another correspondent, "I will not say a word of Lord Mansfield's Judgement in the case . . . until we meet, save only that his Lordship's administration was suitable to the times. The able Dunning set out on the Defendants part by declaring that he was no advocate for Slavery, & in my humble opinion he was not an Advocate for his Client nor was there a word said to the purpose on either side." To Laurens, the idea that English law might prevent a master from recovering his slave was comical, merely a sign of the (corrupt) times.[20]

Just one month later, Laurens rushed to London to arrange for a slave named Cato, the property of a friend and former business partner, George Appleby, to be put on board a ship bound for Savannah, from where he would be sent on to Charles Town, with instructions to take "proper precautions" to prevent Cato's "Elopement." Cato, perhaps, had learned of the Somerset case; if so, Henry Laurens made sure he could not take advantage of it. More tellingly still, Laurens left behind, when he returned to Charles Town in November 1774, the slave Scipio, whom he had brought from Charles Town to attend to him personally. Scipio had first surprised him, on their arrival in 1771, by insisting that he now be called Robert. Laurens complied and, at first, was quite pleased with Robert, who "hitherto has behaved very well and promises fair to continue good and dutiful." In the letter that first mentioned the Somerset case, Laurens added that "my man Robert Scipio Laurens says, the Negroes that want to be free here, are Fools. He behav'd a little amiss one day, and I told him I would not be plagued by him. If he did not choose to stay with me, to go about his Business. He said he would serve no body else, and has behaved excellently well ever since." But by 1774, Robert no longer served Laurens and had gotten into a scrape with the law, apparently for stealing a ham. Laurens wrote to his friend Appleby, who had learned about Robert's troubles, saying not to worry: "His Value will not be very great even if I recover him. He is a sad Rascal, unprincipled, ungrateful, & never will be better."[21]

In November 1774, Laurens boarded the packet *Le Despenser* at Falmouth, without Robert. He arrived home on December 11, though not before a scare when his ship struck a shoal at the mouth of Charles Town's harbor in rough water near midnight while being piloted by "an unskillful Young Man." The crew got the ship off the shoals, saving Laurens and the rest of the passengers from having to swim or make it to shore in a small boat, "ten or twelve Miles from Shoar & seven long hours of Night before us." After leaving behind the ungrateful Robert, it must have been doubly pleasing to Laurens to arrive finally at his Charles Town mansion to be greeted by his old domestic servants, Stepney and Hagar, with apparently genuine expressions of devotion.[22]

"The Children of Israel were delivered out of the hands of Pharo"

On January 9, 1775, a month after Laurens arrived back in Charles Town, he was elected one of thirty delegates from the city to the new General Provincial Committee. When this body met two days later, it renamed itself South Carolina's Provincial Congress, and, for the next year, it effectively exercised virtually all powers of government in the colony. The roll of delegates reflects the power of the wealthy merchants and planters who had long dominated South Carolina's politics. In addition to Laurens, there was John Izard, in the fourth generation of Izards to serve in the colony's legislature. There also were John, Thomas, and Edward Rutledge; Charles and Charles C. Pinckney; Thomas and Daniel Heyward; and Arthur, Thomas, and Henry Middleton— each a future signer, or close relative of a signer, of the Declaration of Independence or the U. S. Constitution. Most of the members of the legal, but now largely irrelevant, Commons House of Assembly had been elected to the Provincial Congress, but the Congress was almost four times the size of the Commons House. The additional members were largely upcountry planters and farmers or skilled artisans and small businessmen from Charles Town, none of whom would have been elected to the assembly before the democratization that had accompanied the rising resistance to British policies in the past decade. One of the most important of the new members was Daniel Cannon, the carpenter-builder, leader of the Sons of Liberty, and member of the earlier committees set up to enforce nonimportation agreements. Others included James Brown, another carpenter turned contractor; Peter Timothy, printer and publisher of the *South-Carolina Gazette;* Theodore Trezevant, a tailor; Michael Kalteisen, a wood merchant and wagon master; and the brothers John and Simon Berwick, owners of tanyards and ironworks.²³

The Provincial Congress chose Charles Pinckney as its first president. It approved the resolutions of the Continental Congress and endorsed the embargo on trade with Britain including, after some debate, the exception made for rice, the main source of the colony's income. It authorized Pinckney to appoint, if necessary, a "Secret Committee" "to procure and distribute such articles" as might be needed for the public safety "and other necessary purposes." It reappointed Gadsden, the Rutledges, Lynch, and Middleton to serve as the colony's representatives at the Second Continental Congress, due to open in Philadelphia on May 10. After calling for a day of fasting and prayer on Friday, February 17, they adjourned until June, authorizing the still-existing General Committee of Charles Town to call them back into session earlier, if necessary.²⁴

On February 17, the speaker of the Commons House led its members into St. Philip's. There they heard, "with great seriousness," a "very good patriotic" sermon from the Reverend Robert Smith, rector of St. Philip's, a sermon praised by Henry Laurens as "the best I ever heard from his reverence." The Reverend Smith, who after the Revolution became South Carolina's first Episcopal bishop, focused on the need to fear God and obey his commandments; he used the history of the Jews to remind his audience of the good that flows from proper obedience and the evils that result from disobedience. He mentioned the "mighty things that God had done for [the Jews] in Egypt" but reminded his listeners that, "after every general revolt from God," the Jews found themselves "groaning under Burthens, afflicted by Tyrants, oppressed by Conquerors." It was right, he assured them, to ask the blessings of the Almighty in the conflict with "our Mother Country," but only as long as the Americans were motivated, not by "the unreasonable thirst for power, or factious discontent," but by "the sole Defence of undoubted rights."²⁵

Within days of Smith's sermon, the grand jury in Charles Town met to discuss another sermon, one given by an Englishman who had recently crossed the Atlantic on the *Mermaid,* arriving on December 28, 1774, just two weeks before the first meeting of the Provincial Congress. He was David Margrett, a man of African descent who had been sent to preach the gospel to Africans in America and who brought with him ideas about the relation between slavery and liberty, and the lessons of God's relationship with the Jews, that differed markedly from those heard by Laurens and his fellow representatives in St. Philip's.[26]

The roots of Margrett's mission went back more than three decades, to the first appearance in America of George Whitefield, the evangelical preacher from England. Whitefield's message had had a profound effect on two South Carolina brothers, Hugh and Jonathan Bryan, owners of large plantations near Port Royal, south of Charles Town. Taking to heart Whitefield's criticisms of slave owners, the Bryan brothers had sponsored preaching to their own slaves and to those belonging to their neighbors. Their local Anglican pastor complained that, while slaves were being converted in great numbers, they were being "taught rather Enthusiasm, than religion," that they claimed "to see visions, and receive Revelations from heaven and to be converted by an Instantaneous Impulse of the Spirit." Hugh Bryan himself wrote a long letter in 1740 to the *South-Carolina Gazette,* calling "Insurrections of our Slaves," as well as disease, drought, and a recent devastating fire in Charles Town, "God's just Judgements . . . upon us."[27]

Examining some of Hugh Bryan's journals in February 1741, a committee of the Commons House of Assembly found "several Passages that deserve the Notice of the civil Magistrate and which, being published amongst the People, may prove of the most dangerous Consequence to the Peace and Safety of this Province." The committee was unwilling to put these passages in print, but the following month, the grand jury in Charles Town charged Bryan with writing "sundry enthusiastick Prophecies of the Destruction of *Charles-Town,* and Deliverance of the Negroes from their Servitude: And that by the Influence of said *Hugh Bryan,* great Bodies of Negroes have assembled together, on Pretence of religious Worship, contrary to Law, and destructive to the Peace and Safety of the Inhabitants of this Province." In a letter to her father, nineteen-year-old Eliza Lucas spelled out the contents of the journal in more detail: Bryan had predicted that "African hosts" would destroy most of South Carolina "by fire and sword." (She wrote also about Bryan's account of his encounter with an "Angel of Light" who had told him to cut a rod from a tree and use it to part the waters of a river; his attempt to follow these instructions ended badly when his brother had to pull him from the river, where he was "splashing and splutering . . . up to the Chinn.") Sober-minded Anglicans might dismiss the prophecies, but as Lucas wrote, they "dreaded the consiquence of such a thing being put in to the head of the slaves and the advantage they might take of us." Indeed, stories soon circulated that Hugh

Bryan's prophecies were part of "SECRET DESIGNS contrary to the Peace and Tranquility of the Government," and that he had even "furnished spare Arms for such Design." The grand jury in Charles Town called for punishment for planters whose religious enthusiasm seemed likely to turn slaves to visions of liberation.[28]

Whatever their religious convictions, neither Whitefield nor the Bryans meant to attack slavery itself. Whitefield would later learn to appreciate the advantages of owning slaves when the Bryans made him the gift of a South Carolina slave plantation to support an orphanage he had founded in Bethesda, Georgia. He rationalized that the ancient Hebrews had owned slaves and that Africans brought to America as slaves would actually benefit, since they could now be converted to Christianity. Hugh Bryan, for his part, apologized for his excesses and soon satisfied himself with working to convert his own slaves, not to free them.[29]

Two decades after Whitefield's first visits to South Carolina, Governor William Henry Lyttleton was informed that a free black man named Philip Johns was spreading a dangerous religious message in Prince William Parish, not far from the Bryans' properties. Johns, Lyttleton later concluded, had been inspired by the behavior of the Reverend Richard Clarke, rector of St. Philip's Church in Charles Town. Clarke, "of much learning but of an overheated imagination," had convinced himself by close study of the Bible that the end of time was near. He predicted that "Some great Calamity" would befall South Carolina in September 1759. In early 1759 Clarke let his beard grow and began to walk the streets of Charles Town, "crying, Repent, Repent, for the Kingdom of Heaven is at hand." Then, he precipitously resigned his office and departed for England. Almost immediately afterward, Philip Johns was heard preaching to slaves in Prince William Parish that "he had seen a Vision, in which it was reveal'd to him, that in the month of September the White People shou'd be all under ground, that the Sword shou'd go through the Land, & it shoud shine with their blood, that there shou'd be no more White King's Governors or great men but the Negro's shoud live happily & have Laws of their own."[30]

Magistrates in Prince William examined Johns and sentenced him to a whipping and branding, but he persisted with his prophecies. In June 1759, according to a slave named Prince (formerly owned by Johns himself), Johns claimed that "God Almighty" had given him work to do, as shown in a "written paper," and that, when the corn was laid by, the Indians would come and assist the blacks in "killing all the Buckraas." Pursuing the case, a white deputy in the parish heard that another free black man, John Pendarvis, "reputed to be a person of credit and property," had purchased guns and ammunition for this planned insurrection. The Governor's Council, investigating further, heard testimony that the plot involved seizure of arms from a country store, followed by a march on Charles Town. Johns had "communicated his Design to the most sensible Fellows throughout the Province, and even in Charles-Town, and recommended to them to do the same." Johns was sent back to Prince William, put on trial again, and, this time, executed, in August 1759. This reminder of the latent potential of the Christian message to inspire slaves to rebellion was one reason most slave owners felt little enthusiasm for converting their slaves.[31]

Although there is considerable evidence for the spread of Christian ideas among slaves, few South Carolina slaves joined the state Church of England; the most careful study estimates that only 3 to 5 percent of the colony' slaves in the 1770s were members of Anglican congregations. It was to address this deficiency that David Margrett had been sent to the colonies, his mission one fruit of the final act of George Whitefield's own life. Whitefield had continued to travel back and forth between Britain and North America; he was in Massachusetts when he died in 1770. In his will, he left all the property (including slaves) of the orphanage at Bethesda, Georgia, to Selina Hastings, the Countess of Huntingdon. The countess, born in 1708, accepted Methodism in 1739 and, after being widowed in 1746, devoted the rest of her life, and much of her considerable fortune, to efforts to evangelize unchurched Britons and those who lived in "the back settlements and among the Heathen Nations." She built chapels, supported ministers, and opened a seminary of her own, Trevecca, to train young men for the ministry; Whitefield preached the sermon at Trevecca's opening. After Whitefield's bequest, she dispatched the Reverend William Piercy and several Trevecca students to take charge of the orphanage and preach the Gospel to Indians, Africans, and poor whites.[32]

One of the countess's protégés was the Afro-Englishman David Margrett. Margrett's origins are unknown, although he claimed to have escaped from slavery. His name does not appear on a surviving list of Trevecca's students, but there is no doubt that the countess was supporting his evangelical efforts in England, since a letter from "your Ladyships unworthy servant, David Margrett" to "My very dearest ever hon'd Lady" survives in her papers. With uncertain spelling but in a neat hand, Margrett wrote that he was "ashamed that I should trouble your ladyship because I am but a Poore unworth cretor." He had been "Exceedingly tempted by the devil who tells me . . . I am yet in my Sins and tempts me to Leave the Preaching and Prayings." When he preached, however, "many of my hearers were afected Exceedingly," and "it rejoiceth my heart to see sinners flock Like doves to the window and many of my own Complection." To the countess and to the Reverend Piercy, Margrett seemed ideally suited to work in America, where, Piercy wrote, "the Lord is carrying on a most blessed work among the poor Africans." In Charles Town, this blessed work was being much advanced by "Faithful" Thomas, a slave "called to the ministry" by the preaching of his owner, the Reverend John Edwards. Piercy encouraged the countess to send over "the African Student" to "teach & instruct the poor Negroes"—that, is the slaves—at the Bethesda orphanage. He assured her that thousands of "those poor dark & benighted Savages" were ready to be instructed.[33]

The countess, convinced, sent Margrett off to London merchants to be properly outfitted with linen shirts and suits, handkerchiefs, gloves and hats, sheets and pillowcases. In late 1774, along with David Cossom and other Huntingdon students, Margrett sailed on the *Mermaid* to Charles Town. Immediately after they arrived, the countess's representatives in Charles Town arranged for Margrett to preach to slaves at the home of Patrick Hinds, a friend to the cause. Hinds was not rich, but like other white Carolinians, he depended on slavery. He specialized in "Negro shoes," and he owned slaves himself. He had bought a slave—probably his first—in 1757 from Henry Laurens. Being a "poor Industrious shoemaker," he had purchased, cheaply, a "Negro . . . full of Sores" in hopes of curing him "by an aplication of Proper Remedys." He soon discovered, though, that this African arrival was "an Idiot." Hinds asked the captain of the slave ship to take the slave back but was refused, leaving him with a "boy" who was "not worth a Groat." Laurens wrote to the Lancaster merchants who had financed the voyage, asking them to consider an abatement of the price, given that Hinds was "very much to be pittied" for having purchased "such a Loathsome Carcass."[34]

By 1775, Hinds was prospering enough to own a large lot on the edge of the city, perhaps including a tanning operation. When Hinds allowed David Margrett to preach in this space, which could accommodate many slaves, he no doubt expected Margrett to model his behavior on that of the Reverend Edwards's "Humble, Faithful & Sincere" slave, Thomas, who "perseveres in the way of the Lord." Thomas, Edwards, and David Cossom all cautioned Margrett about South Carolinians' feelings and fears about their slaves and urged him "not to speak anything respecting their outward condition." Margrett, however, clearly shocked by his observations in Charles Town, delivered a message dealing decidedly with this world, not the next. As reported by one man, Margrett preached to his audience of slaves that "the Jews of old, treated the Gentiles as Dogs & I am informed the People of this Country use those of my Complection as such." It was not so in England, he assured them—perhaps thinking of the decision of Lord Mansfield in the case of James Somerset: "Thank God! I am come from a better Country than this." He reminded his hearers that "the Children of Israel were delivered out of the hands of Pharo & he & all his Host were drowned in the Red Sea and God will deliver his own People from Slavery."[35]

This was not at all what the countess, or Piercy, or John Edwards, or Patrick Hinds had in mind. "They do say," Edwards explained, that "such expressions made use of by a Person of his Colour in a Conventicle of Negroes woul'd hang him under our Negro Law." Nor was the message welcomed by whites in Charles Town, just now meeting to protect their own liberties from Parliamentary oppression. Word quickly spread across town, and Cossom and his wife, Elizabeth, hustled Margrett to a boat bound for Georgia. Edwards wrote to Piercy "to Caution [Margrett] in [the] future" and to "beg you will not suffer him to return here again." The next month, Charles Town's Grand Jury cited Patrick Hinds "for entertaining and admitting Negro Preachers in his House and on his Grounds, where they deliver Doctrines to large Numbers of Negroes, dangerous to and subversive of the Peace, Safety and Tranquility of this Province."[36]

✦

In the spring of 1775, a decade of disputes and ideological conflict seemed to be approaching a climax. Public pronouncements from England, not only from leaders in Parliament, but also from King George III, gave no hint of compromise on the fundamental issues, and the Provincial Congress's authorization of a "Secret Committee" charged with preparing to defend the public safety was a thinly disguised acknowledgment that the next stage of the dispute might be armed conflict. Henry Laurens, always the reluctant revolutionary, wrote to his son that "chances are many against my Seeing a happy period" ahead. Still, Laurens hoped that "those Seeming Threats from the Ministry, will rather animate us, wisely to resist against & counteract the impending blow, by Submitting, if it must be so, to temporary inconveniences. & even to poverty & distresses in preference to Slavery."[37]

What Laurens, along with his fellow white South Carolinians, failed to see was how the conflicts of the past decade had their sometimes secretive shadows in the rising hope among those who were actually, not metaphorically, enslaved. After white South Carolinians had rallied in the streets against the hated Stamp Act in 1765, blacks had turned out in the same streets not long after, "crying out *'Liberty.'*" When Carolinians defended their resistance with an appeal to the rights of nature, allies of slaves had insisted that Africans, too, "are by nature equally free and independent, equally susceptible of pain and pleasure, equally averse from bondage and misery, as Europeans themselves." When whites prayed to the God of the Israelites to support them in their "Defence of undoubted rights," blacks prayed to the same God to "deliver his own People from Slavery," as he had delivered the Jews. Now, as South Carolina patriots prepared for armed conflict, might their own slaves be doing the same?

PART II

Liberty's Trials

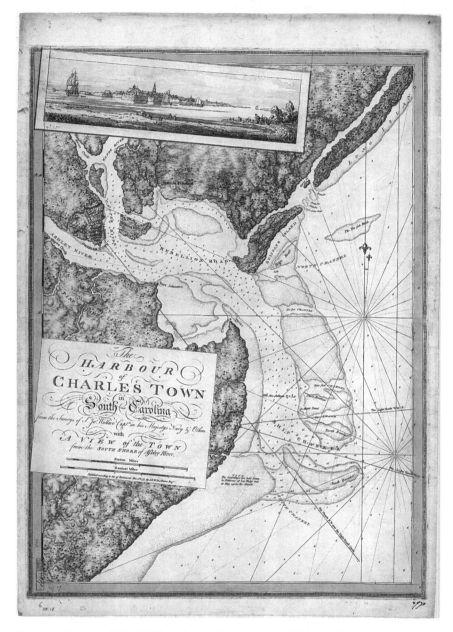

Figure 14. A map of Charles Town harbor from *American Neptune,* the great nautical atlas compiled for the Royal Navy by Joseph Des Barres. This is from the 1777 edition. The channel for large ships is marked at the lower center-right. (HARVARD MAP COLLECTION)

CHAPTER FOUR

"A plan, for instigating the slaves to insurrection"

"The Dread of Instigated Insurrections at Home"

O N MAY 3, 1775, well-wishers gathered on a Charles Town wharf to see off Christopher Gadsden, Henry Middleton, Thomas Lynch, and the Rutledge brothers, Edward and John, on the *Lloyd*, the Philadelphia packet, heading for the opening of the Second Continental Congress. (Lynch and Edward Rutledge would still be in Philadelphia in July 1776 to sign the Declaration of Independence.) In the two months since the Provincial Congress had appointed them, tensions had escalated, not only between the patriots and the royal government, but also within the patriot ranks. In March, the General Committee of Charles Town divided sharply on the question of whether to allow Robert Smythe, a local merchant, to unload furniture and horses he had imported from England for his own use. A small turnout of the General Committee agreed that this would not violate the embargo, but crowds of men, most of them artisans, turned out in the streets to prevent what they saw as a breach of nonimportation, threatening to slay the horses if they were landed. In a tumultuous meeting with hundreds in attendance, Christopher Gadsden urged the General Committee to reverse its decision, which it did by a single vote. Edward Rutledge and Thomas Lynch, on the opposite side of that argument from Gadsden, now, at least, were united with him in their determination to support American rights in Philadelphia. None of them yet knew that Americans in Lexington and Concord, Massachusetts, had, on April 19, already fallen in battles against British troops that had marched from Boston to seize stores of powder.[1]

That same day, waiting to enter the harbor as the delegation boarded the *Lloyd* was the ship *London,* just arrived from its namesake city. On board was a letter that would alarm South Carolina's leaders perhaps even more than the news—when it finally arrived—of Lexington and Concord. The letter was addressed to Henry Laurens from his friend Arthur Lee, who had been living in London for seven years and from whose pen had poured out pamphlets, letters, petitions, and essays defending American rights and denouncing the perfidious actions of Britain's corrupt politicians. Just a year before, Laurens, himself in London, had paid Lee to publish a defense of South Carolina's Commons House of Assembly in its disputes with British authorities. Now, Lee claimed to know that "a plan was laid before the Administration [of Lord North], for instigating the slaves to insurrection."[2]

Could it be true? Could even the British authorities stoop this low, actually urge America's slaves to rebel just to restore their own eroding power? The letter itself has been lost, but it no doubt echoed that of Arthur Lee's brother William, who, on March 6, had written to Robert Carter Nicholas in Virginia with a claim of proof of just such a plan: "unquestionable authority" had informed him that Virginia's governor, Lord Dunmore, had written to Lord Dartmouth, head of the Board of Trade, "that the negroes have a notion the king intends to make them all free, and that the Associations, Congress and Conventions [of the Americans] are all contrivances of their masters to prevent the king's good intentions towards them and keep them still slaves; that from this circumstance, it is probable they will rise," distracting their masters "from opposing the ministerial measures." Such a notion was certainly plausible as a belief of slaves; stories circulate among the poor and oppressed in many places and times of a "good king" whose intentions are being thwarted by evil advisers. South Carolinians might also have heard that Lord Dunmore had told local leaders in Williamsburg, Virginia, in April that if the colonists resisted his authority with arms, he might be "forced . . . to arm all my own Negroes and receive all others that will come to me whom I shall declare free." (It was a policy he would put into practice the next fall.)[3]

In fact, Dunmore had written nothing like this to Dartmouth, and Arthur and William Lee were merely speculating about the plans of Lord North's ministry. But, for Charles Town's patriot leaders, slaveholders to a man, it rang true, because in Charles Town, "it was already known" that the slaves "entertained ideas, that the present contest was for obliging us to give them their liberty." They recalled, especially, the visit to Charles Town, just four months earlier, of the free black preacher David Margrett, who had raised an uproar by comparing South Carolina's slaves to the Jews held in bondage in Egypt. Since then Margrett had been living and preaching to slaves at an orphanage in Bethesda, Georgia, owned by the Countess of Huntingdon, the English supporter of evangelical ministries.[4]

By coincidence, the Reverend William Piercy, the supervisor of the orphanage, was in Charles Town in the first week of May 1775 (he was on the way to Philadelphia). At first, as he wrote to his sponsor the countess, he had been delighted to see that "the work of the Lord still goes on gloriously in this Town among the poor Slaves, thanks to the work of Mr. Edwards's slave Thomas," whose "great piety as well as great gifts the Lord has given him not only command attention from those of his own color, but also makes him very useful." But soon Piercy learned that events in Charles Town were threatening David Margrett once again. Since going to Georgia, Piercy wrote, Margrett had been "led again by the Devil into the same snare" of preaching about this world, not the next. According to Piercy, Margrett's "pride seems so great, that he can't bear to think of any of his own colour being slaves, tho' he has confessed that he was only a run-away slave himself." Once more, he "not only severely reflected against the Laws of the Province respecting Slaves but even against the Thing itself: he also compared their State to that of the Israelites during their Egyptian Bondage & summed up the whole with this Remark that he did not doubt but that the Lord wou'd deliver his People (meaning the Slaves) from their Taskmasters as he did the Jews."[5]

By May 1775, Margrett apparently had decided that he, himself, might well be the new Moses who would lead his enslaved brothers and sisters to freedom. "Nothing could have happened of a more distressing nature, we are so surrounded with blacks, or have given me greater pain," wrote Piercy, "as my soul so much longed for the instruction & salvation of your Slaves. I don't indeed know what Judgment to form either of his words or conduct since he has been at Bethesda, but the whole has been the most alarming & brought me into the greatest reproach as well as Censure from the Governor [of Georgia] & all the white people. We have been under a continual apprehension of an Insurrection among the Slaves from his conduct & discourses to the negroes. And this upon such strong grounds as have almost distressed me to death both day & night."[6]

Charles Town's whites may have been unaware of what Margrett was doing in Georgia, but when Arthur Lee's "secret letter" to Henry Laurens arrived on May 4, Margrett's preaching in Charles Town back in January immediately came to mind. Here, most certainly, was an emissary from Britain, who just months before had been in town, telling the slaves that God would soon free them. On May 7, "A Gentleman" came to inform Piercy "that the People are determined to send a party of men to Georgia & take David & should they lay hold of Him he will certainly be hanged for what he has delivered, as all the laws are against Slaves. The people are continually apprehensive of an Insurrection among the Slaves and insist upon it that he was the first cause. In all their town meetings this affair has been upon the Carpet & they seem more & more terrified with the consequences." Piercy hurriedly sent word back to Georgia, and before a party of South Carolinians could come for him, Margrett was on his way back to England, and permanent safety, on the ship *Georgia Planter.*[7]

On May 8, the same day that Piercy finished his letter, the brigantine *Industry* arrived in Charles Town from Salem, Massachusetts, with copies of the first newspaper reports of the battles between British troops and American militia at Lexington and Concord. The details seemed to confirm their fears that the British would stop at nothing to crush American resistance. The report, copied in the *South-Carolina and American General Gazette,* compared the redcoats' "cruelty" to "what our venerable ancestors received from the vilest savages of the wilderness." They had burned and pillaged as they went, and "it appeared to be their design to burn and destroy all before them"; worse was "the savage barbarity exercised upon the bodies of our unfortunate brethren who fell. . . . Not content with shooting down the unarmed, aged and infirm, they disregarded the cries of the wounded, killing them without mercy, and mangling their bodies in the most shocking manner." If the British were capable of such atrocities, why would they blanch at a slave insurrection that advanced their wicked purposes?[8]

The elements conspired with this military and political news to increase the gloomy outlook, when, after a mild winter, a week of violent spring storms swept in from the ocean, drowning the low inland swampland and ruining the new rice crop. Patriot leaders could not wait for the weather to improve before they took action. The Charles Town General Committee, now headed by President Henry Laurens, met on May 5 and appointed a "Special Committee" of eleven, charged to plan, as they deemed necessary, "for the security of the good people of this Colony." Three days later, the day they heard of Lexington and Concord, they met again and called for the Provincial Congress to come back into session on June 1. In the mean time the new Special Committee proposed several measures, including the creation of a "South Carolina Association" that would include every citizen willing to sign the following statement:

The actual Commencement of Hostilities against this Continent—the Threats of arbitrary Impositions from Abroad—and the Dread of Instigated Insurrections at Home—are Causes sufficient to drive an oppressed People to the Use of Arms: We, therefore, the Subscribers, Inhabitants of this unhappy Colony, holding ourselves bound by that most sacred of all Obligations, the Duty of good Citizens toward an injured Country, and thoroughly convinced that under our present distressed Circumstances, We shall be justified before God and Man, in resisting Force by Force; do unite Ourselves, under every Tie of Religion and of Honour, and associate as a Band in her Defence against every Foe. And we do solemnly promise, that whenever her Continental or Provincial Councils shall decree it necessary, We will go forth, and be ready to sacrifice our Lives and Fortunes, in attempting to secure her FREEDOM and SAFETY.

And so white Carolinians pledged their resistance, to enslavement by the British, and to their slaves' attempts to secure freedom of their own.[9]

"Hostile attempts that may be made by our domesticks"

Alarms of a British-sponsored slave revolt were spreading up and down the coast and into the backcountry. In North Carolina, people heard that King George "was ordering the tories to murder the whigs, and promising every Negro that would murder his Master and family that he should have his Master's plantation." Panicked whites stepped up patrols and locked up slaves since "an insurrection was hourly expected." Georgia's unhappy governor informed London of "a report which has been propagated that [the] administration have it in view to send over troops to Carolina and at the same time to attempt to liberate the slaves and encourage them to attack their masters." However "absurd and improbable," the report had "nevertheless had an exceeding bad effect." In the backcountry, rumors spread that John Stuart, the Indian commissioner, a supporter of the British administration, was encouraging Catawba and Cherokee Indians to attack, and "at the same time it was given out that the Negroes were immediately to be set free by government and that arms were to be given them to fall upon their masters." Stuart had to flee to St. Augustine to escape inflamed patriots. The colonists were also certain that the story of a plot would spread quickly among the slaves themselves. Two of Georgia's delegates to the Continental Congress explained to John Adams, in a "melancholly Account of the State of Georgia and S. Carolina," that "the Negroes have a wonderfull Art of communicating Intelligence

among themselves. It will run severall hundreds of Miles in a week or Fort-
night." They told Adams that if the British could land one thousand regular
troops, they could readily recruit twenty thousand slaves to their banner.[10]

In Charles Town, white fears escalated as new "facts" appeared, pointing toward conspiracy to incite rebellion. On May 29, the *South-Carolina Gazette*
printed a letter supposedly sent from England to a resident in New York back in
February. The letter asserted that King George was determined to suppress resistance, that he had sent down to the Royal Navy base at Sheerness "seventy-
eight thousand guns, and bayonets, to be sent to America, to put into the hands
of N*****s [Negroes], the Roman Catholics, the Indians and Canadians; and all
the wicked means on earth used to subdue the Colonies." In the same issue,
"Caroliniensis" wrote in, alarmed that the General Committee had refused to
accept immediately some of the proposals of the Special Committee, instead
waiting for the meeting of the Provincial Congress. The writer warned his fellow
colonists that "abject Submission, or a noble Resistance are the only Alterna-
tives. . . . Destruction, or what is worse, the Slavery of all, the Virtue of your
Women, the Blood of your guiltless Children, may be the Price of a few Days
Delay." Worse still, to "close the black Scene—there remains a Sentence which I
cannot, I dare not mention"—the kind of warning meant to suggest mass rape of
white women by slaves. These sensational reports inspired more alarms concerning the pending arrival of the new governor, Lord William Campbell.
Rumors circulated that Campbell was bringing with him on HMS *Scorpion*
fourteen thousand stand of arms to distribute to slaves and Indians.[11]

Whites did not wait for the Provincial Congress to meet before mobilizing
in defense. The news of the "most horrid Barbarities" committed by British
troops near Boston had "caused the boiling of much blood." Their greatest
fear, as merchant Josiah Smith, Jr., wrote to a friend, was "hostile attempts that
may be made by our domesticks, who of late have been taught, (by some
designing Wretches) to believe they will be all sett free on the arrival of our
New Governer, indeed secret Intelligences by the last Ship from London, hath
been convey'd to a Gentleman here, that such an Act of Grace was in con-
timplation among the Cabinet Oppressors." The militia drilled every day and
patrolled the streets every night. Henry Laurens called in the slaves belonging
to his brother James, who was then in London, and "admonished them to
behave with great circumspection in this dangerous times, set before them the
great risque of exposing themselves to the treachery of pretended friends &
false witnesses if they associated with any Negroes out of your family or mine."
The Special Committee looked for evidence of the insurrection plot. Preacher

David Margrett had escaped the noose, but the committee members went about their work, prowling along the bye-lanes and alleys and in the narrow passageways between the stores and warehouses on the wharves, looking for allies, black or white, of their British oppressors.[12]

On Thursday, June 1, 1775, the members of the South Carolina Provincial Congress gathered to meet the imminent (as they thought) twin threats of British invasion and slave insurrection. In a sign of their sense of urgency, members resolved to meet as early as 7:30 a.m. each day—not the leisurely hour of 10:00 a.m., as in the old Commons House of Assembly. As their president, they replaced Charles Pinckney with Henry Laurens. Two weeks later, when the Provincial Congress established a thirteen-member Council of Safety, with executive powers and control over military affairs, Laurens was also selected president of the new council. In this way, in that summer of 1775, Laurens became the most important patriot leader in South Carolina, simultaneously president of the Provincial Congress, the Charles Town General Committee, and the Council of Safety.[13]

The first important item to consider was the call for an "Association" of South Carolinians, as drafted by the Charles Town General Committee three weeks before. After two days of sharp debate, the Provincial Congress agreed to the wording. For the most part, the new Association was an elaboration of the General Committee's version, declaring that, because of "commencement of hostilities" near Boston, the "arbitrary impositions from a wicked and despotic ministry," and "the dread of instigated insurrections," South Carolinians must "UNITE . . . under every tie of religion and of honour, and associate, as a band in her defence against every foe." The central dispute was over the final sentence declaring that any persons (that is, white men) who refused to sign would be held "inimical to the liberty of the colonies." Copies were to be printed and circulated throughout the colony, with every man required to subscribe his name. The carpenter Daniel Cannon, leader among the Sons of Liberty, was appointed to the committee charged with gathering signatures in Charles Town. The Association would be, not just a call to defend liberty, but a way to brand as an enemy any who refused to support the "patriots" (as they called themselves) now in control of the city.[14]

The second order of business was to prepare the colony's defenses against invasion and insurrection. The Provincial Congress appointed thirteen members to a committee "to consider of ways and means for putting the colony in a posture of defense" and, on the following afternoon (June 4), appointed a committee of five, with Thomas Bee as chair and Daniel Cannon as a mem-

ber, "to make enquiries on the subject" of "insurrections of slaves." (Back in
1739, when Thomas Bee was just an infant, his father had led the white militia
that had defeated the Stono rebels.) Over the next four days the congress
banned rice exports (providing for the colony to purchase rice from planters
and store it in public magazines) and authorized the raising of two regiments
of infantry and a third of mounted rangers. The congress organized this
armed force, deciding on bonuses, pay scales, and allowances for uniforms
and rations and selecting, by ballot, officers of the three regiments, right down
to the twenty-nine lieutenants. The congress rejected more radical proposals
to fit out a merchant ship as a man-of-war, to seize HMS *Tamar*, a Royal
Navy ship then in Charles Town harbor, or, most drastically, to sink in the
shipping channel obstructions that would block the harbor to oceangoing
ships. They did, however, agree on the more limited measure of forbidding
pilots to bring any man-of-war or troop transport over the bar.[15]

Henry Laurens was among those who opposed the most radical measures; he argued that to declare all nonsigners of the Association "inimical to
liberty" would be a calumny against those who, despite their love of liberty,
considered the time not yet right for a threat to take up arms. He thought the
blocking of the harbor might destroy the city's commerce for a full generation, and he was convinced that paying excessive salaries to the officers and
men of the new regiments might bankrupt the colony. He wrote to his son,
John, that they might as well tell the prime minister, Lord North, "You need
not My Lord be at expence or trouble to humble the Carolinians they are
effectually ruining their own country."[16]

On June 8, one week after the congress convened, Charles Town's people
witnessed the consequences of dissent from the new regime. According to
Michael Hubart, he had been visiting a friend on King Street on June 2, just
as the Provincial Congress was debating the wording of the Association,
when James Dealey burst in with the "good news" that arms were on the way
"to be distributed amongst the Negroes, Roman Catholics, and Indians." (No
doubt Dealey had read, or at least heard about, the letter in the *South-
Carolina Gazette* on May 29, alleging that the king was sending thousands of
arms to America for just that purpose.) When Hubart objected to the idea
that "Roman Catholics and Savages should be permitted to join and massacre
Christians," Dealey thumped his chest and swore that he was a Roman
Catholic; "he had arms, and would get arms, and use them as he pleased."
Dealey, accompanied by a second man, Laughlin Martin, then followed
Hubart to his home, threatened to "cut off his head," and compelled him to

apologize. Martin called for drink and toasted "Damnation to the [General] Committee, and their proceedings." Dealey and Martin had thus openly defied patriot authority and "threatned vengeance against the whole Country by exciting an Insurrection." (It surely didn't help that they were Catholics.) Hubart sent his account of this encounter to the Committee of Correspondence, which passed it to the "Secret Committee," appointed back in February. William Henry Drayton, its chairman, endorsed Hubart's report with the words "SECRET, tar and feather him."[17]

Rather than take direct responsibility for meting out this punishment, the Secret Committee called on "some of the lower people" to do so for them. A crowd set up a "judge,"called witnesses, and sentenced Dealey and Martin to the ritual humiliation only recently invented by Americans further north as punishment for dissent—the "Suit of Cloathing, of the true American Manufacture," as one Charles Town editor called it. The two men were stripped, coated with tar, doused with feathers, and drawn through the city's main streets in a cart. The crowd then put them aboard a ship bound for England, although Martin, a wharf manager "of Some Credit in Town," was allowed to return to shore after promising an abject public apology. The apology duly appeared in the *South-Carolina Gazette: And Country Journal*. In it, Martin admitted to "having spoken unjustly, and having behaved myself in a very criminal Manner, touching the Association lately entered into by the good People of this Colony." He confessed his sorrow "for such shameful Conduct, well deserving exemplary Punishment." As one loyalist wrote sarcastically to London authorities, "this very *well-timed* piece of Justice was attended with the happiest effects, no one since daring even to think of refusing to swallow any thing that may be offered." Some prominent men had been reluctant to sign on to the Association; soon the only local holdouts were "almost to a Man Kings Officers whose conduct therefore drew no Censure."[18]

As the Provincial Congress deliberated and the Charles Town crowd suppressed open dissent, Thomas Bee's committee undertook investigation of the feared slave insurrection, a far more dangerous prospect, in whites' eyes, than dissent by a few white malcontents. At 6:00 p.m. on Wednesday, June 14, Bee presented the committee's report. Although the text has not survived, its contents can be gleaned from a June 18 letter of Henry Laurens to his son. "Trials of Several Negroes Suspected & charged of plotting an Insurrection have been conducted," he wrote. "Two or three White people" had been imprisoned "upon Strong Negro Evidence." "Among the most Criminal," Laurens added, was "Jerry the pilot."[19]

"THOMAS JEREMIAH (a Free Negro)"

"Jerry the pilot" was Thomas Jeremiah, a free black man who was, as much as
Henry Laurens himself, a product of the opportunities presented by Charles
Town's place in the Atlantic system of trade. On the rivers and harbor that
made the city's existence possible, black Carolinians had more control of their
own lives than anywhere else, and Jeremiah had flourished in that world.
Some blacks sailed on the big oceangoing ships and brigs, many more on the
boats in the local maritime and riverine traffic. Small schooners were popular
for coastal traffic because these two-masted vessels were easy to control with a
small crew, big enough to sail in open water, but still shallow enough in draft
to maneuver among the islands and bays along the coast. Henry Laurens, for
example, owned the *Baker*, crewed by four slaves, to sail the Cooper River to
his Mepkin Plantation, and the *Wambaw*, crewed by five slaves, to communicate with his Wambaw Plantation farther north. Black crews also guided the
canoes and pettiaugers (in South Carolina, the most commonly used corruption from the Spanish *piragua*, for the dugouts favored by Carib Indians) that
most planters used to bring rice down river and take back provisions and
manufactured goods. The canoes were not the slim boats familiar to us today
by that name but substantial craft, usually carved of cypress logs, sometimes
made by combining two logs to make a larger boat that might be more than
twenty feet long. Perriaugurs were bigger still, typically made of three logs
and up to forty feet long. Most were fashioned by skilled plantation slaves
after completion of daily agricultural tasks. Blacks also dominated the fishing
trade—both buying and selling fish in Charles Town's streets and markets.
When the commissioners of markets set up a new Fish Market in 1770, they
noted that "the Business of Fishing is principally carried on by Negroes,
Mulatoes, and Mestizoes." Concerned to prevent forestalling and "extor-
tion," the commissioners specified fines for anyone buying fish privately for
resale and for anyone who tried to "persuade People by Word, Letter, Message, or otherwise" from bringing fish to the market or to "persuade them to
enhance the price."[20]

　　Thomas Jeremiah by 1775 had risen to the top of this rough-and-tumble
world and, in the process, had risen about as high as it was possible for a black
man to do in colonial South Carolina. His life was remarkable in many ways.
He was a free man in South Carolina at a time when more than ninety-nine in
a hundred blacks were enslaved, and the law itself "always presumed that
every negro, Indian, mulatto and mustizo, is a slave, unless the contrary can be

made appear." How he came to be free is a question whose answer is lost among the missing documents from South Carolina's early history. He may have been born of a free mother, like his fellow black waterman Scipio Handley. He may have been freed by his owner as a special favor for good service. But if he was like most of the small number of free African-American men in Charles Town, he had bought himself from his master. A few slave owners were always ready to make that bargain, especially since they could get two or three times the value of a slave if the slave himself was the buyer. They just had to agree to allow their slaves to earn money on the side, so they could pay the price.[21]

As a young man, Jeremiah had learned to be a pilot. All the oceangoing traffic that carried out rice and indigo and brought back slaves and manufactured goods depended on the skill of the pilots who guided vessels over the bar through the harbor's narrow ship channel. As the era's standard guide to all things marine explained, "That part of navigation, which regards the piloting or conducting a ship along the sea-coast, can only be acquired by a thorough knowledge of that particular coast, after repeated voyages." Such long experience acquainted pilots with "the time and direction of the tide, knowledge of the reigning winds; of the roads and havens; of the different depths of the water." For nighttime crossings, the light at the top of St. Michael's and the lighthouse on James Island helped, but pilots also had to steer by "the various sorts of ground at the bottom; as shells of different sizes and colours, sand, gravel, clay, stones, ooze, or shingle." The importance of pilots was spelled out in the regulations of the Royal Navy, which charged captains "to treat them with good usage, and an equal respect with warrant-officers," and to make sure they had good hammocks conveniently located "near their duty, and apart from the common men." While the pilot was at work he must have "sole charge and command of the ship; or whatever concerns the navigation: and the captain is to take care that all the officers and crew obey his orders." Not surprisingly, piloting was closely regulated in South Carolina. So essential was it that, to make sure they used licensed pilots, ship captains were required to pay the fee—based on the draft of the ship—even if they did not use one.[22]

By the 1770s, Thomas Jeremiah had worked as a pilot for at least twenty years, until he knew every shoal, every tree, the site of every shipwreck, the places where the sand usually shifted after a big storm. It had been learning by doing. Back in 1755 he had run HMS *Jamaica* on to No Man's Land; Captain Hood was not too happy about that, and the *South-Carolina Gazette*, the local

Figure 15. Nicholas Pocock sketched this "Prospect of Charlestown" in 1767,
with Pocock's own *Lloyd* in the center, and a pilot's schooner on the left.
(NATIONAL MARITIME MUSEUM, GREENWICH, LONDON)

paper, had blamed it on Jeremiah's "carelessness." It was fortunate that Mr. Tucker, Jeremiah's employer and the actual holder of the pilot's license, got the ship off the shoal without damage after unloading its guns and provisions. The next year the paper reported that a merchant ship, the *Brothers Adventure*, "was lost upon our Bar, by the same Fellow (Jerry) who some Time ago ran the *Jamaica* Man of War ashore." But he persisted until, by 1775, he was recognized as "one of the best pilots in the harbor."[23]

Officially appointed pilots were always white men, but those who did the actual work were often black. Indeed, the use of blacks as pilots was so common that the law on pilotage specified that each official pilot should always keep at least one white man at the Sullivan's Island lookouts. The work of a pilot was sometimes dangerous and usually highly competitive; pilots raced across the bar to get to a ship first and claim the right to the fee. Pilot boats had to be fast but also seaworthy, in case of heavy weather. They also had to be easily managed by a single crew member—the apprentice or assistant who would sail out with the pilot, drop him off, then bring the pilot boat back in. For these reasons, pilots favored swift, small schooners, which could be easily managed by two men and tolerably well sailed by one (fig. 15). A pilot boat caught in a storm, though, might be driven far from the harbor, leaving the pilot and assistant to make do in bad weather in the scant shelter of an open "cock-pit" abaft.[24]

Jerry, as whites called him, might have earned his price with his pilot's skills, or he might have earned money by fishing in slack shipping seasons, or perhaps he had been rewarded with cash while earning a "well known" reputation "in extinguishing of Fires" in a city that more than once had seen conflagrations wipe out a major share of its buildings. By the late 1760s he had become a man of considerable property, able to afford to buy more than himself. In 1768 he built, or had built, a "WELL-BOAT, in order to supply the inhabitants of this town with LIVE FISH every day." (A well-boat was a large fishing craft fitted with bulkheads to form a "well" amidships that could be flooded with sea water through holes bored in the bottom, to keep fish alive and fresh in the age before refrigeration.) Jeremiah, perhaps, had been inspired in this entrepreneurial endeavor by the appearance of such a boat (called a "smack") from Philadelphia in 1767, where it sold live fish at Wragg's wharf (fig. 16). The well-boat required a crew, and to maximize profits from this enterprise, Jeremiah did what other Carolinians did: he invested in slaves, purchasing enough for a crew.[25]

Jeremiah, in the 1770s, was a mature man, a skilled pilot, a fisherman, a merchant, and a slave owner, well known and at least somewhat respected on the Charles Town waterfront. That respect may be what saved him from considerable pain and humiliation in 1771, when he got into a scrape with a white ship captain, Thomas Langen, in Berkeley County, up the Cooper River. Convicted of assault, "the said Thomas Jerry" was "Sentenced to lie in the stocks One hour & receive ten Lashes between the hours of Eight & Ten." Jeremiah asked for pardon from Lieutenant Governor Bull, and Bull did indeed "Pardon Remit and Release, the said Thomas Jerry, or by whatever other name he is called."[26]

The next year Jeremiah found an anchor that had been lost in the harbor and used his slave crew to bring it up. Then he advertised in the *Gazette:* "TAKEN UP . . . between *Hard* and *Gadsden's* wharf, by THOMAS JEREMIAH (a Free Negro) an ANCHOR of about Five Hundred Weight. . . . The Owner may have it again, by applying to him, paying Salvage, and the Expence of this Advertisement" (fig. 17). Raising an anchor weighing five hundred pounds was no simple task. The attached rope had rotted off, so it had been in the water for some time—perhaps it had been noticed by others who lacked the inspiration or ability to raise it to the surface. If no one claimed the anchor—worth about

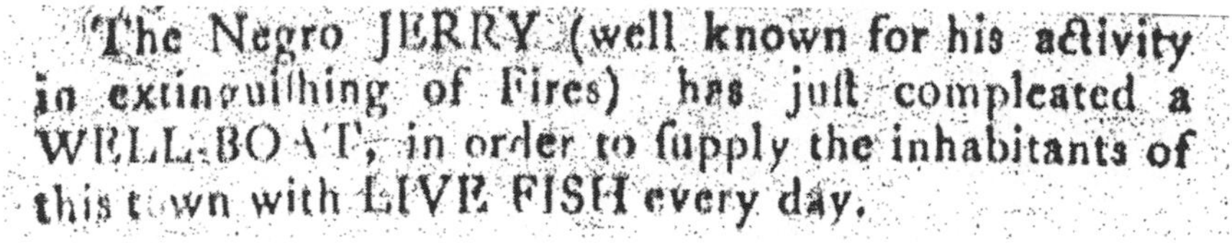

> The Negro JERRY (well known for his activity
> in extinguilhing of Fires) has just compleated a
> WELL-BOAT, in order to fupply the inhabitants of
> this town with LIVE FISH every day.

Figure 16. The *South-Carolina Gazette* informed readers about Thomas Jeremiah's new
fishing boat on June 20, 1768.

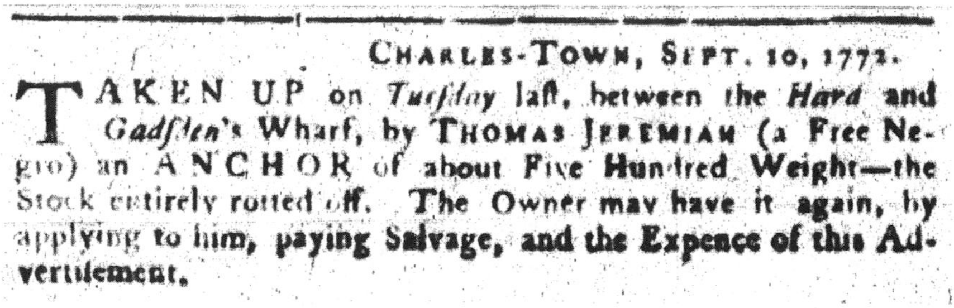

> CHARLES-TOWN, SEPT. 10, 1772.
>
> TAKEN UP on Tuesday laft, between the Hard and
> Gadfden's Wharf, by THOMAS JEREMIAH (a Free Ne-
> gro) an ANCHOR of about Five Hundred Weight—the
> Stock entirely rotted off. The Owner may have it again, by
> applying to him, paying Salvage, and the Expence of this Ad-
> vertifement.

Figure 17. Thomas Jeremiah placed this advertisement for a recovered anchor in the
South-Carolina Gazette on September 10, 1772.

£9 sterling, or almost one-third the value of an adult slave arriving from
Africa—Jeremiah could sell it off. But the name on the advertisement is
revealing in itself. In the only document we have that definitely came from his
own hand, he was not "Jerry," the diminutive sort of name typically used for
slaves, one of the dozens of ways in which whites, in every personal encounter,
could subtly confine Africans to the status of inferiors. He was, instead,
"THOMAS JEREMIAH (a Free Negro)," businessman and jack-of-all-trades on
the water, ready to deal with the owner of this lost anchor. He was obviously a
man of ambition and determination, "in a very thriving situation," and in one
estimate, "universally acknowledged to be remarkably sensible and sagacious."
He was also a man of pride, who owned slaves to work his boats and to serve
him and his wife at home. His rise in South Carolina showed that the colony
could be, even for a black man, "pre-eminently a good poor man's country."
Observers in Charles Town estimated his wealth at £600 to £1,000 sterling
(the latter equal to about $200,000 in 2009). Some black South Carolinians
may have inherited more wealth, in the form of plantations and slaves, from
their white fathers, but as measured by what he had earned in the sweat of his
brow, Thomas Jeremiah was probably, in 1775, the richest man of African
descent in British North America.[27]

"The War was come to help the poor Negroes"

How did Thomas Jeremiah come to be implicated in a slave insurrection? Two slaves had offered the most damning testimony. On June 16, Jemmy, a slave owned by a Mr. Peter Croft, said that ten weeks earlier he had been on Prioleau's Wharf—the site of the Fish Market—with "one Thomas Jeremiah, a Free Negro," who had told him "He had something to give Dewar a run away Slave belonging to Mr Tweed; and wished to see Him, and asked Jemmy to take a few Guns to the said Dewar, to be placed in Negroes hands to fight against the Inhabitants of this Province, and that He Jeremiah was to have the Chief Command of the said Negroes; that He Jeremiah said He believed He had Powder enough already, but that He wanted more Arms which He would try to get as many as He could." The second statement came from Sambo, who said "that about 2 or 3 months ago being at Simmons Wharf, Jerry says to Him Sambo do You hear any thing of the War that is coming." When Sambo answered no, Jeremiah replied, "yes there is a great War coming soon—Sambo replies what shall we poor Negroes do in the Schooner—Jerry says set the Schooner on fire, Jump on Shore, and Join the Soldiers—that the War was come to help the Poor Negroes."[28]

What should Thomas Bee's committee make of these testimonies? Two conversations on the waterfront, which was Jeremiah's turf; two accounts that did not exactly mesh, though they did echo the alarms, both long-standing and recent, of whites in Charles Town. That a "Free Negro" boatman like Jeremiah would have contacts with runaways was a commonplace fear and certainly plausible. Surely, he would have been aware of a looming "great War," as he watched Charles Town bustle to prepare for one. Sambo's reference to "the Schooner" suggests that he might have worked with Jeremiah as a pilot, perhaps as the second man in his pilot boat who dropped off Jeremiah on the ship to be piloted, then returned to the pilot's waiting station on Sullivan's Island. Or was Sambo—his owner was never identified—one of Jeremiah's slaves? Perhaps so. In any case, it seems plausible that Sambo was recalling a real conversation about a coming war with Britain.

Most of the specifics of Jemmy's testimony are harder to credit. Why would a slave owner—a substantial slave owner, as Jeremiah was—have reason to organize a slave rebellion? How could he, regardless of intent, gather so much scarce gunpowder as to have "enough," especially when the patriots themselves were faced with a dangerous shortage of powder? What stands out more than the alleged "facts" in Jemmy's testimony are the ways in which those "facts" matched whites' fears. For years, whites had raised alarms about "nocturnal rendezvouses" and "intriguing meetings" of runaways and other slaves, of discussions in "private committees; whose deliberations were carried on in too low a voice." Just five months earlier, in January, the free African preacher David Margrett, arriving from England, had told slaves that slavery was unjust; that in England a black man was treated with respect; that a new Moses would free America's slaves, as the first Moses had freed the Jews long ago. In early May, Arthur Lee's letter to Henry Laurens had warned of British "plans" for an insurrection, and within a week of that letter, Lee's warning had been transformed in the popular white imagination into something more concrete: that "our domesticks . . . of late have been taught . . . to believe they will be all sett free on the arrival of our New Governer." Perhaps the new governor himself, Lord William Campbell, who was expected in Charles Town at any moment, would arrive with British guns stored on board his naval transport, HMS *Scorpion*, ready to distribute "amongst the Negroes, Roman Catholics, and Indians," as James Dealey and Laughlin Martin were claiming. One can easily imagine that white interrogators may have fed these fears to Jemmy, Sambo, and other slaves in the form of leading questions until the requisite accusations were forthcoming. According to the law, slaves were to "suffer death as a felon," not only if they "raise or attempt to raise an insurrection in this Province," but if they were "accomplices, aiders and abettors." Jemmy and Sambo had a powerful incentive to pick up, and to confirm, their interrogators' darkest suspicions while minimizing their own direct involvement. Slaves knew that their judges could reduce a sentence or even pardon them if they showed, for example by testifying against others, that they themselves "deserve mercy."[29]

Then, too, Jeremiah was a pilot, a skill that could be put to traitorous uses when the Provincial Congress was debating whether to block the shipping channel to keep out British men-of-war. In fact, one of the charges against him (though not reflected in the surviving slave testimony) was that "Jerry said 'if the British ships come here, he would pilot them over Charlestown Bar.'" Another charge was that he planned to set fire to the city as part of the insurrection. The possibility of arson by slaves was a long-standing fear of whites, and it was a capital crime for a slave to set fire even to a stack of rice or corn. In 1741, and again in 1754, slaves were burned to death in Charles Town for arson, and many whites suspected that the "Great Fire" of 1740, which had destroyed a large area of the city, had been set by slaves. If Jeremiah was "well known for extinguishing fires," he might easily turn his skills as a firefighter against Charles Town.[30]

Further testimony was sought from a woman owned by Baptist minister Oliver Hart and a man owned by attorney Joshua Ward, who supposedly "could make very ample discoveries." As the investigations proceeded, however, some clearly began to doubt the reality of a plot, and before the end of June, the white suspects had been set free, perhaps because the only evidence was "Negro Evidence," not accepted against white men in court. Thomas Jeremiah himself was released from "close confinement," though he was still locked up in the Work House. Had there been nothing more than loose talk among slaves on the waterfront? Bee's committee seems to have found it difficult to get freeholders to volunteer to serve, along with two justices of the peace, on a "Negro" court to try the suspects. Some whites were beginning to believe that "there appears very little foundation" for their fears of an insurrection. Bee's committee was leaning toward having "one or two Negroes" simply "Severely flogged & banished."[31]

As Bee and others wavered about what to do, Henry Laurens intervened. To Laurens, perhaps the most damning evidence against Thomas Jeremiah was, not the testimony of Jemmy and Sambo, but the testimony of his own character. Jerry was, in Laurens's opinion, "a forward fellow, puffed up by prosperity, ruined by Luxury & debauchery & grown to amazing pitch of vanity & ambition." He may have reminded Laurens of his own boatman Abraham, "Sly and artful," "active, alert and Strong," a man who had given him much trouble. As a free man, Jeremiah could not be compelled to offer the "gratitude" Laurens expected, and felt he deserved, from his slaves. But although Jeremiah, as a "Free Negro," was beyond the reach of a master, he was not beyond the reach of the Negro Act. When Laurens asked the investigating committee on what grounds they could simply whip and banish "one or two Negroes," he got "the old answer, why they don't appear to have been so guilty as to deserve death but must receive Some punishment for example Sake." Laurens was appalled at this relaxation of the precise terms of the law. If the accused were innocent, very well then, let them go, but if they deserve any punishment at all, then "nothing less than Death Should be the Sentence."[32]

CHAPTER FIVE

"The Young King was about to alter the World, & set the Negroes Free"

In His Majesty's Service

A S CHARLES TOWN'S patriot elite debated the fate of Thomas Jeremiah, His Majesty's Ship *Scorpion* arrived outside the Charles Town bar. On board were the new governor of South Carolina, Lord William Campbell, and his family. Some radicals had urged that pilots be forbidden to bring the *Scorpion* past the bar, but more moderate figures like Henry Laurens prevailed, and on the evening of June 17, 1775, the governor's ship was guided into the harbor. In its hold were not the thousands of arms for slaves and Indians that Carolinians had feared but elegant furniture, china, and textiles for Lord William's home, fit for the same Atlantic-wide world of refinement to which Charles Town's gentry belonged.[1]

Listed in a meticulous inventory, and among the most valuable possessions, were portraits of Lord and Lady William by the Irish painter Nathaniel Hone (figs. 18, 19). The beautiful Sarah Campbell looks straight at the viewer with the hint of a smile, a ring of pearls on her slim neck, a lace shawl over a dazzling, low-cut, lace-trimmed, orange-red dress (perhaps the point lace "suit" of the inventory, valued at £53, roughly $10,000 in 2009). Her left hand rests on a young whippet hound. In his portrait, Lord William looks off to his right—perhaps to conceal damage from a boyhood injury to one eye. A cascading lace collar adorns his elegant embroidered waistcoat.[2]

For the governor's home on Meeting Street there were two mahogany four-poster beds, several less expensive bedsteads, three mahogany dining tables, two mahogany desks (the most costly a "Large Elegant Lady's Writing Desk" valued at £40), an "elegant Harpsichord" (£84), and a cello. A carved

Figure 18. Lord William Campbell brought this portrait, painted by Nathaniel Hone, with him to Charles Town when he arrived on the HMS *Scorpion* in June 1775.
(COURTESY OF THE CAMPBELL-JOHNSTON FAMILY)

Figure 19. Nathaniel Hone also painted this matching portrait of Sarah Izard Campbell.
(COURTESY OF THE CAMPBELL-JOHNSTON FAMILY)

chimneypiece would prove too large for any of the rooms in the house (fig. 20). There were also three chests packed with silver plate worth nearly £600, several dozen place settings of china and Queen's Ware dishes, a hundred knife-and-fork sets (some with "Black Handles Tipped w[i]th Silver"), plus hundreds of bottles of wine, beer, and ale, and more still in pipes and hogs-

Figure 20. Campbell and his wife moved into this house on
Meeting Street, owned by Sarah Campbell's cousin,
Elizabeth Izard Blake. (Library of Congress)

heads. A miscellany of Lord William's "Cloaths Lace Ruffles, Swords, Fire
Arms &c" filled a large wardrobe, valued altogether at nearly £500.[3]

The most valuable piece of furniture (£100), a "Large Mahogany Library,"
seventeen feet long, housed the Campbells' 436 volumes, themselves of considerable value. Some met the practical needs of a naval officer and government official: two editions of French pilot books; *Statutes of the Admiralty;* a
collection of *Treaties between Great Britain & Other Powers;* a *Geographical
Grammar;* and several dictionaries. An intriguing "Mathematical Manuscript
by Ld Willm Campbell" himself, implausibly valued at more than £5, suggests
wide-ranging intellectual curiosity. There were travel accounts of Russia, the
Nile, and the Pacific, and a few religious works, including a New Testament, a
prayer book, and three volumes of sermons by orthodox Anglican divines. A
scattering of classics included Xenophon, Virgil, and Plutarch. More common

were works of history: Richard Cambridge's *Account of the War in India between the English and the French* (Lord William was a veteran of that conflict); Edmund Burke's *European Settlements in America;* Charles Rollin's *Ancient History;* Nathaniel Hooke's *Roman History;* a *History of Algiers;* the *Life of Marlborough.* And most numerous of all were the works of literature to be found on the shelves of gentlemen and ladies throughout the eighteenth-century Anglo-Atlantic world: several volumes of Samuel Johnson's *Idler* and *Rambler;* works of Milton, Swift, and Pope (as well as Pope's edition of Shakespeare's works); Laurence Sterne's *Sentimental Journey* and *Tristram Shandy;* Tobias Smollet's *Peregrine Pickle;* Dryden's plays; six volumes of *The Arabian Nights.* An enlightened interest in philosophy is evidenced by a *Concise History of Philosophy* and collections of the works of Jean-Jacques Rousseau in thirteen volumes and Voltaire in thirty-five volumes.[4]

If most of these books could be found in private libraries of Charles Town's gentry and in the growing collection of the Charles Town Library Society, what is missing suggests a good deal about the differences between British and American versions of what was, in most respects, a single cultural world. There are no volumes by Locke, Montesquieu, or John Trenchard and Thomas Gordon, the four writers on politics and philosophy most commonly found in Carolina's private libraries. Instead were books by the Scottish philosopher and historian David Hume, including his *Essays* and his eight-volume *History of England,* a conservative counterpoint to the likes of Trenchard and Gordon, critics of Britain's political establishment.[5]

William Campbell was of Clan Campbell of Argyll, in the southwest Highlands, long one of the most powerful Scottish clans and, in the mid-eighteenth century, a leading force in British politics. Archibald Campbell, Tenth Earl of Argyll, had backed the "Glorious Revolution" of 1688 that overthrew James II in favor of William and Mary, and in 1701 he was rewarded by the grateful new monarchs, who elevated him to become the First Duke of Argyll. John Campbell, the Second Duke, was among the strongest supporters in Scotland of the Act of Union of 1707 that joined Scotland and England (with Wales) in the single monarchy of Great Britain. This history did not make the Campbells popular in Scotland; far from it. In 1692 the forces of the First Duke, in the "Massacre at Glencoe," had slaughtered dozens of men from the Clan Donald, opponents of William and Mary. The Act of Union itself was widely unpopular in Scotland, and many resented the way that John, the Second Duke, had maneuvered approval through the Scottish Parliament.[6]

The Campbells' leadership in supporting the Union and, especially, in resisting repeated attempts to restore the Stuarts to the British throne, was as much military as political. The Second Duke, known as "Red John of the Battles" because of his long and distinguished military career, commanded the army at Sherrifmuir that defeated the son of the deposed and exiled James II, who had returned in 1715 and raised an army to try to recapture the throne. John's dual role in politics and the army was memorably celebrated in a couplet by Alexander Pope: "Argyle, the State's whole thunder born to wield / And shake alike the Senate and the Field." (Jonathan Swift, on the other hand, dismissed him as an "ambitious, covetous, cunning Scot.")[7]

Since the Second Duke had no male heirs, at his death in 1743 his title passed to his brother Archibald. The Third Duke continued the family tradition of combining military and political power. He had been on the field at Sherrifmuir with his brother; in Parliament he controlled a distinct Scottish faction that supported the ministry of Robert Walpole. Two years after Archibald became duke, Bonnie Prince Charlie, the grandson of James II, led the second, more famous Jacobite invasion (so called after the Latin form of "James"). The Campbells were strong backers of the Crown during this attempt to overthrow King George II. Returning from France, the Bonnie Prince gathered an army in Scotland and had a surprisingly easy path south into England before he was forced to retreat north. General John Campbell, cousin of the Third Duke, was in charge of security in the western Highlands while the main British army crushed the invaders at Culloden. General Campbell's son was on the field at Culloden, watching as the British cavalry chased down the fleeing troops of the Bonnie Prince and "made terrible Slaughter of them." The Jacobite army suffered perhaps two thousand dead, King George's forces just three hundred. Prince Charles escaped back to France, but the Jacobite threat was decisively ended.[8]

General John Campbell married Mary Bellenden, a celebrated beauty and friend of Alexander Pope, "so agreeable and engaging," according to one contemporary, that he never heard anyone who knew her "who did not prefer her as the most perfect creature they ever knew." Not in the line of direct descent from the First Duke of Argyll, John Campbell would, ordinarily, have lived out his life simply as a military man. He did not even live in Scotland, instead building a mansion, of classic Palladian design, at Combe Bank in Kent, southeast of London. But because his cousin Archibald had no legitimate male heirs, John succeeded him, in 1761, as Fourth Duke of Argyll. William, the future governor of South Carolina, was born in 1736, the last of the Fourth Duke's six children (his mother died giving him birth). William grew up in a wealthy noble family at the center of British politics, and, as the son of a duke, held the honorific title of "Lord," but, as "a Younger Brother without a Fortune," he had no serious prospects of inheriting either the title, or much property, from his father.[9]

Given the Campbell tradition, one obvious career path was through the military, but instead of the army, where commissions sold for a high price, William entered the Royal Navy. In the navy, far more than the army, advancement required merit; incompetence in officers on a ship at sea could easily lead to disaster. Connections could get a man into service under a commander-patron—or, rather, a boy into service, since most officers started as lowly servants before the age of fifteen—but even a gentleman's son like Campbell spent years literally learning the ropes, working the guns on the lower decks and climbing the spars along with ordinary seamen. Before a man could be commissioned as a lieutenant, he had to spend at least six years at sea, at least two years in the navy at the rank of midshipman, reach the age of twenty, and pass an examination in seamanship. A lieutenant who survived the diseases and accidents that killed nearly a third of young officers, and was fortunate to have superior officers willing to recommend him, could move up the ranks, but even then, success in action was ordinarily a requirement for eventual command.[10]

William Campbell was sixteen when he entered the navy in 1752 as an able seaman on the *Penzance*. He transferred to the *Tyger* and sailed under Captain Thomas Latham east to India to protect the ships, assets, and interests of the British East India Company. When war between France and Britain broke out in 1756 and quickly spread to the Indian subcontinent (the French Compagnie des Indes was a major competitor to the British company), Campbell was in the little force that sailed up the Hugli River in support of troops led by John Clive. In the first six months of 1757, Campbell experienced the recapture of Calcutta, the capture of the French factory at Chandernagore, and the decisive defeat of the much larger army of the nabob of Bengal at Plassey. Campbell then sailed under Rear Admiral George Pocock, whose squadron, in 1758 and 1759, three times engaged a French fleet. Campbell was wounded twice in these battles; by the last of them, he had transferred to the *Yarmouth*, Pocock's flagship. These conflicts in India opened the way to Britain's later military and political conquest of the subcontinent.[11]

In 1760, when Pocock was called home, Campbell sailed with him on the *Yarmouth*. At the end of 1760, he passed his lieutenant's exam, demonstrating that he could "Splice, knot, Reef a Sail, &c.," and in December, he won his lieutenant's commission. Four months later, he served in the fleet that captured the French island of Belleisle (Belle-Île-en-Mer) in the Bay of Biscay. In a rapid rise, he was promoted in January 1762 to commander, and in August to captain and command of HMS *Nightingale*, a small ship of twenty-four guns. For several months he escorted convoys of merchant ships across the Atlantic. In early 1763, the *Nightingale* was stationed in Charles Town's harbor, and in April that year, in St. Philip's Church, the Reverend Robert Smith presided at Campbell's marriage to seventeen-year-old Sarah Izard.[12]

Peace with France was agreed in February 1763, and Campbell, with little prospect of further promotion, resigned from the navy and returned home with his young wife. His father, recently ascended to the dukedom, chose him to stand for his home constituency, Scottish Argyllshire, in Parliament, and Lord William served in the House of Commons for two years. He allied himself with Henry Seymour Conway, another soldier-politician, who served as secretary of state for the southern department (and thus for the American colonies). Conway was also William Campbell's brother-in-law, husband of his sister Eleanor. Although individual votes on bills in the Commons were not recorded, it is almost certain that Campbell voted for the American Duties Act of 1764 and the Stamp Act of 1765. When it became apparent that enforcement of the Stamp Act would be impossible, Conway worked for its repeal. Lord William Campbell in all likelihood cast his vote in favor of repeal in the spring of 1766, marking himself as one of the friends of America in Parliament, but he also agreed with the vast majority of members that Parliament (as expressed in the Declaratory Act) held ultimate authority over the colonies, including the authority to tax.[13]

When the governor of Nova Scotia died suddenly in 1766, Lord William, with support from his father the duke, successfully lobbied for the position, resigned from Parliament, and served in Nova Scotia until 1773. While colonies to the south were embroiled in the escalating conflicts with the British ministries, he was proud to report to London that Nova Scotia's general assembly demonstrated no signs of "that Licentious principle, with which the Neighboring Colonies are so highly infected." But Campbell was not entirely happy in Nova Scotia. He had trouble with his eyes, and his youth in Kent and long service in the Indian Ocean had left him ill-prepared for Nova Scotia's harsh winters. In 1771, he petitioned the colonial secretary for a leave:

> The indifferent state of my health, & particularly the weakness of my eyes, owing to long service in hot climates, & a wound formerly received in my left eye by an Iron spike, lay me under the necessity of requesting your Lordship to intercede with His Majesty in my behalf, that I may

obtain His Royal leave to return to England, or that I may be at liberty to go for some time to such part of this continent, as may be judged fittest to releive me from the ill effects which the continuance so long in this cold climate has brought on me.

During his seven-year term as Nova Scotia's governor, Campbell spent a total of two years out of the colony, visiting Boston, among other places, to recover his health. When he learned of the resignation of South Carolina's governor, Lord Charles Greville Montagu, in 1773, he petitioned for the job. His brother John, who had succeeded his father to become the Fifth Duke of Argyll, lobbied hard for him, and in 1773 William Campbell was appointed South Carolina's royal governor. Because he first went to England, it would be two years before he and his family arrived in Charles Town, Sarah's birthplace.[14]

Lord William was a Scot at a time when Scots were unpopular in the colonies, in part because one of King George's Scottish advisers, Lord Bute, was blamed for "wicked" British policies. South Carolina's Christopher Gadsden even suggested that the troubles in America were part of an elaborate plot designed to return the Stuarts to the throne, and one member of South Carolina's Commons House of Assembly specified in his will that his daughter would lose her inheritance if she married a Scot. When news of Lord William's appointment reached the colony, "Craftsman" wrote, in the *South-Carolina Gazette,* "You are soon, my Countrymen, to have a Scot Governor. If you have a Scot Assembly . . . the Lord have Mercy on you!"[15]

But no one could accuse a Campbell of Jacobite sympathies, and Lord William was not only intimately acquainted with those at the center of British power but had extensive experience as a naval officer, a member of Parliament, and a colonial administrator. Unlike his predecessor, who had become a colonial governor at age twenty-five with no qualifications other than being the second son of the Duke of Manchester, Campbell was a mature man who had made his way by genuine and substantial service. And yet, what perhaps best prepared him for the South Carolina governorship was his wife, Lady William, the former Sarah Izard. Sarah's great-grandfather, the first Ralph Izard, founder of Carolina's Izard dynasty, had arrived in the fledgling colony in 1682. His two sons, Walter and the second Ralph, produced a long line of wealthy and politically powerful descendants—eleven Izards over four generations, including three of Sarah's uncles and two of her brothers, served in the Commons House of Assembly. Sarah's own father, also named Ralph, grandson of the first Ralph, married into another prominent family, the Blakes.[16]

Born about 1746, Sarah was one of six children, four of whom lived to adulthood. No documents in Sarah's hand have turned up, but she probably received an excellent education, since her father instructed his executors to make sure that "all" his children received a "Liberal Education" from his estate. When he died in 1761, he left a great fortune: a Charles Town mansion, six plantations, 340 slaves, and nearly £10,000 sterling (roughly $2 million in 2009) due from some three dozen debtors. He bequeathed most of the land, including the Charles Town house, to one of Sarah's brothers; one plantation to another brother; and one plantation jointly to Sarah and her sister, Rebecca. The personal property, including the slaves that made up the bulk of the estate's value, was divided equally among the four children, the will specifying that slave marriages not be broken up in the division of property. Sarah's share left her, at her marriage, with "one of the most considerable fortunes in the province."[17]

When Sarah married, she retained control of her substantial inheritance. The estate's three executors concluded a marriage settlement with Captain Campbell specifying that her property, estimated at £50,000 Carolina currency, or about £7,000 sterling, would continue as a separate estate, not liable for her husband's debts. She was to receive a direct annual payment of £100 sterling, to be spent as she wished "without the controul or intermeddling of the said William Campbell," and on her death, the estate would go to her surviving children, not to him. The marriage was Campbell's entreé into the Carolina aristocracy, as it had been the young and beautiful Sarah Izard's into the gentry of Great Britain.[18]

Before Campbell left for South Carolina, he spent two years in London, attending to personal affairs and doing his best to ease the way for a successful governorship. He courted the several Carolinians in the city, meeting on more than one occasion with Henry Laurens, and they explained the most contentious current dispute between the Commons House of Assembly and the British administration over the so-called Additional Instruction. This directive from the ministry to the South Carolina governor ordered that he veto all revenue and spending bills that did not include certain restrictions on how the money could be spent. The Commons House had obstinately refused to undertake any business while the "Instruction" was in place; only recently it had resolved that "with a Firmness becoming a Free, and United People, founded on the deepest Sense of the Duty they owe their Constituents ... this House will never insert the Clause recommended in the Instruction dated 14th April 1770, and we trust no Assembly will ever be found in this Province so regardless of the most Essential Rights of the People ever to do so."[19]

When Laurens first heard rumors that Campbell would be the new governor, he had commented only that "no body mentions it with Cordiality," but now Campbell listened carefully to him and other Carolinians, who convinced him that the "Instruction" might bring down his own governorship. Campbell told Laurens that he was "heartily disposed to remove the obnoxious Instruction & smooth the way for Entring upon his government." Laurens reported to a friend in South Carolina that Campbell had "used his utmost endeavour & the Interest of his powerful Friends upon this occasion & his Lordship assured me a few minutes ago that he had now a fair prospect of Success."[20]

In a long letter to the Earl of Dartmouth, Campbell explained that he had made himself "Acquainted in the best manner in my Power with the Nature, & Extent, of the Disquietudes now subsisting" in the province, and he had learned that affairs there were "in such a State of Disorder & Confusion, as to render the carrying on the Business of Government, & his Majesty's service almost impracticable, with any degree of Satisfaction to His Majesty, or the Person He Honours with that Command." Still, he had been assured "by several Gentlemen of Credit, & Character, from that Colony, now in London, that if it was possible to have that Instruction with drawn, the Publick Business would be immediately restor'd to its usual Channel." He promised to "put a Negative upon any such indecent Insult to Government, & invasion of the Privilidges of the other Branches of the Legislature should it ever be again attempted."[21]

With the help of his influential friends, including his brother-in-law Henry Conway, Campbell's lobbying succeeded, and in July, Laurens reported that "Lord William has certainly been very Industrious in procuring a Suppression of the King's Instruction of the 14 April 1770, & to his Lordship & the influence of his powerful friends we are indebted." Campbell's arrival in South Carolina would be delayed because of his wife's pregnancy, but "in the mean time he will be extremely glad of opportunities to Serve our Province & desired me to Say So to any of my friends." During the delay, Campbell arranged to purchase a plantation of 750 acres on the Savannah River, complete with more than eighty slaves. He named it, after the Campbell family seat in Argyll, Inverary. It suggests that he might have seen South Carolina not just as the next posting in a career as a British official but as a permanent home.[22]

"A set of desperate and designing men"

When Lord William finally disembarked in Charles Town on June 18, 1775, no one was happier about his arrival than William Bull II, the lieutenant governor and acting governor. The Bull family had long been among the colonial elite.

Both Bull and his father, William Bull I, had spent long stretches acting as governor while official royal governors were in England or otherwise not in residence. William Bull II had earned the gratitude and support of his fellow Carolinians by his deft handling of many controversies. Recognizing the intransigent nature of Carolinians' defense of their perceived rights and, especially, the obstinacy of the Commons House of Assembly, he had refused to press the claims of king and Parliament too strongly. He had written to his superiors in London, in March 1775, to explain why he had not vetoed the appointment of delegates to the Second Continental Congress by the Commons House (which had rubber-stamped the choices of the extralegal Provincial Congress). As all power was now in the "popular scale," any attempt to thwart the Commons House would have produced a "fruitless altercation" and "exposed me to useless insult and thereby reflected some indignity upon my gracious Sovereign." He pointed out candidly that "authority and reason unsupported by real power are too weak to stem the torrent of popular prejudices." There was little to do but hope that "men of property" would finally realize the dangers they had unleashed in "the many-headed power, the people." He trusted that Lord William "will meet with more happiness and success in maintaining the King's authority" than he himself had been able to do, admitting that his own endeavors to "maintain the supremacy of Great Britain over every member of the British Empire" "have been in vain."[23]

When the previous governor, Charles Montagu, had arrived back in 1766, he had been greeted by booming cannon and pealing church bells, crowds cheering him as he walked, with a large retinue, from the waterfront to the State House two blocks away, then back to Granville's Bastion on the waterfront. At each stop, Montagu's official commission was read aloud to the crowd. A large dinner followed at Dillon's Tavern, at Broad and Church Streets. But when Campbell arrived, Bull retreated to his country estate and failed to appear as the new governor was rowed from the *Scorpion* to the landing place at the foot of the handsome Exchange Building. Campbell did go through the same formalities as had Montagu, with his commission read from the second story of the Exchange, then at the State House, and finally at Granville Bastion. But no church bells rang out, and the only cannon to salute him were at Fort Johnson, manned by the British soldiers, and on HMS *Tamar*, a small sloop of war in the harbor. The local companies of grenadiers, artillery, and light infantry duly lined up and escorted him, but otherwise his retinue consisted of only fifteen or so, nearly all royal placemen. "The citizens, for the most part, preserved a sullen silence."[24]

Nor was there a splendid dinner at Dillon's. Instead, the Campbells were entertained at the King Street mansion of the slave merchant Miles Brewton, husband of Sarah Campbell's cousin, Mary Izard Brewton. The Brewtons would host the governor's family until their Meeting Street house—the property of yet another cousin, Elizabeth Izard Blake, then living in London—was ready for them. Alexander Innes, Campbell's secretary, who had been in Charles Town for several months, had presumably already told his lordship what Innes had earlier written to London: that South Carolina "hardly falls short of Massachusetts in every Indecency, Violence & Contempt to Government," that the Provincial Congress had "taken the reins of government into their own hands," and that the new governor "must be contented to remain for some time a Spectator of Indecencies & Outrages, he can neither prevent nor punish." Should Campbell have had any doubts about this, they must have been erased that evening, when he and Innes went for a walk about town. At the State House on the central square at Broad and Meeting Streets, they saw a member of the Artillery Company on the nightly watch, still in effect to prevent mischief by slaves. Campbell and Innes sought to pass by on the sidewalk between the State House and one of the guns, but the sentinel warned them his orders were "to suffer no person to pass that way." An indignant Innes protested that this was the new governor, but the sentinel replied, "I am not to know the Governor." Lord William and his secretary were bumped from the sidewalk into the unpaved street.[25]

Two days later, the Provincial Congress adopted a statement addressed to the new governor, justifying the seizure of power by an elected, but otherwise illegal, group. When its delegation—including, awkwardly, Campbell's host, Miles Brewton—arrived to present this statement, perhaps in the beautiful second-story hall where Brewton hosted his fabulous dinners, an extraordinary scene occurred. William Henry Drayton, the member of the delegation apparently selected to read the statement to the governor, exchanged polite bows and nods with Lord William while Drayton explained why Carolinians "had taken up arms against his authority."[26]

The Provincial Congress's statement began with assurances that Carolinians were still "loyal subjects" and with the hope that Lord William would "receive no unfavourable impression of our conduct," then barely touched on specific grievances ("they have been so often represented, that your Excellency cannot be a stranger to them"). The statement continued: the "usual means of defence against arbitrary impositions" had failed. Although the congress's members had "no love of innovation" or desire to alter the constitution, and certainly "no lust of independence," the king's "wicked" ministers had been guilty of "slanderous informations and wicked Counsels, by which His Majesty has been led into measures, which, if persisted in, must inevitably involve America in all the calamities of Civil War." A "long succession of arbitrary proceedings," "apprehension of instigated insurrections," and "commencement of hostilities by the British troops against this continent" had driven Carolinians to "associate" and to take up arms. The congress's statement concluded with the hope that Campbell might "make such a representation of the state of this colony, and of our true motives, as to assure His Majesty, that in the midst of all our complicated distresses, he has no subjects in his wide extended dominions, who more sincerely desire to testify their loyalty and affection, or who would be more willing to devote their lives and fortunes to his real service." As for themselves, they preferred "Death to Slavery."[27]

Lord William's first response to this astonishing greeting was regret that he had agreed to meet the delegation. He no doubt would have liked to get some advice from the king's friends in the province as to a response, but that was hardly available. Lieutenant Governor Bull, the governor complained, "remained at his country house about 12 miles from town without favoring me with the smallest attention or giving the least assistance to government." The Governor's Council had fallen into such disrespect and disarray that only three of the councillors were even willing to attend meetings, and one of these was too sick to do so. Campbell thus turned, instead, to Miles Brewton for advice on whether to issue an indignant rejection of the statement or take a less confrontational tone. He decided on the latter. He said that he recognized "no representatives of the people of this province, except those constitutionally convened in the General Assembly." Further, it was "impossible during the short interval since my arrival, that I should have acquired such a knowledge of the state of the province, as to be at present able to make any representation thereupon to His Majesty." Whatever "representation" he did make would be designed to "promote the real happiness and prosperity of the province."[28]

Campbell was more candid in letters to General Thomas Gage in Boston and to the Earl of Dartmouth in London. He told Gage (on July 1) that, with "equal Surprize, & concern," he had found that South Carolinians yielded nothing to Boston "in the violence of their measures, & contempt of all Legal Authority." The resolutions they had adopted were "of a very daring, & dangerous measure"; the address presented to him was "one of the most extraordinary Addresses that ever was offer'd to a Kings Governor"; the Association they had "fabricated" was "absolutely treasonable" and appeared to have been signed by "every one in the Province" except for a few officers of the king. Those who refused to sign faced "all the fury of a desperate, and vindictive Mob." To Dartmouth (July 2), he said that the address was "of a very extraordinary and criminal nature." He half-apologized for not answering it "in such terms as it merited" but had decided that such a response might strengthen the "violent faction" that wanted to plunge the colony immediately "into open and actual rebellion." He had given up his "own feelings" in order to promote "the interest of my royal master." He held out some hope for the future, but, for the moment, "the people of the best sense and greatest prosperity as well as the rabble" had been led down a path of resistance "by a set of desperate and designing men." Still, he had learned that the proposals of the most "daring incendiaries" had been rejected and that more moderate men seemed to have the upper hand. In private conversations, some leading men had assured him that Americans were "heartily disposed now to a reconciliation; every Man of common Sense wishes it." He begged for more substantial support, if not in the form of British regiments, then at least in the form of one or more armed vessels anchored in the harbor to patrol the coast to prevent smuggling. Without that, he could not even be sure of sending mail without its being opened by the rebels; indeed, he learned later that the patriots had seized mail from the post office even while he was composing this letter.[29]

A week later, the Commons House of Assembly met for the first time since the spring. Since nearly all of its members sat also in the extralegal Provincial Congress, the meeting of the Commons House could do little more than provide a facade of legal government; in fact, it scarcely did even that. Campbell sent the Commons House a message about his "grief and disappointment" at the state of affairs: "the legal administration of justice obstructed—government in a manner annihilated—the most dangerous measures adopted—and acts, of the most outrageous and illegal nature, publically committed with impunity." He entreated them, as "the only legal representatives of the people in this province," to deliberate with "coolness, and moderation." The Commons House replied by blaming the king's ministers for "the present dangerous and dreadful situation"; they rejected his "severe censures" on measures taken simply to protect "the liberties of generations unborn." They denounced, in particular, any idea that their grievances were "small or unknown." Campbell replied that the two sides saw things "in so different a point of view" that only the "Great Sovereign of the Universe" could prevent disaster. The Commons House promised to redeem any paper money issued by the Provincial Congress to prevent "instigated insurrections of slaves" or "depredations from Indians," and then adjourned from day to day without doing any business. The Commons House asked Campbell to adjourn the body until November, but, mainly to annoy them, he refused. It was in the Council of Safety, the Secret Committee, and the General Committee that the members of the Commons House did their real work of running the colony.[30]

To Campbell, a child of nobility who had carved out a successful career in the Royal Navy, as a colonial administrator, and as a member of Parliament, the "King-in-Parliament" was the only sovereign and the only protection for the rights of British subjects. Resistance to Parliament's authority was subversion of the constitution. If South Carolina itself had prospered, and if its people were free, it was only because they had been protected by the wise legislation of Parliament and the sacrifices of such men as himself in the king's service. To the Americans, Britain was the Mother Country, the source of their culture and of the constitution that protected their rights; the king was their defender against hostile powers. But they saw themselves as the true rulers of South Carolina. In an outpost of the empire, in a difficult environment, they had not only survived but also created a world of refinement while governing themselves for many decades with little interference from London. Campbell's exchanges with South Carolina's patriot elite exposed these two visions of the nature of the British Empire and two conceptions of British liberty, from "so different a point of view."

"An Insurrection intended"

As Governor Campbell and South Carolina's colonial elite disputed, the stark fear of a slave insurrection in the colony had faded. Thomas Jeremiah and the slave Jemmy still languished in the Work House, but no trials went forward. After the Provincial Congress ordered every white man to take arms and ammunition with them to church (the Stono Rebellion of 1739 had occurred during Sunday services), Henry Laurens ridiculed it as a foolish measure, sure to be ignored and thus bring the congress itself into contempt. By this time, he thought, there "appears very little foundation" for any fears about a slave rebellion. Ten days later Laurens wrote to his brother that "the Rumour & Whisper of Insurrections are no more heard," although everyone stayed "constantly" on guard; "I am sure we have nothing to fear from them." Charles

Town merchant Gabriel Manigault wrote similar comments to his grandson, then in London: "We have been alarmed by idle reports that the Negros intended to rise, which on examination proved to be of less consequences than was expected." Even radicals shared this opinion; thus William Henry Drayton, always pushing for more "energetic" measures, wrote, on July 4, to the colony's delegates in Philadelphia: "As to our apprehensions of the negroes and Indians, they have all passed over. Indeed, we now find that we had nothing to fear from the former, and the latter show the most friendly disposition towards us."[31]

But at this moment, with "nothing to fear," came news of a new insurrection threat, from the Chehaw River neighborhood of St. Bartholomew's Parish, about forty miles south of Charles Town. The Chehaw was one of those sluggish tidal streams whose swamps had been converted into rich rice plantations, a land of live oaks and alligators. Blacks outnumbered whites there by five to one and, in midsummer, when whites who could afford it had left for healthier places, probably by ten to one. Thomas Hutchinson, in a letter written July 5, reported to the Council of Safety that local planters in the Chehaw River region had learned that "Several of the Slaves in the neighborhood, were exciting & endeavouring to bring abt. a General Insurrection." Interrogations of slaves, especially of one Jemmy, a slave of John Wells (not the Jemmy in the Work House), had produced a list of more than a dozen bondsmen, belonging to six different masters, who had been "preaching for two Years last past to Great crouds of Negroes in the Neighborhood of Chyhaw, very frequently." Many of these meetings had taken place on the property of George Austin, absent in England, whose plantation had suffered from runaways who had been stealing and killing Austin's stock. Jemmy told the magistrates that at "these assemblies" he "had heard of an Insurrection intended & to take the Country by Killing the Whites."[32]

As happened so often in such scares, there was a search for a white man at the bottom of things; whites were loath to believe that their slaves could, on their own, think such dangerous thoughts. Now, they blamed John Burnet, a Scot who "hath been a long time preaching to the above Named Negroes & many others very frequently." Burnet had told the slaves, so Jemmy claimed, "that they were equally intitled to the Good things of this Life in common with the Whites." But the immediate instigator of the scare was George, a slave of Francis Smith. George had preached that "the old King" had received a book from the Lord, "by which he was to Alter the world (meaning to set the Negroes free) but for his not doing so, was now gone to Hell, & in

Punishmt—That the Young King, meaning our Present One, came up with the Book, & was about to alter the World, & set the Negroes Free."[33]

Here, once more, was a dangerous mixture of Christian hope and earthly dreams of freedom. Neither is it surprising that these ideas would rise in the neighborhood of Chehaw. It was not far from the plantations of Hugh and Jonathan Bryan, just a few miles downstream, in St. Helena, where, thirty-five years earlier, slaves had preached to "great Bodies of Negroes" who had "assembled together, on Pretence of religious Worship, contrary to Law, and destructive to the Peace and Safety of the Inhabitants of this Province." Hugh Bryan himself, at that time recently converted by the itinerant minister George Whitefield, had speculated in his journal that "African hosts" would destroy the colony by "fire and sword." In 1759, a free black man, Philip Johns, had been executed after making similar prophecies in neighboring Prince William County. It had been revealed to him, Johns had claimed, that the "White People should be all under ground, that the Sword should go through the land, & it should be no more White King's Governors or great men but the Negro's should live happily & have Laws of their own." Johns had told his listeners that he had a "written paper" in which God had revealed his plans.[34]

George's prophecies of 1775 were similar to earlier ones, but this time they were informed by knowledge of the burgeoning revolt against the king who ruled over their own masters. Was there a connection between the "paper" held by John and the "book" George preached about? Was it a mere coincidence that King George II had died in 1760, shortly after Johns's prophetic sermons? If slave masters were rebelling against a new, "Young King," it might be because the Young King "came up with the book" and was indeed about to "Alter the World, & set the Negroes Free." And perhaps news had filtered down from Charles Town, or up from Savannah, about the preaching of a black man named David who had been telling all the slaves that in England even black men were free and that God would bring the poor Africans, as he did the Israelites of old, out of bondage.[35]

Hutchinson did not mention the date when he first heard about George's sermons, but, he explained, he "Apprehended such as were said to be the Principal leader of their Infernal designs, & imediately after convened a Court of Justices & Freeholders" to try them. Witnesses identified fifteen slaves, including two women, as not merely listeners but preachers, at slave gatherings, demonstrating the depth to which this subversive Christian message had penetrated the slave quarters. Local white planters were furious with Burnet, who "had often been told his Conduct was extremely Obnoxious to the People" but who had "persisted & continued incorrigible." With Burnet, though, they were up against the limits of South Carolina law, because no white man could be convicted of a crime on the basis of a black man's testimony. The court thus sent Burnet to Charles Town under guard to be confined in the barracks across from the Work House and interrogated by the Council of Safety. Burnet strongly denied any complicity in an insurrection plot and said he knew nothing of "the pretended Book," though he did admit preaching to slaves in the past and to praying with them "in the woods and in private Places without the Knowledge or Permission of their Masters." He swore that he had no more in view than "the Salvation of those poor ignorant Creatures." Far from inciting them to insurrection, he had sought to "reconcile them to that Lot in Life in which God had placed them, and to impress upon their Minds; the Duty of Obedience to their Masters." Deciding that Burnet had been guilty of no more than a "Tincture of Enthusiasm" that had led him into dangerous practices, the council let him off with a promise to be careful in the future, and he left for Georgia. The slaves in the Chehaw neighborhood did not fare so well. Most were whipped, but, as Thomas Hutchinson reported to the council, George, the man who knew about the book, "under the disagreable necessity to Cause Exemplary punishmts," had already been hanged.[36]

At almost the same moment as Carolinians received this reminder of the dangerous ideas that were circulating among the slaves, on July 4, the *Scorpion* man-of-war prepared to depart from Charles Town and sail north. Captain John Tollemache discovered that several of his crewmen had stayed in the city and had volunteered for the new regiments being raised by the Provincial Congress. They had refused to come back on board. When he asked for assistance in recovering these deserters, the patriots in turn refused. Partly in retaliation, and partly to make certain that he could return safely to Charles Town's harbor when he wished, Tollemache decided to take with him his pilot, "a black fellow who is by far the best pilot in this harbour." Should the patriots go so far as to knock down the lighthouse and cut down the trees that served as channel markers, this pilot had "marks of his own by which he will carry in any vessel in safety in spite of what they can do." The pilot guided the *Scorpion* over the bar on July 4, and it sailed for Boston, leaving behind a distrustful ruling party, a beleaguered governor, and another black pilot still locked up in the Charles Town Work House.[37]

CHAPTER SIX

"Dark, Hellish plots"

"The Glorious Cause of Freedom"

THE AMERICANS' CONFLICT with the Mother Country showed no signs of abating as the summer progressed, and Henry Laurens feared a "bloody" result. "I do not retreat as danger approaches," he wrote to his son John, in London, in July. "I only pray that God will enable me in every trial to do my Duty." He held out hope that King George would "put aside" his bad ministers and that harmony would be restored. Laurens was working intensely throughout the month, meeting daily, including Sundays, with the Council of Safety, and sometimes twice a day. Afterward he composed and copied letters deep into the night. He was spared the hot, sticky weather typical of Charles Town in July; sea breezes, as he wrote John, had brought fresh air and cooling rains almost every day, and "we have entred July with as much temperance as reasonable beings" could expect. The crops were recovering after the deluges of May, and his garden was a delight, with "vast increase of Mocking Birds, Grapes plentiful, Peaches Ripe sooner & Nectarines better than common & very fine, Figs Damsons & Plumbs in abundance." Even Stepney, the elderly slave gardener, was staying sober.[1]

While Laurens contemplated his garden, Thomas Jeremiah and the slave Jemmy remained imprisoned in the Charles Town Work House, no doubt also grateful for the moderate temperatures. The Work House had been built in 1738 to hold, on one hand, those too poor or ill to support themselves and, on the other, "lewd, idle, and disorderly" persons to be shackled and whipped, as the warden thought appropriate. After the colony built a new poor house and hospital nearby, the Work House was left as a "House of Correction" for "fugitive Seaman & Slaves" and "a Place for correcting of Slaves," especially those whose masters loathed punishing slaves themselves. The atmosphere was, no doubt, odorous and fetid, and the cooling showers would have been a blessing.[2]

Though the Work House was "for correcting of Slaves," Thomas Jeremiah was not a slave but an affluent businessman with slaves of his own. Those facts mattered less than his African descent. In the Work House with him and Jemmy were the usual collection of recaptured runaways and slaves sent for punishment. Cato, captured in June, was there, a man of the "Papaw country," "about 45 Years of Age, 5 feet 2 inches High, has his Country Marks on his Forehead," as was another Jemmy, from Angola, who "has his Country Marks on both his Sides, and branded on his left Breast." Both were "New Negroes," African-born, with patterns of scarification that marked them, literally, as members of specific African cultures. On July 4, three more fugitives were brought in after being captured "in the Creek nation," perhaps by Indians looking for a reward. Ben, a "stout fellow," five feet, seven inches tall, and Glasgow, tall and slim, "with his country marks on his face," had run away in Georgia; Joe had run away "from a Mr. Hickey otherwise unknown." Other slaves followed: Gibb on July 14; Bram on July 20; Mashey, a woman, on July 21. Thomas Jeremiah, "Free Negro," had spent a lifetime climbing out of the conditions that most American blacks were consigned to; now he was forced to share his space with African- and American-born men and women who had failed in their own attempts to escape those conditions. As they waited to learn their fates, he and Jemmy could hear the lashings of slaves sent in by their owners for punishment.[3]

The Council of Safety, meanwhile, confronted a pressing problem, a shortage of powder, both for the colony of South Carolina itself and for shipment north in response to an urgent request from the Continental Congress in Philadelphia. A joint force from South Carolina and Georgia had intercepted powder on its way to Savannah, perhaps, they feared, intended for the Indians, and the council arranged to have it brought into Charles Town for reshipment to Philadelphia. The council also commissioned a daring mission to seize powder from the *Betsey,* a British merchant ship positioned outside the bar at St. Augustine, Florida. At the same time, the council worried about conflicts at home that were harder to manage with military strikes, including discontent among white men in the upcountry districts who had, until recently, played little role in South Carolina's politics.[4]

For most Americans and Britons, South Carolina was almost synonymous with rice and slaves; together they had made the colony's trade prosperous and its white population rich. By 1775, however, three-fourths of the colony's white population lived, not in the low-country rice swamps, but in interior districts of small farms. South Carolina's generous policy of land grants to new settlers had enticed German, Swiss, and Welsh immigrants to sail to Charles Town and move to this "back country." Even more immigrants, especially Scots-Irish from Ulster, had come down from Pennsylvania and Virginia, through the Shenandoah Valley, looking for fertile tracts on which to build individual farmsteads. Although some backcountry farmers owned slaves, and although the rise of indigo as a commercial crop had sharply raised the demand for slaves there, overall, no more than one in five of the upcountry population was enslaved, and the threat of a large slave insurrection must have seemed remote.[5]

Many backcountry settlers were, in consequence, far less concerned than the aristocrats of Charles Town with the accusations of American "enslavement" by Parliament; they felt greater loyalty to Britain and its king. The Germans there had no history of living under a parliamentary regime and no historic claim to the "rights of Englishmen," and with their lands granted in the name of King George, they feared that disloyalty might cost them their most important right, the right to their farms. The Scots-Irish had more familiarity with British history but little experience with South Carolina's long struggles over local rights and privileges. Indeed, as of 1765, the entire backcountry was represented by only two members in the Commons House of Assembly; not until the Provincial Congress met in January 1775 did the region get more than token representation. Worse still, until recently, the backcountry had lacked even the most basic institutions of government: effective courts and law enforcement. Justices of the peace had dealt with small disputes; otherwise it required a time-consuming and expensive trip to Charles Town to sue someone or prosecute a serious crime. When a wave of robberies and banditry broke out in the 1760s, substantial landholders in the region organized themselves as "Regulators" to enforce order through vigilante violence. Legislation had been passed to establish courts throughout the backcountry, but the courts had been delayed by disputes, over the tenure of judges, between the Commons House of Assembly and the authorities in London. One leading supporter of the Regulators, Anglican minister Charles Woodmason, complained openly about lowcountry leaders who made "such Noise about Liberty! Liberty! Freedom! Property! Rights! Priveleges! And what not; And at the same time keep half their fellow [white] Subjects in a State of Slavery."[6]

On July 3, 1775, with the Germans' disaffection with the patriot cause well known, the Council of Safety commissioned two German-speaking patriots to go to settlements at Saxe Gotha "to explain to them the present situation of American affairs." They soon returned, however, their mission unsuccessful. More troubling were reports of active resistance to the patriots from farther west, in Ninety-Six District, where some local notables, such as the militia leader Colonel Thomas Fletchall, opposed any armed resistance to the British. Fletchall was joined by former Regulator Moses Kirkland, who, at first, had been sympathetic to the resistance movement against Britain, but then switched sides.[7]

On July 14, Henry Laurens, as president of the Council of Safety, stayed up late laboring over a letter to Fletchall; the many phrases crossed out or inserted in his draft copy are signs of the importance and delicacy of this communication. He began by reminding Fletchall of the perils at hand. Britain was seeking to force colonial submission to acts "founded in injustice." Worse, there were dangers from disunity and from the "insidious acts of false Brethren" at a time "when this Colony in particular is alarmed by threats of Invasions by the British Soldiery, of instigated Insurrections by our Negroes, of inroads by the Neighbouring Tribes of Indians." Surely, reports that Fletchall "is not a freind to the cause of Liberty" must be false. Surely, Fletchall would "join with the freinds of the Glorious Cause of Freedom in Defence of the liberties of the whole British Empire." Surely, he and his militiamen would add their signatures to the Association agreed upon in June by the Provincial Congress, calling on South Carolinians to join together as a "band" in defense of their rights. Laurens closed with reassurances—perhaps he was reassuring himself as well—that patriots were not enemies of King George; they wanted simply restoration of "Constitutional Law when every Man may again eat of the fruit of his own Vine, may sit under his own Fig Tree, when his person & his property will be out of the reach of foreign Invaders & secured under the Protection of a Protestant Prince of the Royal Line" and of "his Legal Representatives chosen by himself." Perhaps as he penned these words he was looking out at the vines and fig trees in his own garden.[8]

By the time Fletchall received this letter, he had already cooperated with Moses Kirkland to seize some ammunition from a patriot force at the court-house at Ninety-Six. His response to Laurens, dated July 27, was hardly reassuring. He had gone to every militia company in his regiment to have the text of the Association read aloud to the assembled men, but not one man had signed. Fletchall reminded Laurens that "we never had any Representitives[.] Not one man in fifty Ever gave any Vote for any Such Thing." His message concluded: "I am Resolved and do utterly Refuse to Take up arms agt my King." His regiment had circulated and signed a set of resolutions as an alternative to the Association, asserting that the king had "not acted inconsistant with & Subversive of the Principles of the Constitutions of the British Empire." Of course, they wanted "to Live in Peace & true friendship With the rest of Our Country men," and they were "Ready & Willing at all times to assist in defending the Province in Order to Oppose and Suppress the incurtions of Indians[,] insurrections of Negroes, Or any Other Enemy which may or Shalle Invade this Province or unlawfully disturb the good People thereof." But they would obey no laws "but the Statutes of great Britain which are of force here, and the Acts of the general Assembly of this Province" (and not, by implication, acts of the Provincial Congress). They were "determined not To take up arms against [the king] but to bear true Allegiance as formerly." The statement could well be interpreted as more of a threat than an offer of "true friendship," as it claimed.[9]

To counter this dangerous threat of division among white Carolinians, the Council of Safety authorized a new delegation to travel through the backcountry "to explain to the people at large" the reasons for the conflict with Great Britain, to "quiet their minds" and to convince them of the importance of unity "in order to preserve themselves and their children from slavery." These emissaries, departing Charles Town on August 2, were William Henry Drayton, perhaps the most radical of Charles Town's patriot leaders, and two ministers, William Tennant, Presbyterian, and Oliver Hart, Baptist, since only a minority of backcountry whites belonged to the Anglican Church. In one area settled principally by Germans, no one showed up to hear their arguments; "their Countrymen were so much averse to take up Arms as they imagined against the King, least they should lose their lands; & were so possessed with an idea that the Rangers [that is, mounted militia] were posted here to force their signatures to the Association, that they would not by any Arguments be induced to come near us." Meeting with a regiment of rangers, Drayton "harangued" them on "their duty and obligation, to oppose and attack any British troops, landing in this Colony," but a mutiny almost broke out the following night after he informed them that the cost of any supplies provided by the patriot authorities would be deducted from their pay. At another gathering, Oliver Hart watched as Fletchall told his followers that "the people below wanted them to go down and assist them against the Negroes," but that only a "Fool" would do that.[10]

"No Stone has been left unturned"

Lord William, aware of the discontent in the backcountry, began to see it as his one hope to rally support to the king's government. The Governor's Council, dwindling in numbers, was held in such "low estimation" that no one would accept a place on it; Lieutenant Governor Bull, with decades of experience in dealing with recalcitrant local leaders, was still holed up at his country estate and had not even sent Campbell copies of official papers. The Commons House of Assembly did no business other than exchange petulant communications with the governor. When Campbell asked it to consider some sort of revenue bill to cover public debts, the Commons House harkened back to old disputes, complaining that he had referred to them as the "lower house" of the legislature. As he wrote the Earl of Dartmouth in London, Campbell had decided not to dissolve the Commons House, on the grounds that this would have "inflamed the minds of the people, weakened government, and riot, anarchy, and confusion could not fail of being the consequence." He explained to Dartmouth that he now understood that his hopes for "temper and moderation," nurtured by his meetings with Carolinians such as Henry Laurens back in London the previous year, had been misplaced. He now met "with nothing but violence and frenzy." The actions of the patriot party proceeded, not "from a mob fired by oppression," but rather from "a concerted plan and firm determination of a powerful party to establish an independency," a party "ripe for any violence." On top of everything else, on July 7 had come word of the Battle of Bunker Hill on June 17 outside Boston, the Pyrrhic victory in which the British had suffered heavy losses. Campbell could scarcely believe reports of the battle, but unless a more accurate version came from British sources, or unless General Gage could send word of some sort of "severe correction" to the Americans, the news would simply embolden his opponents. "It is hardly possible to conceive," he complained, of "a situation more irksome than mine is at present, scarce a shadow of authority left."[11]

Still, a ray of hope remained. He had written to General Gage on July 2 that almost "every one in the Province" had signed the Association, but he had learned that the patriots' "boasted unanimity" was "notoriously false."

Their "intolerable tyranny" had given much offense; efforts to *"oblige"* people to subscribe to the Association had "stirred up such a spirit in the back part of this country, which is very populous, that I hope it will be attended with the best effect." He had received expressions of loyalty from "very respectable people" from Camden and Ninety-Six who claimed to represent the "sentiments of some thousands in those districts" who had designed a "counter-association." Surely, it would be hard for the Americans to defend their country "where their slaves are five to one, to say nothing of the disaffection of many of the back-country people and of the Indians."[12]

Campbell knew, apparently from Moses Kirkland, all about the "counter-association" Colonel Fletchall had circulated among his men, with its pledge not to take up arms against the king. On August 7, William Henry Drayton and William Tennant, still in the backcountry, wrote to the Council of Safety that "Moses Kirkland is gone to Town to the Governor," expecting to get from Campbell instructions to "counteract & oppose the Provincial proceedings." Thomas Fletchall later said that he did get "Orders from Lord William Campbell to hold himself and his regiment in readiness to support any disturbances offered to Government," and to "apply to Mr. Alexander Cameron then Superintendent to the Creek and Cherokee Indians for assistance in case it was required." Drayton and Tennant gave orders to provincial troops to arrest Kirkland, if they could find him, and take him to Charles Town to be interrogated about his suspicious behavior. The patriots never managed to arrest Kirkland, and he continued to stir up opposition to their plans until mid-September, when he sneaked into Charles Town in disguise, met with the governor, and slipped aboard HMS *Tamar* in the harbor.[13]

The rise of dissent from white South Carolinians provoked patriot leaders into a renewed sense of urgency. The most extreme of them, such as William Henry Drayton and Arthur Middleton, favored drastic measures to put the harbor "into the best posture of defence" by destroying the landmarks used by harbor pilots and by sinking vessels in the harbor channel. The Council of Safety's more moderate members, including Laurens, defeated these "ruinous" proposals. To Laurens, the more immediate threat was, not a British invasion, but divisions at home, the "defection to our Cause" in the backcountry by men like Thomas Fletchall, who might march on Charles Town in support of the king. "Ministerial Emissaries"—especially North Carolina's governor Josiah Martin—"have been exceedingly diligent in that quarter," he wrote to his son. "No Stone has been left unturned by [the] Administration & by their Creatures, to disunite us poor distressed Americans. —Insurrections of our Negroes attended by the most horrible butcheries of Innocent Women & Children—Inroads by the Indians always accompanied by inhuman Massacre—Civil discord between fellow Citizen & Neighbour Farmer, productive of fraud perjury & assassination, are all comprehended within their plans, & attempts have been made to carry them all into Execution."[14]

"Every humane breast must be filled with horror from the bare recital, [and from] Indignation against our common Enemies," Laurens added in the same letter, assuring his son that he had proof. There was the letter of Indian Commissioner John Stuart to his deputy Alexander Cameron, written months ago, and recently found in Stuart's letterbook in Georgia. Stuart had urged Cameron to prevent Americans from "alienat[ing] the affections" of the southern Indians from the king and to "use your influence to dispose those people, to act in defence of his Majesty and Government, if found necessary." What could this "defence" mean except Indian attacks on white settlements and farms? So, too, there was the June 26 letter from North Carolina's Governor Martin to a member of his council, stolen from the mails, in which Martin had said he would consider calling on Negroes for support if the colony went into open rebellion ("Nothing could ever justify the design, falsely imputed to me, of giving encouragement to the negroes, but the actual and declared rebellion of the King's subjects, and the failure of all other means to maintain the King's Government"). Martin had since repeatedly called Americans "rebels," and it must follow that he "thought it expedient to encourage an Insurrection" and allow "the Negroes to butcher their Masters." Laurens had also seen several letters from Lord Dartmouth to Martin and to Governor James Wright of Georgia, written in the spring and seized from the Charles Town post office, containing assurances that London intended to enforce Parliament's rights in the colonies, if necessary, by "drawing the sword." Lord Dartmouth was, by reputation, a deeply pious man, but, Laurens asked, "are these dark Hellish plots for Subjugating the Colonies, consistent with Lord Dartmouth's religious tenets?"[15]

The patriot party, faced by the rising threat in the backcountry, began to crack down on dissent in Charles Town itself. First, the Charles Town General Committee, on July 11, summoned for interrogation the few men, about two dozen in all, who had refused to sign South Carolina's Association. Since Laurens was still president of the General Committee as well as president of the Council of Safety, it fell to him to chair these sessions and ask the questions. "It was an affecting circumstance to me," Laurens wrote his son. "I considered the trial in its nature & in its extent & possible consequences; I addressed each Respondent with a demeanour which I beleive did not displease him, nor did it derogate from the dignity of the people who had laid their Commands on me."[16]

Perhaps the most prominent, and to the patriots most worrisome, among the dissenters was William Wragg, "of a very respectable standing in the Colony, being a gentleman of liberal education; much esteemed for his social virtues; and possessing a large and independent fortune." In the entire decade-long controversy over British policies, Wragg had stubbornly opposed open resistance in the colony. He had published several critiques of the nonimportation movement back in 1769 and would countenance no defiance to the king in view of "his gratitude for the honorable notice his Majesty had been pleased to take of him" (Wragg had earlier been offered, but declined, the post of chief justice in South Carolina).[17]

Nearly all the rest of the "Non-Associators" were royal officials. Dr. George Millegen, surgeon for His Majesty's forces in the province, left an account of his interrogation. Millegen had arrived thirty years earlier as a volunteer in King George's War (1744–1748) and remained ever since. He had been approached twice, most recently by "Daniel Cannon, a house carpenter, and Edward Weyman, clerk of St Philip's Church," and asked to "subscribe to this lying Association paper"; both times he had refused. Summoned to appear on July 23, he avowed his full support for "the civil and religious rights of mankind," but once more refused to sign.

> Thirty eight years ago, I began to eat the King's bread when it was impossible for me to earn it, and near thirty years ago in November 1745 I entered His Majesty's service a volunteer and then dedicated my life to him and my country. I have continued in the service from that time under different commissions with, I hope, an irreproachable character, and as I have now the honour of a commission from His Majesty. I intend, God willing, to be true to the trust reposed in me. Therefore, gentlemen, allegiance as a subject, gratitude as a man, honour as a gentleman, and my duty to the King as an officer, all forbid my joining your Association.

To Henry Laurens and others, "patriotism" might mean loyalty to the American cause and, in particular, to the decrees of the Provincial Congress. To Millegen, though, patriotism meant support for the king (both the person and institution), who protected the liberty of his subjects and to whom he owed ultimate loyalty. Charles Town's leaders, and the popular crowd they called upon to suppress dissent, were the true enemies of liberty. Other royal officials likewise refused to sign, even though, according to the governor, "repeated hints had been given out of doors that those petty tyrants expected great deference and respect if not absolute submission to their mandates."[18]

As the Council of Safety and the General Committee debated over the next four weeks what to do with these uncooperative men, local leaders turned their attention to the other threat from within, the colony's black population. Perhaps they felt it necessary to send a clear message to any slaves who might be contemplating resistance. Perhaps they were feeling pressure from Charles Town's white artisans, laborers, and petty shopkeepers, who had filled the ranks of the new regiments and who were willing to enforce their opinions with direct intimidation. Perhaps they simply felt that it was time to bring to a close an anomalous situation, with supposed insurrectionists indefinitely confined. Whatever the reason, about the time William Wragg and others were answering Laurens's questions, the patriots decided to bring Thomas Jeremiah and the slave Jemmy to trial.[19]

"The noblest monument, and firmest Bulwark of their liberties"

If the right not to be taxed by any but one's own representatives was the most important point of Americans' conflict with the British administration, the right to a trial by jury was close behind. But neither the free Thomas Jeremiah nor the slave Jemmy could receive a jury trial in the city of Charles Town.

In 1769 the *South-Carolina Gazette* reprinted resolutions of the Boston Town Meeting assailing taxation without representation and protesting the expanded reach of Admiralty Courts, operating without juries. "Next to the Revenue itself, the late extensions of the jurisdiction of the Admiralty, are our greatest grievance." These courts could assess forfeitures of goods and penalties "not by a jury . . . but by the civil law and a single judge!" To accept their jurisdiction in America would place a "brand of disgrace upon every American" and virtually repeal a key guarantee of the Magna Carta: *"No Freeman shall be taken or imprisoned,"* or deprived of his property or liberties, or outlawed *"or any other wise destroyed . . . but by lawful judgment of his Peers."* Trial by jury, the Boston resolution continued, had been for centuries Britons' "noblest monument, and firmest Bulwark of their liberties." This language echoed Sir William Blackstone's recently published *Commentaries on the Laws of England* (1765–1769), which had become, almost immediately upon its publication, the most influential work in both Britain and the colonies on the common law. "The trial by jury," Blackstone had written, "is also that trial by the peers, of every Englishman, which, as the grand bulwark of his liber-

ties, is secured to him by the great chartere." It "has been, and I trust ever will
be, looked upon as the glory of the English law." Henry Laurens, in his
pamphlets of 1767–1769, quoted and paraphrased Blackstone extensively
while arguing that "the History of [our] Ancestors" shows that they esteemed
trial by jury as "the *Palladium* of their Constitution . . . [and] their unalienable
Birthright."[20]

The Boston resolutions and Laurens's pamphlets were concerned with
the rights of property owners not to be deprived of property by arbitrary
decisions of judges. But, as Blackstone had written, if the right to a jury trial
had "so great an advantage over others in regulating civil property, how much
must that advantage be heightened, when it is applied to criminal cases!" For
the "antiquity and excellence of this trial, for the settling of the civil property
. . . will hold much stronger in criminal cases; since, in times of difficulty and
danger, more is to be apprehended from the violence and partiality of judges
appointed by the crown, in suits between the king and the subject, than in
disputes between one individual and another, to settle the metes and bound-
aries of private property."[21]

For criminal cases, indeed, the law had placed an extra barrier "between
the liberties of the people, and the prerogative of the crown," in the form of
the grand jury, which must indict before a person could even be put on trial.
In unlimited monarchies, the Crown might "imprison, dispatch, or exile any
man that was obnoxious to the government," at its will and pleasure, but in
England, Blackstone wrote, "no man should be called to answer to the king
for any capital crime, unless upon the preparatory accusation of twelve or
more of his fellow subjects, the grand jury: and . . . the truth of every accusation, whether preferred in the shape of indictment, information, or appeal,
should afterwards be confirmed by the unanimous suffrage of twelve of his
equals and neighbours, indifferently chosen, and superior to all suspicion." To
protect the liberties of England "this palladium" must remain "sacred and
inviolate," especially from "secret machinations, which may sap and undermine it; by introducing new and arbitrary methods of trial, by justices of the
peace, commissioners of the revenue, and courts of conscience."[22]

To be sure, the concept of trial by jury, like that of "no taxation without
representation," was a mix of myth and reality. The original guarantee of trial
by jury in the Magna Carta was not intended to be universal but was limited
to members of a small range of elite groups. Even when trial by jury for felony
cases was later extended to all Englishmen (and women), courts were heavily
biased against the poor. Most English trials were very short, averaging per-

haps a half-hour each, without lawyers or professional prosecutors; jurors might consult for mere minutes, without leaving the courtroom, before pronouncing the verdict. Given the nature of the criminal law, with its emphasis on the protection of property, and the criminal trial, with its seemingly hapless defendant and highly influential judge, one pointed analysis has argued that the outcomes of felony trials in eighteenth-century England (that is, those for which the penalty was hanging) were a product of "class favouritism and games of influence," that the criminal law was in effect a "conspiracy" (though an unconscious one) of the elite. Even if many of the accused were not sentenced to hang, and many others were saved from hanging by a pardon, such apparent leniency simply operated to enforce the "hegemony" of the ruling elite by convincing the poor that the rule by their betters was legitimate.[23]

Others, however, have shown that trial by jury gave real protection to many poor men and women accused of serious crimes. Blackstone was correct that even the poorest man or woman could not be executed unless indicted by a grand jury and convicted by a unanimous petty jury. Although jurors were not literally the "peers" of the poor (they were supposed to own property) who most often appeared in the dock, neither were they rich; they came "almost exclusively" from the middling group of property holders, such as artisans, small farmers, and shopkeepers. Examinations of trials in Britain show that these juries often acted with great independence. Of all those accused of murder in one English jurisdiction in the era of the American Revolution, only about one-fourth were found guilty and executed. As the author of another careful study of English criminal trials (including both capital and noncapital crimes) concluded, "Most sentencing and pardoning decisions were almost certainly based on universal and widely agreed criteria rather than on 'class favouritism and games of influence.'"[24]

This deep-rooted tradition of trial by jury, not in ideology alone, but to a significant extent in practice, was perhaps even stronger in South Carolina than in England. South Carolina law, for example, called for an elaborate procedure to select impartial jurors, involving a child selecting slips of paper of "equal size and bigness" from a six-drawered box, and, unlike English law, guaranteed the right of the accused in felony cases to see the charges against him or her in advance and to have counsel during the trial. This makes all the more stark the nature of the trials conducted under South Carolina's slave code, known as the Negro Act. Passed in 1740, in the wake of the Stono Rebellion, the act proclaimed goals both practical (the extent of masters' power over slaves "ought to be settled and limited by positive laws"; slaves must "be kept in due subjection and obedience") and humanitarian (owners should "be restrained from exercising too great rigour and cruelty over them"). Among its many provisions were those establishing crimes for which slaves were responsible and the forms and procedures for their trials. Slaves—although property—could be held responsible for any act considered a crime in England, plus a range of others: striking any white person (except in defense of his or her owner); being absent from home without a "ticket"; refusing to submit to questioning about a ticket by "any white person"; wearing clothing made from other than a specified list of cheap textiles; or buying and selling goods without permission from a master. Several "crimes," unknown in England, were felonies in South Carolina and thus punishable by death, as, for example, burning a stack of rice or a barrel of tar; stealing another slave; giving anyone poison; and a third conviction for striking a white person.[25]

As for Thomas Jeremiah's alleged crime, the act required that "every slave who shall raise or attempt to raise an insurrection in this Province, [or] shall endeavor to delude or entice any slave to run away and leave this Province, every such slave and slaves, and his and their accomplices, aiders and abettors, shall, upon conviction aforesaid, suffer death." Thomas Jeremiah, though not a slave, nonetheless came under the terms of the act because it treated all Negroes as if they were slaves, specifying that "crimes and offences committed by free negroes . . . shall be proceeded in, heard, tried, adjudged and determined by the justices and freeholders appointed by this Act for the trial of slaves, in like manner, order, and form."[26]

That "manner, order, and form" fell far short of the standards enshrined in the common law. For capital cases, the court consisted of five to seven men: two justices of the peace and three to five other property owners (if the act did not specify that they would all be white, it was because any other option was unthinkable). As the author of a contemporary compilation of South Carolina law noted, the jurisdiction in these cases was "of a mixed nature, the office of a judge and jury being blended together." After taking an oath to judge "truly and impartially," these men would together hear the accusation, examine witnesses "and other evidences," and determine the matter "in the most summary and expeditious manner." A simple majority of the court, rather than the unanimity required of a regular jury, was sufficient for conviction. The weight given to evidence given by slaves, who were not allowed to give their testimony under oath, was "left to the conscience of the justices and freeholders."[27]

Perhaps nothing about South Carolina surprised Josiah Quincy, Jr., visiting from Massachusetts in 1773, more than the nature of these trials. Quincy had come to the southern colonies in 1773 partly for his health (tuberculosis would kill him in two years) and partly as an ambassador from the Massachusetts Committee of Correspondence. But he was also a lawyer and legal scholar, the first attorney in America to compile and publish law reports, and he spent several days in Charles Town copying material from Edward Rutledge's handwritten reports. In the notebook Quincy kept while studying for the bar, an exemplary document in the history of legal education, he had invoked David Hume's praise for "the Institutions of Juries, admirable in itself + the best calculated for the Preservation of Liberty + ye administration of Justice, that ever was devised by the wit of man." "Nothing contributes more, than the institution of tryals by Jury, to the support of that equity + Liberty, for which the English Laws are justly celebrated." Quincy practiced what he preached. The most celebrated criminal trials in recent colonial history had been those of British soldiers and officers involved in the infamous Boston Massacre of 1770, when several Bostonians had been shot down in the streets. In this case, the defense was conducted by lawyers, and John Adams, to the considerable benefit of his historical reputation, not only volunteered to defend the soldiers but got them off either with full acquittals or with convictions on a reduced count of manslaughter. Adams's assistant in this case was the twenty-six-year-old Josiah Quincy, Jr., considered a legal prodigy, chosen by Boston's patriot leaders to help demonstrate that Americans were a people ruled by law, not vigilante justice or mob action.[28]

Moreover, in Massachusetts, many of the procedural protections of the law were extended to both free blacks and slaves. To be sure, those of African descent were not fully equal under the law; one historian has compared their legal status to that of white women. Still, in Massachusetts, blacks "received the protection of the King through the rights to sue, witness, and petition and received justice in the same courts as white citizens." Both slaves and free blacks pressed these advantages in the era of the American Revolution. They signed petitions against slavery to both the colonial legislature and to British authorities, and they sued in court for freedom. Indeed, it was ultimately judges, pronouncing judgments in such suits, that effectively ended slavery in Massachusetts immediately after the Revolution. (In these suits, John Adams several times represented the slave owners defending their property rights—a fact seldom mentioned by his biographers.)[29]

In Charles Town in 1773, Quincy was shocked by what he learned of the colony's Negro Act.

Two justices and three freeholders might and very often did *instanter* upon view or complaint try a negro for any crime, and might and did often award execution of death, issue their warrant and it was done forthwith. Two gentlemen present said they had issued such warrants several times. This law too was for *free* as well as *slave*-negroes and mullatoes. They further informed me, that neither negroes or mulattoes could have a Jury; that for killing a negro, ever so wantonly, as without any provocation, there could be nothing but *a fine;* they gave a late instance of this; that (further) to *steal* a negro was death, but to *kill him* was only fineable. Curious laws and policy! I exclaimed. Very true, cried the company, but this is the case. [30]

On August 11, two justices of the peace and three other property owners convened a court to try and judge Thomas Jeremiah and the slave Jemmy. For the most part, such justices, few with any legal training, decided only minor civil and criminal disputes; cases with more at stake went to courts in Charles Town. Only in trials under the Negro Act were justices called upon to make judgments on cases of life or death. In *The Practical Justice of the Peace and Parish-Officer, of His Majesty's Province of South Carolina,* a former chief justice of the colony, William Simpson, urged that, in all trials of Negroes held under the act, "a record of such trials seems highly necessary." If such records were indeed made, few survived from the colonial period, and as with the great majority of such cases, no official records of the trial of Jeremiah and Jemmy have been preserved.[31]

The names of two members of Jeremiah's and Jemmy's court are known. John Coram, one of the justices, was a retail dry goods merchant. Though never a major leader, he had been active in the patriot movement at least since 1769, when he had been named to the committee of thirty-nine charged with enforcing the nonimportation agreement of that year. Daniel Cannon, among the "mechanics" of Charles Town who had risen to political influence during the past decade, was one of the freeholders. A "carpenter" in most sources, he had, by the 1760s, become a contractor and sawmill owner; his crews, including numerous slaves, built grand houses for the city's rich and worked on the new poorhouse and hospital. He had been a leader of the Sons of Liberty and the Wilkes Club, formed by mechanics to support the cause of John Wilkes, who had been imprisoned in London for "libeling" the king. After the Sons of Liberty emerged, Cannon filled several important positions in Charles Town, among them street commissioner, commissioner for public markets, fire master, and vestryman of St. Philip's Church. Like Coram, he served on the 1769 committee to enforce nonimportation. He was elected in January 1775 as one of the city's thirty representatives to the Provincial Congress and, in March, served on the grand jury that investigated the subversive preaching of the free black Englishman, David Margrett. In June, Cannon was appointed by the Provincial Congress to Thomas Bee's committee to investigate the threatened insurrection. As a politically powerful leader of the mechanics and a member of the investigative committee that first fingered Thomas Jeremiah, Cannon may well have been the dominant member of the court.[32]

The two key witnesses against Jeremiah were Jemmy, himself on trial as co-conspirator, and the slave Sambo. Coram had recorded the testimony of both back in June, and presumably in the August trial both reiterated their claims: Sambo, vaguely, that Jeremiah had told of a "great War coming soon" "to help the Poor Negroes"; Jemmy, in more damning detail, that Jeremiah asked him to take "a few guns" to "Dewar a run away slave," that slaves were preparing "to fight against the Inhabitants of this Province," and that Jeremiah himself would "have the Chief Command of the said Negroes." According to one source, at least one other witness (not named) backed up the charges. The members of the court could ask whatever questions they wished of Jeremiah, Jemmy, Sambo, and any other witnesses, though we have no way of knowing if they did. Two sources suggest two additional specific charges, one, that Jeremiah had said, "If the British ships come here, he would pilot them over Charlestown Bar"; the other, from decades later, that Jeremiah planned to "set fire to Charlestown."[33]

It is certain that Jeremiah vigorously denied all charges. There is one intriguing, and, at the same time, frustrating, statement about the trial, from Henry Laurens, that "Jerry when he was first confronted by Jemmy, positively denied that he knew his person—that he knew the Man—although upon enquiry it clearly appeared that they were old acquaintance & nearly allied by Jerry's connection as a husband to the other Man's sister." Intriguing, both because it tells us that Jeremiah *was* married and because it hints at a personal motive behind Jemmy's testimony—was there animosity between the two brothers-in-law, one free, the other enslaved? Frustrating, because this is *all* the sources reveal about these personal matters. We do not know the name of Thomas Jeremiah's wife, or whether she was free or still enslaved, or whether the couple had children. Other free black men in Charles Town had purchased family members, including wives; some had freed their wives and children. (Children born to a still-enslaved mother were slaves by law and belonged to the mother's owner; children born to a free woman were free from birth.) Was his wife a faithful visitor to his cell? Did she appeal, in his behalf, to influential whites, even Lord William Campbell? There are no answers in the surviving records.[34]

Nor is there evidence that Jemmy's testimony was motivated by anything other than his own hopes for a pardon and an understandable desire to live. Laurens's statement that Jeremiah denied even knowing Jemmy is, as with much of the other surviving claims, quite problematic. It is hard to believe that Jeremiah could have thought that he could get away with denying that he knew his own wife's brother. Yet, if Coram, Cannon, and the other members of the court believed he had lied, it would have strengthened their sense of resolve in deciding against him. Their decision was unanimous. Guilty, for both Thomas Jeremiah and Jemmy.[35]

The law left to the court, not only the finding of guilt or innocence, but also the determination of the punishment. While allowing consideration of mercy "as in their discretion shall think fit," the law also limited that discretion, insisting that in every case in which more than one slave was "concerned" in an "attempt to raise an insurrection," at least one "shall be executed for example, to deter others from offending in the like kind." The court's judgment did not stop at the sentence of death; the law further authorized them to inflict "such manner of death, and at such time, as the said justices, by and with the consent of the freeholders, shall direct, and which they shall judge will be most effectual to deter others from offending in the like manner." They might, for example, sentence both Jeremiah and Jemmy to be burned at the stake (as two slaves had been burned in 1769 in Charles Town, for poisoning). They did not go that far, sentencing both to be hanged one week later, on August 18. Afterward, though, their bodies were to be taken down and burned. There would be no grave to memorialize these condemned rebels.[36]

—•—

CHAPTER SEVEN

"Justice is Satisfied!"

"It was not in our Power . . . to prevent it"

ON THE AFTERNOON of August 12, 1775, the day after Thomas Jeremiah's trial, a rowdy crowd surged through the streets of Charles Town, hauling on a cart the forlorn figure of George Walker, a British gunner at Fort Johnson, naked, tarred, and feathered. According to Arthur Middleton, one of the members of the Council of Safety who favored extreme measures, Walker's "crime" was "nothing less than damning us all." Walker gave a rather different version of the events. As he later claimed, he had been on board a ship in the harbor when the captain demanded that he "drink damnation" to King George. When he refused, he was put ashore and quickly surrounded by a "mob of Rebels" who "insisted on his drinking some treasonable and rebellious Toasts against his Majesty's person & Government." Walker was given a "sham trial" at the base of the Exchange. Found "guilty" of "insolent speech," his punishment was to be stripped, tarred and feathered, and carried through the city streets for five hours. He was then given another chance to damn the king but instead defiantly "drank damnation to the Rebels." The enraged crowd then carried out the sentence, not only covering him with tar and feathers, but pelting him with stones and "filth" picked up from the streets, injuring a rib and an eye. From 2:00 that afternoon until 7:00 in the evening, the crowd pulled him through the town, stopping at the houses of Governor Campbell, members of the Governor's Council, and other Tories, applying more tar and feathers at every stop. At the house of Fenwicke Bull, who was reviled for once trying to bribe a jockey to throw a horse race, "they stopt, call'd for Grog; had it; made Walker drink D——n to Bull, threw a bag of feathers into his Balcony, & desired he would take care of it 'till his turn came; & that he would charge the Grog to the Acct of Ld North."[1]

That same afternoon, another loyalist, the royal surgeon Dr. George Millegen, visiting his mother-in-law, had gone to sit under the shade of her balcony. As he had himself written more than a decade earlier, the summer heat could be brutal in Charles Town, especially when the winds came from the south and the air was "sultry and suffocating." In the worst stretches—as in the memorable summer of 1752—"Refreshing Sleep was a Stranger to our eyes, and though we lay on thin matresses upon the floor, with all the windows and doors open, we were constantly bathed in Sweat. . . . Dogs sought the Shade and lay panting, as if they had long pursued the Chace; poultry drooped the wing, and breathed with open throats." Then everyone suffered "an excessive Dejection of Spirits, and Debility of Body."[2]

Though it was hot that August 1775, Charles Town was getting daily thunderstorms, the air "ventilated and renewed as it were, by these temporary agitations," and if Millegen was feeling "dejection of spirit," it may have been less from the weather than from the summons he had received the previous day to appear, once more, before members of the Charles Town General Committee. Millegen had refused to sign the pledge of "Association" demanded by local patriots, but, unlike most of the Non-Associators, he had been known as a part of Charles Town society for three decades. Since his army service during King George's War, he had served as a surgeon for both South Carolina's provincial troops and regular British forces. He had made a good living as a physician in Charles Town, "beloved, & respected by all ranks." He was married in St. Philip's, the mother church of Anglicanism in the colony, and he joined the private Charles Town Library Society. It was Millegen who had written the society's "Advertisement," proclaiming the determination of the members to prove themselves "worthy of their Mother-Country, by imitating her Humanity, as well as her Industry, and by transporting from her the Improvements in the finer as well as in the inferior arts." In his *Account of the Situation, Air, Weather, and Diseases of South Carolina*, published in 1763, Millegen had praised the colony's gentry ("more numerous here than in any other Colony in North-America") as dressing with "Elegance and Neatness," as "sensible, spirited, and open-hearted," and as exceeding most people in "Acts of Benevolence, Hospitality, and Charity." South Carolina's ladies were "genteel and slender," their air "easy and natural," their manners "free and unaffected." Indeed, he later wrote, South Carolina was "the most thriving Country perhaps on this Globe, and might have been the happiest"—but for the "Demon of rebellion" that had "banished humanity from among them, with every other virtue."[3]

On that evening of August 12, the Demon of rebellion paid Millegen a visit. The mob pulling George Walker on a cart suddenly appeared, heading for his house, but found him instead, three doors away, under the balcony of his mother-in-law's home. Millegen's "small sword" offered little protection against the "outrageous mob," which was, as he later wrote, "hissing, threatening and abusing me." "Here is the scoundrel Millegen." "Put him into the cart with the other." "He is the greatest villain of the two." "Seize the scoundrel and bring him to the cart." The crowd hesitated as Millegen put his hand to his sword. Suddenly his wife, who had been in a back room, "flew into my arms and fainted away." Men "poured into the house and almost terrified to death" his mother-in-law, Mrs. Watson. The jeering and shouting crowd swarmed around Millegen as he carried his wife to his own house down the street. They forced open the gate to his yard, as a female slave ("a faithful creature") came to his assistance, only to be "knocked . . . down several times." Millegen managed to push the intruders out and lock the gate. It was now 7:00 p.m., and the mob carried Walker back to the waterfront and put him under the town pump for an hour, before dumping him off Beal's wharf into the harbor. He was picked up and carried to safety by a friendly boat. The men in the crowd had made their point: "There was scarce a non-subscriber [to the Association] who did not tremble."[4]

The next day, Millegen's friends urged him to leave the city; the day after that Governor William Campbell gave the same advice. But Millegen was determined at least to face the General Committee on the day he had been summoned for, Tuesday, August 15. The committee had decided to ask the Non-Associators to swear "on the Holy Evangelists of Almighty God" that they would not "by word, deed, or writing, attempt to counteract or oppose the proceedings of the people of North-America and particularly in this province." Henry Laurens, committee president, found the whole procedure distasteful and embarrassing, but he was spared participation because the General Committee delegated the hearings to a small subcommittee. Millegen, again, refused to bend. Millegen had, in July, freed his slave, Thomas Gullan, for a token payment of £5 in South Carolina currency, "in consideration of the favor and affection which I have for and bear towards" him. He told his wife good-bye before his hearing on August 15, and immediately after the interrogation he was taken by canoe out to the *Tamar* man-of-war in the harbor, never to set foot in Charles Town again. To Arthur Middleton, a member of the subcommittee that interrogated Millegen, the incident was amusing. He wrote to William Henry Drayton that Millegen wanted to avoid George Walker's fate, or, as he put it jocularly, he "had an unconquerable Dislike to the mode of Cloathing lately adopted in these scarce times."[5]

That same Tuesday, Lord William Campbell sent a message to the Commons House of Assembly, which was meeting daily and adjourning without conducting any business. He had never seen a tar-and-feathering before the Saturday crowd came to his house with George Walker in tow. "I have been a Spectator," said his message, "of outrages I little expected ever to have seen in this place," and especially the "barbarous outrage committed in the Streets of this Town on a poor, helpless, wretched, individual, with the particular circumstances of Cruelty, & Insult." Regretting that he "neither can protect, nor punish," he asked the Commons House for help "in this dreadful emergency" in enforcing the laws. Or would they rather admit that "all Law, & Government is at an end?" He also asked for assurances that his own family would remain safe "& that its Peace is not in any danger of being invaded."[6]

The Commons House asked Henry Laurens to draft a reply, which he labored over during the next two days. Everything, he wrote, was the fault of "the oppressive hand of an Arbitrary Ministry" that had driven the people of South Carolina "to the most unhappy extremities." As for George Walker, Charles Town had been "enraged by the daring & unprovoked Insolence of a person who although he was supported by the public & eat the Country's Bread had openly & ungratefully uttered the most bitter Curses and Imprecations against the People of this Colony & of all America." They had, Laurens wrote in his draft, "Tared & feathered him," but, crossing that out, he substituted "after a slight Corporal [punishment] had Carted him through the streets." A revealing, almost apologetic, admission followed: "This we confess was an Outrage: at the same time, your Excy must do us the Justice to own it was not in our Power nor within the line of our Duty to prevent it." In the final, and official, version of the reply, the Commons House itself edited this last point: "It is not in our power in such cases, to prescribe limits to popular fury." The Commons House did add a tepid apology that Campbell had suffered insults and feared that his family was in danger. It concluded with a warning in the form of advice that "your Excellency's wise and prudent conduct, will render such apprehensions groundless."[7]

"Perfectly resigned to his fate"

In the midst of these sometimes chaotic events, life continued as usual for most people in Charles Town—at least those who were white. Every night, members of the Corner Club met at Dillon's Tavern, at Broad and Church, to drink "in an Ocean of froth & folly." Provincial soldiers kept up their nightly patrols, and any slaves about kept quiet. The Atlantic shipping trade had ground to a near-complete halt, but then August had always been relatively quiet, with the slave trade slowed by hurricane season and the new rice crop still in the fields.[8]

At the Work House, Thomas Jeremiah and Jemmy had new company, Sango, "about 4 feet 10 inches high, has a scar over his right Eye, and a Brand on his left Breast. . . . Taken up at Goose Creek 13 Miles from Town." The days to the hanging were dwindling. As the condemned waited, however, some of Charles Town's influential men began to express an interest in their case, then concern, then full-bore support. To be sure, Henry Laurens claimed that Jeremiah had "many friends among people of his own Colour." These "friends," perhaps among the city's small number of other free blacks and the slaves who knew him and his family, may have been appealing privately to important whites, though no surviving sources say this. But two important white men were taking "uncommon pains" in their behalf. These were the rectors of the two Anglican churches in the city, the Reverend Robert Cooper of St. Michael's and the Reverend Robert Smith of St. Philip's.[9]

Most ministers of Britain's state church, of which the king himself was head, were loyalists, not patriots, in the American Revolution. One such, the Reverend Mr. Bullman, assistant minister at St. Michael's, in 1774 had denounced from the pulpit the spirit of the times, when "every idle Projector, who cannot, perhaps, govern his own household, or pay the debts of his own contracting, presumes he is qualified to dictate how the State should be governed," and "every silly Clown, and illiterate Mechanic, will take upon him to censure the conduct of his Prince or Governor." Each, he advised them, should "keep his own rank, and . . . do his own duty, in his own station, without usurping an undue authority over his neighbour, or pretending to censure his superiors in a matter wherin he is not himself immediately aggrieved." A majority of the congregation, many of them the very mechanics Bullman insulted, promptly voted to dismiss him, and he had left the colony in the spring of 1775. The Reverend Mr. Cooper was himself suspected of Tory sympathies, and in 1776, he, too, would leave South Carolina for England.[10]

The Reverend Robert Smith, however, shared with the planters, merchants, and well-to-do mechanics who filled his pews in St. Philip's a "common indignation at the conduct of the [British] Ministry." That was one reason he had been chosen to deliver a sermon on February 17, 1775, a day set aside by the patriots, meeting in the Provincial Congress, for "fasting, humiliation and prayer, before Almighty God devoutly to petition him to inspire the King with true wisdom, to defend the people of North-America in their just title of freedom." Again, on July 20, designated by the Second Continental Congress as a day for "fasting, humiliation, and prayer," Smith had preached in St. Philip's pulpit "a sermon suitable to the occasion." No one could doubt on whose side the Reverend Mr. Smith stood.[11]

People noticed, then, when both rectors, Smith and Cooper, visited Thomas Jeremiah in the Work House, and when Smith returned there repeatedly. Jeremiah professed to be a Christian, and these visits were appropriate for men who faced imminent death, but as Laurens noted, such visits had, even for white prisoners, usually been "left to the Dissenting Ministers" such as the Baptist Oliver Hart. But the purpose of the visits was not only to offer Christian consolation but also to elicit confession and penitence, thus confirming the justice of the sentence and removing any lingering doubts about guilt or innocence. Thus, the crowd was pleased when, in 1769, Dolly, a slave about to be burned to death for poisoning, "made a free confession, acknowledged the justice of her punishment, and died a penitent." It was disappointed when Liverpoole, the "Negro Doctor" accused of giving Dolly the poison, did neither before he, too, was burned at the stake. By explaining God's willingness to forgive a repentant sinner, together with divine power to punish in awful fashion those who refused, a minister could bring great authority to this quest for confession.[12]

The Reverend Mr. Smith, as he himself later explained, "attended this black as much from a desire to ascertain the reality of an instigated insurrection as from motives of humanity," and, accordingly, "used every argument, every art," probing for contradictions, seeking to draw out a confession. But in vain. Jeremiah adamantly denied his guilt and declared his complete innocence. "His behaviour was modest," the rector told Governor Campbell, "his conversation sensible to a degree that astonished [me], and at the same time he was perfectly resigned to his unhappy, his undeserved fate. He declared he wished not for life, he was in a happy frame of mind and prepared for death." The Reverend Smith had neither wanted nor expected such a response. Smith then questioned the slave Jemmy closely, and separately. Jemmy recanted his entire testimony. He had been told, so Jemmy said, that giving testimony was the only way he could avoid punishment, and in any case, the court had told him that they contemplated nothing more than whippings for those accused. (This admission, by Jemmy, indeed, echoes the complaint of Henry Laurens, back in June, that the court had planned simply to whip some of the accused and let them go.)[13]

Just when Lord William learned about Thomas Jeremiah and his trial is not known. He knew when the August 11 trial took place, and he knew of the conviction. He also knew that this supposed crime was connected to earlier rumors that he was part of the planned insurrection and had planned to arrive the previous June with thousands of arms in the hold of his ship, to distribute to the slaves. As governor, he was the only person in the colony to whom appeals from a sentence could be made, and he waited for some sort of petition to arrive. But none came. Finally, he asked John Coram, one of the justices of the peace in the trial, to lay before him the precise charges and the evidence the court had heard. On Wednesday, August 16, Coram complied, bringing copies of the statements made by the two accusers, Jemmy and Sambo.[14]

"My blood run cold," Campbell later wrote, "when I read on what grounds they had doomed a fellow creature to death . . . [and I] expressed to the justice in the strongest terms my sense of the weakness of the evidence, and entreated that for his [that is, Coram's] own sake and that of his fellows he would get a petition signed by him." As reported later by Coram to others, Campbell's words had been direct indeed: "the People should consider what might be the Consequence of executing him upon such Evidence in case the times should alter." Campbell adamantly denied using this language—essentially a threat that the patriots might, in the future, deserve a similar sort of summary trial for their own rebellion—but the reports of it, spread by Coram to others, "greatly affected the minds of those to whom it was repeated." These latter words, from the pen of Henry Laurens, were, in fact, an understatement. Campbell's own version was that "my attempting to interfere in the matter raised such a clamour amongst the people as is incredible, and they openly and loudly declared if I granted the man a pardon they would hang him at my door." From "a man of the first property in the province who had always expressed great friendship"—probably Miles Brewton, his first host and his relative by marriage—Campbell heard a similar warning about "the dreadful consequences that would attend my pardoning him," with the vivid conclusion that it "would raise a flame all the water in Cooper River would not extinguish."[15]

"A Case of Blood"

Campbell, refusing to give up, asked his attorney general, James Simpson, and the judges on the Court of General Sessions (the regular criminal court of the province) to provide legal opinions about the trial, the evidence, and the sentence. These men, accordingly, met with John Coram and Daniel Cannon. They reviewed the written evidence and were told that the court had heard other, oral, testimony as well. Coram and Cannon had questioned Sambo and Jemmy on several occasions, always getting the same story, and, convinced of Jeremiah's guilt, had accordingly sentenced him to be hanged "and then burned to ashes."

Campbell asked these legal advisers to tell him three things: Was Thomas Jeremiah properly tried under the Negro Act, even though he was a free man? Did the evidence support a finding of guilty? Was death an allowable punishment? On Thursday, the six men retired, individually, to think about the case; that evening, they gave their answers in writing. And they were split. Simpson, who had been visited by the tar-and-feather crowd the previous Saturday; Chief Justice Thomas Knox Gordon; and Justices Edward Savage and William Gregory all concurred that the trial was *not* legally proper and that Jeremiah should not suffer death. Justice Charles Mathews Coslett disagreed, and Justice John Fewtrell refused to give an opinion. Yet, even before they began to discuss the case among themselves, they told Campbell their opinions would make no difference, that Jeremiah's death "was determined on" and, moreover, that the execution would be carried out "with particular circumstances of insult" if the governor tried to stop it.[16]

Campbell was, as he later wrote, "almost distracted and wished to have been able to fly to the remotest corner of the earth from a set of barbarians who are worse than the most cruel savages any history has described." Still he persisted. Having learned about the Reverend Mr. Smith's visits to the Work House, he asked Smith to come see him. On Thursday, Smith recounted his story of Jeremiah's steadfast denials of guilt and of Jemmy's confession that his testimony had been false. Determining on one last effort, Campbell asked Smith to write down his account, so he could send it to the court and the patriot leaders. He decided, too, at Smith's request, to issue a pardon for Jemmy—although whites in Charles Town seemed determined to hang Jeremiah, there was apparently no objection to letting Jemmy off. That evening, the governor sent a copy of Smith's statement to John Coram, with a cover note: "Without attempting to comment upon the contents of this paper, I only Send it for your perusal. In a Case of Blood I wave *Ceremony*, I would even give up *Dignity* to Save the Life of an Innocent Man.—Consider it Seriously Sir, lay it before your Brother Justice, & the Freeholders, between God & your own Consciences be it, I take every Holy Power to witness I am innocent of this Mans death, upon your Heads be it, for without your interposition I find I cannot Save him." Coram passed this note along to Laurens, who thought it "a very extraordinary Letter," in effect, accusing Coram and the rest of the court members of "the shedding of innocent blood." One member of the court actually did try to get a petition for pardon signed by the other members, or so Campbell said, but Coram, Cannon, and the rest were unmoved.[17]

A second copy of the Anglican rector's account went, at 7:00 p.m. on Thursday, to Laurens himself, as president of the Council of Safety and of the Charles Town General Committee. It did not reach him until 9:00, at a meeting of the General Committee, where he was presiding. This time Campbell's note was not quite as personal: "I beg leave to inclose a paper for your perusal which has affected me more than words can express[.] Surely Sir I may appeal to your feelings for me as the Representative of Majesty in this unhappy Province, Think Sir of the weight of Blood, I am told I cannot attempt to save this Man without bringing greater Guilt on this Country than I can bear even to think of." Laurens had the papers read to the General Committee, but the committee "utterly refused to take them under Consideration."[18]

Laurens himself thought that "good manners" required a response, so after the committee adjourned, he went home and wrote a reply to Campbell late that night. Claiming—implausibly—to be unfamiliar with the details of the specific evidence against "Jerry," Laurens told the governor that he was satisfied that "the unhappy Man in Question was found Guilty after a fair Legal trial," with a unanimous verdict. He dismissed the Reverend Smith's account of Jemmy's retraction, on the grounds that Jemmy had changed his testimony only "after he secured his own pardon and Reward." This was untrue, since Jemmy was not pardoned until at least a day after he had recanted his testimony to Smith. With "this Colony under the threats of Insurrections," and "strong proofs" against the accused, Laurens wrote, it was "no wonder they are alarmed at the Sound of Pardon to a Man circumstanced in all respects as Jerry is,—especially after the recent Instance of one of their Negro Pilots being illegally carried away by the Commander of one of His Majesty's Sloops of War."[19]

Laurens's last comment, referring to the departure of the *Scorpion* with a black pilot a month before, is revealing for two reasons. It points out the Americans' real fear that Charles Town's black pilots might prove valuable allies to an invading British fleet. But even if true, this violation of the orders of the Provincial Congress was hardly a capital offense. Laurens's reply also reveals a lack of candor. Just a month before, writing to his son John, he had referred to the departure of the black pilot on the *Scorpion* but admitted that Captain Tollemache of the *Scorpion* had been provoked by the colony's refusal to give up some of his seamen who had left his ship to volunteer for the new provincial troops. "I was singular in my opposition to that impolitic measure," he wrote to John, "& expressly foretold the consequence." Writing now to Campbell, he made no such admission.[20]

Laurens's reply reached Campbell late Thursday night. Early Friday morning (execution day), he had his secretary, Alexander Innes, reply to Laurens, correcting Laurens's misunderstanding about Jemmy's testimony and pardon. The Reverend Mr. Smith had heard the recantation by Wednesday at the latest; the application for Jemmy's pardon was not submitted until Thursday at noon and not signed until 6:00 p.m. that day. Even now, Innes claimed, Jemmy would not know that he had escaped a hanging unless John Coram had told him about it. Laurens immediately replied—it was just 7:00 a.m.—and again his response showed confusion about the sequence of events. Having heard, back on Wednesday, from John Coram about Campbell's interest in pardoning Thomas Jeremiah, he had assumed that this was the same date as Jemmy's pardon. He repeated Coram's story about his meeting with Campbell on Wednesday, quoting the supposed remark about what would happen "in case the times should alter." "With regard to Jemmy," Laurens wrote, "he is certainly a liar of the most abominable order of Liars," and he was "at a loss what kind or degree of Credit to give to his Testimony." It was an odd note to conclude on, since it was as much an impeachment of the original testimony as of the retraction.[21]

Innes replied again—immediately—to set the record straight and to explain that "you have mistaken Jemmy for Jerry," that no pardon for Jemmy had been considered before noon on Thursday; "Mr. Smith can satisfy Mr. Laurens in that part if a doubt remains in his breast." Innes stoutly denied that Campbell had made any veiled threats as Coram claimed and just as stoutly defended the governor's motives as proceeding only from "Humanity Justice and Mercy." He closed: "Adieu Sir I beg pardon for detaining you so long the horrid Scene will soon be closed and the Matter decided by that Eternal God to whom all hearts are open & before whom the most Secret thoughts cannot be hid."[22]

Innes was right about the "horrid Scene." Between the hours of 11:00 and 12:00 that morning, Thomas Jeremiah was brought to the green across from the Work House, the same place where Dolly and Liverpoole had been burned at the stake in 1769, for poisoning, and where Williamson Willis, a white man, had been hung in 1773 for "stealing a Negro." (As Josiah Quincy, Jr., had noted, whites could only be fined for killing a slave, but they could be hanged for stealing one.) It was the seventeenth execution in Charles Town in the past decade. Before the daily thunderstorms hit, Jeremiah's body was consumed by fire. He asserted his innocence once more before he was swung off the cart to strangle to death. He "behaved with the greatest intrepidity as well as decency," Governor Campbell later wrote, "and told his implacable and ungrateful persecutors God's judgment would one day overtake them for shedding his innocent blood."[23]

✦

Was he guilty? Did Thomas Jeremiah plan a slave insurrection? Henry Laurens believed it, or so he wrote to Alexander Innes immediately after the execution, in a final response to Innes's communications of that morning. Although he did not doubt that the governor had been motivated by feelings of humanity, justice, and mercy, he said, "I must declare that I also now believe that Jerry was Guilty." "The Scene is closed! Justice is satisfied!"[24]

Two days later, Laurens repeated this claim in another letter to his son John. "Uncommon pains" had been taken to save Jeremiah; the legality of the trial had been "called into question," and one of Campbell's supporters "threw Magna Charta in the Faces of the people." He summarized for his son the sequence of events: the Reverend Mr. Smith's intervention and Jemmy's recantation of testimony; the General Committee's refusal to consider the matter; Laurens's own correspondence with the governor and his secretary. Jemmy's retraction "could have no weight," he insisted, considering that the accusation had been supported by two other witnesses, that Sambo had stuck to *his* story, and that Jeremiah had denied knowing Jemmy, who turned out to be his own wife's brother. "I am now fully satisfied that Jerry was guilty of a design & attempt to encourage our Negroes to Rebellion & joining the King's Troops if any had been sent here."[25]

South Carolina loyalists believed the entire episode had been manufactured to provide an excuse to raise a military force at home that would overawe supporters of the British government, including the governor. To Campbell's secretary, Alexander Innes, the case was a "horrid Conspiracy." Writing a year later, he claimed that the colony's leaders, after the news of battles at Lexington and Concord, "were under the necessity of having recourse to a Plot, pretended to be formed by Government, for an Insurection of the Slaves, to collect the Militia, and furnish a pretence for raising two

Regiments of Infantrie." The story of an insurrection "was industriously propogated, by the Designing, & was credited by and terrified the Weak." For Dr. George Millegen, too, writing aboard a ship the following month, the insurrection scare was no more than a "bugbear." The accusations that "His Majesty's ministers and other servants instigated their slaves to rebel against their masters and to cut their throats" was "credited by the ignorant and unwary." The claim was further boosted by unfounded rumors that some slaves were refusing to work, that others "had obtained arms and were gone into the woods," and that still others had murdered their masters, and all this was used by patriots to frighten whites in Charles Town into signing the Association and to justify the raising of "an armed force to be entirely at their disposal to protect themselves and to intimidate and distress His Majesty's loyal subjects." Thomas Jeremiah had been "a sacrifice to the groundless fears of some and the wicked policy of others."[26]

Some historians who have mentioned the incident have written in full confidence that Jeremiah was planning to lead a slave revolt; others have been more skeptical. Perhaps the only definitive judgment to be made is that we will never know with certainty. My own view is that Innes and Millegen were mistaken in believing the execution part of a cynical plot. Many sources are clear that even sober-minded people like Henry Laurens repeatedly expressed their concerns, in private and in public, about a possible slave insurrection. Their fears were not unreasonable. Whites knew, from both remote and recent history and from their own experience, that many slaves hated slavery and would gladly have overthrown it by violence, if they dared and could. They had seen it attempted in the Stono Rebellion, a living memory for most patriot leaders; in the next few years, they would see many of their slaves flock to British lines and sometimes volunteer to fight with British forces. They had been recently reminded of these dangers, if they needed any reminding, by the preaching of David Margrett in January and of the slave George in July.[27]

At the same time, the evidence against Thomas Jeremiah is, on its face, extraordinarily weak. And there is the man himself, although we can see and hear him now only through the eyes and ears of others. Governor Campbell's incredulity rings true: "It was needless to urge the improbability of a fellow in affluent circumstances, who was universally acknowledged to be remarkably sensible and sagacious, possessed of slaves of his own, entering into so wild a scheme as to instigate an insurrection without support, without encourage-ment (for happily not a shadow of evidence appeared that any white man was concerned)."[28]

Certainly, when closely examined, Henry Laurens's arguments reek of special pleading. He was writing, as he admitted to his son two days after the execution, "to furnish you with a narrative of Jerry's latter history as to enable you in case of need to contradict false reports which may be, among others, propagated to the prejudice of the poor Carolinians whose impolicy &, in many instances, mad conduct, will appear glaring enough without the aid of one Lie." Laurens could admit "mad conduct" among his fellow patriots, but not the lack of courage and virtue that would be implied by deliberately hanging an innocent man. And in his final analysis, it was less the evidence against Jeremiah that told for Laurens than the black man's character and his fear of the consequences of a pardon. As for the former, "Jerry was a forward fellow, puffed up by prosperity, ruined by Luxury & debauchery & grown to an amazing pitch of vanity & ambition—& withal a very Silly Coxcomb—Such Characters are found in all Countries, & Men may be ruined by prosperity when perhaps their whole Estate real & personal would not yield an hundred Guineas." It seems fair to point out that, if this sort of character was a sign of guilt, half of South Carolina's political leaders would have deserved hanging.[29]

As for the fear of the consequences, Laurens admitted to his son that, while "I altogether acquit the Governor" of bad motives, "my regard for him induced me to alarm him. . . . For although I know none of the out of Door Secrets of the people, & carefully avoid Such knowledge, yet I had heard enough to fill me with horror from a prospect of what might be done by Men enraged as Men would have been if a pardon had been Issued." After the example of George Walker, tarred-and-feathered in the streets, Laurens and other patriot leaders had admitted that "it is not in our power . . . to prescribe limits to popular fury." Laurens did not want to see a gallows erected on Meeting Street in front of the governor's house, as had been threatened if a pardon was issued, and surely did not want to see Campbell, a member of a British noble family, dragged into the streets to witness such a vigilante hanging—or even share in it. Also, elections for Charles Town's representatives in the next session of the Provincial Congress, which would meet in November, would take place just ten days after the hanging, and anyone openly opposing the execution might well be rejected by the voters. And yet, to go so far as to acknowledge, not just to others but to himself, that his fellow Carolina patriots were committing what Campbell called a judicial murder, Laurens could not do. It had been the same with his vacillating convictions on the slave trade, and on slavery itself. He could never admit that the world of liberty and justice for men like himself, a world for which he was prepared to sacrifice all, was founded on the denial of liberty and justice to others. In this trial, he had blinked.

"By God and my Country"

The trial and execution of Thomas Jeremiah is a story about America at its founding, but not the kind celebrated on the Fourth of July. When Henry Laurens wrote that supporters of a pardon for Jeremiah had "called into question" the law under which he was tried and "threw Magna Charta in the Faces of the people," he laid bare the conflicting visions of what America was and should be, as well as the conflicting actions taken to fulfill that vision. For Governor Campbell and his few supporters in the colony, the nub of the case was about the rights of Britons, rights that were rooted precisely in the Magna Carta. Thus, Dr. George Millegen wrote that "this man's trial was illegal. . . . this man was free and a Christian and possessed of property to the amount of six or seven hundred pounds sterling, therefore he ought to have been tried by the King's court and by a jury." But to Laurens and other white patriots, Jeremiah's property, religion, and freedom were as nothing in the scales when weighed against the stigma of his African descent.[30]

The same split appears in the legal opinions solicited by Governor Campbell when he was trying so desperately to save Jeremiah. All of his legal advisers, the judges and attorney general, began with the provisions of the Negro Act of 1740, which stated quite clearly that "all crimes and offences committed by free negroes, Indians . . . mulattoes or mustizoes, shall be proceeded in, heard, tried, adjudged and determined by the justices and freeholders appointed by this Act for the trial of slaves, in like manner, order and form, as is hereby directed and appointed for the proceedings and trial of crimes and offences committed by slaves; any law, statute, usage or custom to the contrary notwithstanding." Four of the six advisers proceeded to analyze the issues as an English judge was expected to do: the law being "of a very penal nature, must receive a strict and literal construction." In England, it was not at all unusual for this sort of "strict and literal" view of the penal code to lead to dismissed indictments or overturned verdicts, even in capital cases where the facts themselves were not in dispute—for example, because a name was spelled wrong in an indictment or the precise wording of a charge was incorrect.[31] Turning to the Negro Act, the majority of advisers pointed out that the crucial seventeenth section, specifying that "every slave who shall raise or attempt to raise an insurrection in this Province" should suffer death, did *not* (like other sections of the act) specifically mention free Negroes. They concluded that "the said Jerry being a *free Negroe* and *not a slave* is clearly not within the words of the said 17th Section." If Jeremiah was not covered by the Negro Act clause on insurrections, he would have to be considered "in like manner as a white man." In existing British law, the relevant crime for a white man would be "levying of War" against the king, but an act of Parliament had declared that no one, whatever his alleged words, could be convicted of this crime unless he had committed some kind of overt act.[32]

The dissenting opinion by Justice Charles Coslett agreed with the facts, but not with the conclusion. Granting that any penal law "according to the usual rule . . . ought to be taken strictly," he pointed out that the Negro Act called for its clauses to "be construed most largely and beneficially for the promoting and carrying into execution this Act." To interpret the act any other way was unthinkable, he concluded: "I could not help reflecting, that there was a vast multitude of slaves and free Negroes Mullatoes &c in the Province, and that it might be of the most fatal consequence to the lives and properties of the white Inhabitants, if these fellows once got it into their heads that free Negroes &c were not punishable under this Act for such an enormous crime."[33] It was not just a question of slavery and freedom, or of crime and punishment, but of whites and those who were not white.

When an Englishman or Englishwoman stood trial for a serious offense, except in the rare circumstances of a guilty plea, the clerk asked each how each wished to be tried. The correct answer was "by God and my Country." "My country," here, was the jury itself—the defendant would be judged by his "countrymen."[34] In South Carolina in 1751, Governor James Glen had complained to the Commons House of Assembly that the colony was not properly enforcing the legal requirement that jury members be freeholders—owners of a minimum amount of real property. Propertyless men should not serve on juries, he wrote, because such men, "having no estates either in lands or goods," were not "that Country," but instead, "in the eye of the law, Strangers, a sort of Sojourners among us." Social and economic conditions in America eroded the traditional identification of property holders as the only true members of "the country," and the American Revolution turned out to be a moment when that expansion of meaning became orthodox. It was Thomas Jefferson's rhetorical genius to enshrine a larger notion of who belonged to "the country," when he wrote into America's founding document that "all men" are entitled, not to the classic Lockean formulation of "life, liberty, and property," but to "life, liberty, and the pursuit of happiness."[35]

Thomas Jeremiah was a property holder, a large property holder. He was dependent on no one. But he could not be a "countryman." Nothing illustrates the point better than Henry Laurens's casual comment of 1774, when he had been in London and his servant Robert was accused of theft. Then, he had written to his friend George Appleby that he did not mind so much the loss of the value of a slave, and indeed "would never have regretted the loss of him, if he had bettered his fortune by Staying in England." But, "I confess my wishes are to See the Kingdom cleaned from every one of his Colour." The fate of Thomas Jeremiah illustrates the stark racial limitations—and for him the tragic consequences—of Laurens's visceral understanding of the meaning of Englishness, and thus of America. Thomas Jeremiah might be free, Christian, and a slave owner, but one "of his Colour" could never be an Englishman, and for Laurens, the America being born as a separate nation would be a white man's country.[36]

Epilogue

A FTER HIS EXECUTION, Thomas Jeremiah's name disappeared from the public records of South Carolina. There is no gravesite or memorial tablet. There is no surviving inventory of his property, as usually would have been made for a deceased property owner. Whether this was a deliberate omission or deletion, or simply the result of the destruction of records during the Revolutionary War, is unknown. There is nothing about his wife; we do not know her name or whether she was free or if Jeremiah had purchased her freedom. We know nothing of his children, if any; nothing about his slaves or his fishing boat. Memories of his story among Charles Town's slaves and free blacks were never recorded, as far as is known.

Thomas Jeremiah's story did linger for a time in both South Carolina and in London. At the end of August 1775, Lord William Campbell sent an extensive account of the trial and his failed attempts to save Jeremiah to his superiors in London. His account circulated in London, and John Laurens wrote to his father from there that, if the reports were accurate, "the character of our countrymen for justice and humanity would suffer very much." In Parliament, Lord Sandwich cited Jeremiah's case, in debate on December 15, 1775, as an example of Americans' injustice: after a "mock tribunal," with a "suborned" slave witness, they had "put an innocent free negro to death, attended with every circumstance of cruelty and baseness," just because he had "in an unguarded minute" said if the king's ships came to Charles Town, he would "pilot them safely up." A brief newspaper report of Sandwich's remarks simplified the story further: the Americans had "been so cruel as to . . . murder a free Negro of Property in Carolina, supposed to be a Friend of Government." In a widely circulated pamphlet, *Answer to the Declaration of the American Congress,* the authors cited the execution as an example of the many cruelties inflicted on innocent men by the American rebels.[1]

Thomas Jeremiah was, with few exceptions, erased from South Carolinians' histories of their revolution. The most influential early historian of the colony and state, David Ramsay (Henry Laurens's son-in-law), ignores Jeremiah in his two-volume history of South Carolina in the Revolution; so does William Moultrie in his *Memoirs of the American Revolution So Far as It Relates to the States of North and South Carolina, and Georgia.* In John Drayton's *Memoirs of the American Revolution,* still a valuable source for South Carolina's historians, with many documents whose originals have been lost, Jeremiah appears, literally, in a footnote, as "Jerry," a "Negro man" and pilot, executed for conspiracy to excite an insurrection and to set fire to Charlestown, and because he said that "if the British ships come here, he would pilot them over Charlestown Bar." In Joseph Johnson's *Traditions and Reminiscences* of the Revolution, published in 1851, Jeremiah's story appears but barely survives in a brief and mangled version that gets most of the facts wrong. Not until the 1970s did South Carolina's historians rediscover Thomas Jeremiah.[2]

⋅✦⋅

Barely a month after Jeremiah's execution, Lord William Campbell fled to the protection of HMS *Tamar* in Charles Town harbor. From the *Tamar,* he transferred to the sloop of war *Cherokee* and stayed aboard in the harbor for the rest of the year, communicating as best he could with his family in Charles Town, with London, with the British military authorities in North America, and, from time to time, with the patriots who controlled the city and province. Throughout the fall of 1775, dozens of slaves fled to join him on the men-of-war in the harbor, and others fled to Sullivan's Island, where they were shielded by the protective guns of the British ships. The patriots remonstrated with the masters of the *Tamar* and *Cherokee* for "harbouring and protecting negroes, who fly from their masters to Sullivan's Island, and on board the vessels" in the harbor, and for "daily complaints from the inhabitants on the sea-coast, of robberies and depredations committed on them by white and black armed men, from on board some of the ships under your command." After receiving no satisfaction, in December they launched an attack on Sullivan's Island, killing several runaways, driving off some, and recapturing others.[3]

Sarah Izard Campbell, meanwhile, remained in the governor's mansion on Meeting Street with her three children. She was watched carefully but, for the most part, left alone until December 1775, when the commander of the *Scorpion* man-of-war, recently arrived back in Charles Town, seized a shipment of specie intended for the merchant brothers Samuel and Benjamin

Legaré. In retaliation, the Legaré brothers brought some of their fellow members of the provincial infantry to the Campbell house at night to demand that Lady William turn over "Plate, Jewels, and Valuables." When she refused, they broke into the carriage house and took away the Campbells' carriage and horses.[4]

The Council of Safety, embarrassed by the episode, sent someone to return the carriage and horses, but Lady William indignantly turned the man away; later the council authorized the Legaré brothers to auction off the carriage to recover the value of their seized shipment. Sarah Campbell heard from a friend that the patriots might take her and the children hostage. On December 15, under cover of darkness, they all slipped out of the house to a boat, waiting in the creek behind their house, and were taken to the *Cherokee* in the harbor. Two other canoes, carrying servants and property belonging to the Campbells, were captured that night. One may have been piloted by Scipio Handley, a free black fisherman and fruit seller. Either that night or later, Handley was captured while helping Campbell communicate with the city. He was put in irons, and word came that "he was to be put to Death" for defying the patriots. He survived when he received a file "by the hand of a Friend," filed off his shackles, escaped from the jail, and made his way to St. Augustine.[5]

On January 6, 1776, the *Cherokee* and *Tamar* sailed away with Lord William, his family, and an unknown number of South Carolina runaway slaves. (At least one of those slaves, twenty-year-old Sarah Gordon, later was taken from New York City to Nova Scotia, and permanent freedom, by the Royal Navy.) The South Carolina Council of Safety hoped patriot forces would capture the governor, perhaps on a visit to his Savannah River plantation, and return him to Charles Town, but that did not happen. Lord William would make one last visit to Charles Town. In June 1776, British Commodore Sir Peter Parker and General Sir Henry Clinton decided to occupy Sullivan's Island, at the mouth of Charles Town's harbor, as a base of future operations against the city. They arrived with an armada of nine ships, three thousand troops, and a black pilot, Sampson, for the assault. Campbell, though retired from the navy, volunteered his services, and during the attack of June 28, he was on Parker's flagship, HMS *Bristol*, on the lower gun deck, as in his midshipman days, not at the officers' station on the quarterdeck. The encounter was a triumph for the Americans, a humiliating defeat for the British. The British troops, stymied by unfamiliar and difficult terrain and by the Americans' resistance, never set foot on Sullivan's Island, and the British naval cannonade made little impact on the palmetto-log fort the South Carolinians had constructed. Three British ships ran aground on the shoals. American gunners focused fire on the flagship, the *Bristol,* which suffered more killed and wounded than the entire American side in the battle. One of the wounded was Lord William, who was struck on his left side. Commodore Parker praised his performance and reported that the contusion "has not proved of much consequence."[6]

In fact, Campbell never really recovered from the wound. He returned to England in 1777 and lived with his family at the estate of his sister Eleanor and her husband, Henry Seymour Conway. On September 4, 1778, he died of "a painful and lingering consumption which the physicians thought proceeded from the wounds he received on Sullivan's Island." He was buried at St. Anne's Church in London. Lady William, having lost her estate, and her husband's, to the Revolution, lived on with the Conways for several years, becoming great friends with Conway's daughter, Anne Seymour Damer, traveling with her to France and Italy. She died of an unknown ailment, at the age of thirty-eight, on September 4, 1784—the sixth anniversary of Lord William's death. The Campbell descendants live in Britain today.[7]

Henry Laurens survived the Revolution to see the new United States emerge as an independent country. He was often at the center of developments, but he paid a fearful personal cost. His favorite son, John, with brilliant prospects, was killed in battle at the age of twenty-eight; his own health was damaged; his property was ravaged.

When the Second Provincial Congress of South Carolina met in November 1775, Laurens was not chosen again as president—that honor went to the younger and more radical William Henry Drayton—but he remained as president of the Council of Safety and as a voice of moderation. In February 1776 he criticized Thomas Paine's powerful pamphlet, *Common Sense,* for its call for outright independence and for "those indecent expressions with which the pages abound" (Paine had called King George a "wretch" and "an inveterate enemy to liberty" with "a thirst for arbitrary power"). Laurens was still hoping, if "seemingly against hope," for a reconciliation with "the Mother Country, England."[8]

But Laurens never wavered when the time came to choosing sides between America and Britain, as some of his friends, such as Miles Brewton, had. He helped draft a constitution for South Carolina, adopted in March

1776, and under its terms was elected to the new office of vice president of South Carolina. He was deeply involved in preparations for defense against the assault of Commodore Parker on Sullivan's Island, spending many hours of each day in the saddle in the weeks leading up to the June 28 attack. It was that attack that convinced him, finally, that reconciliation was impossible. When news arrived in Charles Town, on August 2, that the Continental Congress had passed a Declaration of Independence, he accepted it, though not without "a Tear of affection for the good old Country & for the People in it whom in general I dearly Love."[9]

In January 1777, South Carolina's new legislature chose Laurens as a delegate to the Continental Congress. He took up his seat in July, serving on several important committees. When President John Hancock resigned his seat in November 1777, the Congress chose Laurens to replace him. For the next thirteen months he presided over the Congress's deliberations while the new country struggled to support its army and negotiated an alliance with France that would help win its war for independence. Laurens was a strong nationalist and staunch supporter of George Washington against his critics, and he became entangled in several of the bitter partisan conflicts that roiled the Congress; at one point he threatened to kick the clerk of the Congress.[10]

In 1779, the Continental Congress chose Laurens to go to the Netherlands to negotiate a loan of $10 million. He left Philadelphia on the brigantine *Mercury* in August 1780 but made it only as far as Newfoundland, where the ship was captured by the British navy. His trip across the Atlantic ended, not in Amsterdam, but in London, where he was sent to the Tower on "suspicion of high treason." He spent fifteen months in the Tower, much of the time in close confinement and with limited access to visitors, and suffered with severe gout. His old friends in Britain, especially his slave-trading partner Richard Oswald, urged him to turn his back on the American cause, promising that he would be well rewarded. It was an offer he never considered, but he did twice petition for release on parole. After his case was taken up by such figures as Edmund Burke, he was freed on December 31, 1781.[11]

The Continental Congress appointed Laurens the following spring to the commission charged with negotiating a treaty of peace with Britain, but since other members—Benjamin Franklin, John Adams, and John Jay—were already in Paris, at work on the treaty, Laurens decided to stay in Britain to try to convince influential men that the war could end only with the absolute independence of the United States. He spent much of the time in Bath, site of the old Roman baths, trying to recover his health. He had his portrait painted by John Singleton Copley. He traveled to southern France to visit his brother James and daughters Martha and Polly, who were spending the war there. In November 1782, a message came from the Congress instructing him to go to Paris, but he arrived after the terms of peace had been agreed to and the document drawn up, though not yet signed.

Not until 1784 did Laurens return to America, and it was another year before he made it back to South Carolina. He found his Charles Town mansion almost in ruins, his Mepkin Plantation severely damaged, and one-fourth of his slaves gone, some having escaped to the British, others having died. His Georgia plantations were not worth restoring. He estimated his income at only one-fifth of its prewar level. He retreated to private life, living at Mepkin, his Cooper River plantation, and rebuilding his fortune. He refused political posts, including the opportunity to represent South Carolina at the Constitutional Convention in 1787 (though as a member of the ratifying convention in South Carolina he voted in favor of the new compact). He died in 1792. Apparently because of an acute fear of being buried while still alive, he left instructions for his body "to be Wraped in twelve Yards of Tow Cloth, and Burnt until it be entirely and totally consumed."[12]

✦

In a letter to his son John, then in London, on August 14, 1776, Henry Laurens had described the scene of a few days earlier, when the text of the Declaration of Independence reached Charles Town. South Carolina's president, William Henry Drayton, had led a procession, including the members of every major political body, from the town center to the Liberty Tree. There the Declaration was read "with great Solemnity" before a cheering crowd of thousands. Maybe it was the stirring opening sentences of the Declaration, proclaiming that "all men are created equal" and endowed with rights to "life, liberty, and the pursuit of happiness," that inspired Laurens, in this same letter to his son, to write, in an often-quoted phrase, that "You know my Dear Sir. I abhor Slavery." He was, he said, "devising means for manumitting many of" his own slaves and "for cutting off the entail of Slavery."[13]

It was a remarkable statement from a man who had built a fortune selling slaves and exploiting their labor. Laurens placed all responsibility for slavery on "English Men," writing, "I am not the Man who enslaved them, they are indebted to English Men for that favour." "These Negroes were first enslaved by the English—Acts of Parliament have established the Slave Trade in favour of the home residing English & almost totally prohibited Americans from reaping any share of it—Men of War Forts Castles Governors Companies & Committees are employed & authorized by the English Parliament to protect regulate & extend the Slave Trade—Negroes are brought by English Men & sold as Slaves to Americans—Bristol Liverpoole Manchester Birmingham &ca. &ca. Live upon the Slave Trade." He had, Laurens continued, been "born in a Country where Slavery had been established by British Kings & Parliaments as well as by the Laws of that Country Ages before my existence"; the "Christian Religion" had not opposed slavery, but "I nevertheless disliked it." His own slaves, he was sure, "all to a Man are strongly attached to me," but now "the day I hope is approaching when from principles of gratitude as well as justice every Man will strive to be foremost in shewing his readiness to comply with the Golden Rule."

> I am not one of those who arrogate the peculiar care of Providence in each fortunate event, nor one of those who dare trust in Providence for defence & security of their own Liberty while they enslave & wish to continue in Slavery, thousands who are as well intitled to freedom as themselves.—I perceive the work before me is great. I shall appear to many as a promoter not only of strange but of dangerous doctrines, it will therefore be necessary to proceed with caution, you are apparently deeply Interested in this affair but as I have no doubts concerning your concurrence & approbation I most sincerely wish for your advice & assistance & hope to receive both in good time.

Laurens admitted, in this letter, that not only the "avarice of my Country Men" but also "my own" would present difficulties. The admission almost leads one to overlook the series of rationalizations that denied his own enthusiastic, and enormously profitable, participation in the slave trade and the exploitation of slaves on his plantations. This would be especially so if he had subsequently made serious efforts to fulfill his promise of emancipation. In fact he did nothing.[14]

Laurens had asked his son for "your concurrence & approbation," but he knew he would get both, because by this time, John, far more than his father, had become an outspoken critic of slavery. While attending school in Geneva, John had apparently absorbed the antislavery arguments of Enlightenment writers, and among his good friends in London were such men as John Bicknell and Thomas Day, who had collaborated on a famous sentimental antislavery poem, "The Dying Negro." He wrote back to his father with an enthusiastic endorsement of "the equitable Conduct which you have resolved upon with respect to your Negroes." Arguments in favor of slavery, he added, were "absurd," coming from those who "consider'd only their own Advantage." Admitting that there might be problems in advancing people too suddenly from slavery to freedom—as had been done in ancient Rome, he thought—this was only because "we have sunk the Africans & their descendants below the Standard of Humanity, and almost render'd them incapable of that Blessing which equal Heaven bestow'd upon us all." Emancipation might require a gradual plan to bring the slaves "to the happy State" of freedom.[15]

It was John, and not Henry Laurens, who would make a real effort—the most determined by any white man in the southern colonies—to bring freedom to slaves during the Revolution. John Laurens returned to South Carolina in 1777, in time to accompany his father north from Charles Town to Philadelphia and the Continental Congress that summer. He became an aide to George Washington and a fast friend of Alexander Hamilton, another of Washington's young aides. Six months later, in the dark winter of Valley Forge, John Laurens proposed that his father give him, in advance, part of his inheritance in the form of able-bodied slaves, so that he could train them as soldiers and lead them in battle, thus starting them on the road from "abject Slavery" toward "perfect Liberty." Henry Laurens responded with cautions and a recitation of caveats: there would be too few healthy adult men to form a good military force; without support from other slave owners, it would be an exercise in "Quixotism"; not one person he had consulted had approved of the idea; it would be cruel to the Negroes to force them to exchange "circumstances not only tolerable but comfortable" for the dangers of the battlefield. But John pressed on; later he would convince both George Washington and the Continental Congress to support a far more ambitious idea, to emancipate three thousand South Carolina slaves and put them in a regiment that he would lead.[16]

A reluctant Henry Laurens was dragged along by his son's enthusiasm, but he never was truly convinced. Like his more famous contemporary Thomas Jefferson, he could denounce slavery in the abstract without ever approving of any concrete proposal to end it, and this remained his attitude for the rest of his life. From time to time he offered faint echoes of his earlier forthright declaration that he "abhorred" slavery. In 1785 he wrote—perhaps notably, to a foreigner—that "to recover and save the honor of the Country, an abolition of slavery by wise and progressive measures is necessary." But a careful reading of that letter shows that the "honor" at stake lay in the willingness of the new nation to pay its debts, not in the existence of slavery itself. In

1783, when in London after the preliminary peace treaty had been signed, Laurens wrote to South Carolinian William Drayton suggesting what he might mean by "wise and progressive measures": it might be possible to emancipate slaves, but only on the condition that the Negroes "may and ought to continue a separate people, may be subjected to special laws, kept harmless, made useful and freed from the tyranny and arbitrary power of individuals." Those of African descent were always to him a "separate people." The best they could hope for was to be "subjected to special laws" and kept "harmless" but "useful," in effect, slaves of the white community at large rather than of individual masters.[17]

When Laurens returned to South Carolina, he kept his slaves working on his plantations, as always—not only not freeing them, but even tracking down and returning to Charles Town at least one slave, Frederic, who had evacuated with the British in 1782 and gone to New York City. Examples of slave resistance such as this could not shake his belief that his slaves were "happy" and loved him, as they ought to do. And if they showed their ingratitude by misbehavior, why, then, he would tell them, "I shall conclude you don't love me & will sell you." Of his nearly three hundred slaves, he freed just one slave, a carpenter named George, at his death.[18]

✦

John Laurens's own plan for a regiment of three thousand free blacks was defeated by overwhelming majorities in South Carolina's assembly (Congress had required its endorsement). Responding to the proposal, Christopher Gadsden, the old South Carolina radical, wrote to Sam Adams that "we are much disgusted here at Congress recommending us to arm our Slaves, it was received with great resentment, as a very dangerous and impolitic Step."[19]

In August 1782, John was killed in a "paltry little skirmish" outside of Charles Town, long after it was obvious that the war would soon be over. Hundreds, perhaps thousands, of Carolina slaves did achieve freedom during the war, but their liberators were the British, not the Americans. When the British occupied Charles Town in 1780 after a siege, their commander, Sir Henry Clinton, promised freedom to "Every Negro who shall desert the Rebel Standard." Perhaps three thousand responded, including several of Henry Laurens's slaves; many of them eventually died of smallpox and other diseases or were recaptured, but about twelve hundred left with the British in 1782 as free men and women, most going on to Jamaica or Nova Scotia.[20]

Henry Laurens received the crushing news of the death of his beloved child in November 1782, just as he was about to embark for Paris to join Adams, Franklin, and Jay in the peace negotiations. Adams remarked in his journal, after Laurens's arrival, that he "was very happy, that Mr Laurence came in, although it was the last day of the conferences. . . . His Apprehension, notwithstanding his deplorable Affliction under the recent Loss of so excellent a Son, is as quick, his Judgment as sound, and his heart as firm as ever. He had an opportunity of examining the whole [of the treaty draft], and judging, and approving." Laurens did arrive in time to get one more provision added to the preliminary articles of peace. Since there was already a good copy of the entire text, ready for signing, the clerk had to insert the new words, literally, between the lines. They stipulated that the British forces would leave without "carrying away any Negroes, or other Property of the American Inhabitants." One of the British negotiators, Laurens's slave-trading friend Richard Oswald, surely approved, since Oswald himself owned a considerable number of slaves in America. John Adams, too, approved. He wrote in his journal that "the Article which [Laurens] caused to be inserted at the very last that no Property would be carried off, which would most probably in the Multiplicity and hurry of Affairs have escaped Us, was worth a longer Journey." Even for this son of New England, black slaves were merely property that might be "carried off," inhabitants of America, perhaps, but not themselves Americans.[21]

Afterword
Thomas Jeremiah and the Historians

THE REDISCOVERY OF Thomas Jeremiah, his trial, and his execution was part of the broader recovery of African-American history inspired by the Civil Rights Movement. John Donald Duncan devoted several pages to Jeremiah in his 1971 dissertation, but it was a 1978 essay by Peter H. Wood that did the most to bring Jeremiah to the attention of historians: "'Taking Care of Business' in Revolutionary South Carolina: Republicanism and the Slave Society."[1] Since Wood's essay, other historians of South Carolina have incorporated Jeremiah's story into their own work. Robert M. Weir added important details about Jeremiah's life in his *Colonial South Carolina: A History,* and Walter J. Fraser, Jr., recounted his execution in a history of Charleston. Philip D. Morgan, in his studies of slavery in South Carolina and Charleston, provided essential context for the story, as did, in a different way, analyses of the relationships between slavery, political culture, and the coming of the Revolution in South Carolina, by Robert Olwell and William R. Ryan. More specialized studies of colonial slave law and capital punishment also have used the case to illustrate particular points.[2]

Eventually, Jeremiah's story made its way into larger syntheses of the era of the Revolution, especially those interested in showing the Revolution from the vantage point of common people. Notable among these are Sylvia Frey, *Water from the Rock;* Gary B. Nash, *The Unknown American Revolution;* Ray Raphael, *A People's History of the American Revolution;* and, most broadly, Marcus Rediker and Peter Linebaugh, *The Many-Headed Hydra: Sailors, Slaves, Commoners, and the Hidden History of the Revolutionary Atlantic.* The appeal of Jeremiah's story for these historians is obvious. It is dramatic, and it fits well into an emerging understanding of the American Revolution as a time of both promise and contradiction for black freedom. Promise, because the egalitarian impulse so memorably articulated in the opening passages of the Declaration of Independence seemed to point to the end of chattel slavery. Contradiction, because slavery did not end. Indeed, that egalitarian impulse did not end slavery even in the personal life of Thomas Jefferson, the man who drafted the Declaration. It is also clear that, even if most white Americans failed to embrace emancipation as a logical consequence of their own battle against "enslavement" by the British government, slaves themselves did do so. Throughout the colonies, some slaves (and free blacks) fought for the Americans, and others for the British; some sued and petitioned for freedom; tens of thousands simply escaped from their masters. In the sweeping accounts of the Revolution "from the bottom up," Jeremiah is a representative of the restive black population—free and enslaved—that sought its own liberty during the Revolution. Thus, in Nash's account, Jeremiah is "a fisherman and boat pilot who . . . hoped to be the agent of deliverance for thousands of slaves," while to Rediker and Linebaugh, he is part of the "motley crew" of slaves, sailors, and laborers in the American Revolution, who were in turn part of an Atlantic-wide resistance to the rise of capitalism. If William Campbell appears at all in these accounts, it is as a bystander and witness to events.[3]

Recent works by Simon Schama and Cassandra Pybus have seen Jeremiah's story in somewhat the same light, but from the perspective of the British side of the Revolution. Schama and Pybus are interested in the ways that British forces became, in effect, a force for slave liberation, sometimes unintentionally but other times deliberately—especially when, at the end of the war, the Royal Navy carried thousands of runaway slaves to freedom in Nova Scotia, London, and elsewhere. Schama pays particular attention to Campbell's attempt to save Jeremiah, and the governor figures as a harbinger of British policies and an early example of actions that eventually produced abolition, first of the slave trade, and later of slavery itself.[4]

I have learned from all of these earlier accounts, some of which I read for the first time while writing a survey of the early history of the U.S. South. I was immediately struck by the drama and poignancy of Thomas Jeremiah's life and death. His story did not make it into my survey, but it did make into my consciousness, and I decided that it was worth trying to present a full account of the case to a wider audience. As I read and re-read these previous treatments of the case, however, I was struck by discrepancies among them, in both the facts and the interpretations of the story. The discrepancies were not usually major—they involved, for example, somewhat different versions of the chronology of the events or minor variations in names and dates. There were also, inevitably, different choices about which facts to include and which to omit. As I worked with the primary documents, I found it easy to understand how earlier accounts could disagree. The most informative primary sources are, not only small in number, but also retrospective and highly partisan. Even participants in the events were at times mistaken about details, and many of their references to crucial events are maddeningly vague about time and place. This strengthened my determination to tell as full a story as I could, while basing my own version directly on the primary sources. Of new sources I found very few, although some of them were helpful in filling out the account, especially in the case of Lord William Campbell and the visit of the free black preacher, David Margrett, in 1774–1775. For the latter, I was gratified to find a letter in his own hand, not previously cited, signed "David Margrett" rather than "David Margate," as other primary and secondary sources have referred to him. But more important than new sources was the straightforward attempt to understand and explain, as carefully as I could, the sequence of events throughout 1775. For example, although Peter H. Wood, Philip D. Morgan, and Sylvia R. Frey, among others, have noted the link between Margrett's preaching and Charles Town's slave insurrection scare, it was only after reconstructing the precise sequence of events, from his arrival on December 28, 1774, to the panic set off in Charles Town in the first week of May by a "letter from London," did I feel that I understood how close the link actually was.

In the end, the full complexities of the events, together with the limits on our sources, make it difficult to maintain any simple interpretation of Thomas Jeremiah's life and death. Those who see Jeremiah as a symbol of black defiance and resistance usually omit the fact that he was a substantial slaveholder, who used his slaves to profit from commercial fishing. The evidence that he actively sought to organize a slave insurrection is both slim and highly suspect; if anything, the totality of the evidence points to his being a capitalist exploiter of slave labor, more than a part of the "many headed hydra" opposing capitalism. It is not impossible that there were slaves in Charles Town wishing good riddance to Jeremiah.[5] At the same time, it is hard to see Lord William Campbell as a representative of "liberty" against "slavery." Jeremiah was not, after all, a slave, and Campbell himself owned dozens of slaves, as did his wife, Sarah. Nothing in this story is simple; all the main characters are caught in conflicting currents, both personal and ideological.[6]

Even if new evidence about Jeremiah's actions and intentions were to turn up in the future, the meaning of the events would remain difficult to interpret. In the end, the debate over Jeremiah's fate shows how complex and elusive are the meanings of "liberty," and, perhaps more important, how those meanings are created in the actions, and conflicts, of men and women in history. Ambitious, intelligent, arrogant, and successful, Thomas Jeremiah did not need to gather arms or preach revolution to undermine slavery, because his whole life was a refutation of whites' basic justification for slavery, which was that Africans, by their nature, deserved to be slaves. William Campbell was no emancipationist, but Henry Laurens and other patriots could see that Campbell's notion that Jeremiah deserved the liberties of a Briton, regardless of his African descent, was itself a serious threat to slavery. There could be no slavery without slave law, defining the differences between masters and slaves, and in a place like South Carolina, there could be no slave law without laws that distinguished between black and white. Those laws helped to create the very racial differences that whites claimed to find in nature. At its heart, the conflicts between patriots like Laurens and William Campbell, and between the patriots and Thomas Jeremiah, turned on questions about whether a man of African descent really was a "countryman" under the law or whether he must always be a "stranger." The debate was about what it meant to be a Briton and what it might mean to be an American; about *who* could be a Briton or an American; about what freedom itself meant. It was Thomas Jeremiah's tragedy that men like Henry Laurens, in answering these questions, turned their faces away from the implications of their own determined fight for freedom.

Abbreviations Used in the Notes

American Loyalist Claims	Public Records of Great Britain and KTO Microform, *American Loyalist Claims. AO12, Exchequer and Audit Dept.*, Ser. 1: *1776–1831* (London, 1972)
BPRO Transcripts	Transcripts of the Records of the British Public Record Office, mf, SCDAH
CHAP	Countess of Huntingdon's American Papers, Cheshunt Institute, Westminster College, Cambridge
DAR	K. G. Davies, ed., *Documents of the American Revolution, 1770–1783,* Colonial Office Series, 21 vols. (Dublin, 1972–1981)
Drayton, *Memoirs*	John Drayton, *Memoirs of the American Revolution . . . as Relating to the State of South Carolina.* 2 vols. (Charleston, 1821; reprint, New York, 1969)
Early American Imprints	Early American Imprints, Ser. 1: Evans, 1639–1800 (online digitized archive accessed through Dimond Library, University of New Hampshire)
HL	Henry Laurens
NAUK	National Archives of the United Kingdom, Kew
NDAR	William Bell Clark, William James Morgan, and Michael J. Crawford, eds., *Naval Documents of the American Revolution,* 11 vols. to date (Washington, D.C., 1964–)
ODNB	*Oxford Dictionary of National Biography*
PHL	Philip M. Hamer, ed., *The Papers of Henry Laurens,* 16 vols. (Columbia, S.C., 1968–2003)
Ramsay's History	David Ramsay, *Ramsay's History of South Carolina from Its First Settlement in 1670 to the Year 1808.* 2 vols. (1809; reprint, Spartanburg, S.C., 1962)
SC and AGG	*South-Carolina and American General Gazette*

SCDAH	South Carolina Department of Archives and History, Columbia
SCG	*South-Carolina Gazette*
SCG and CJ	*South-Carolina Gazette: And Country Journal*
SCH and GM	*South Carolina Historical and Genealogical Magazine*
SCHM	*South Carolina Historical Magazine* (continues *SCH and GM*)
Statutes at Large	Thomas Cooper and David J. McCord, eds., *Statutes at Large for South Carolina*, 10 vols. (Columbia, S.C., 1836–1841)
WC	Lord William Campbell

Notes

PROLOGUE

1. *Statutes at Large*, 7:400.

2. George Millegen, "Narrative by George Millegen of his Experiences in South Carolina," *DAR*, 11:111. This would have been a secondhand report, since Millegen at this time had taken refuge on a ship in the harbor. Even in London, the trapdoor gallows was a later invention. The use of the cart and the look of the gallows are speculative details based on similar descriptions of hangings in eighteenth-century Charles Town and elsewhere. Sometimes the hanged were "turned off" a ladder set up against the gallows, but by the mid-eighteenth century in England, "felons were more often swung off from carts than pushed off ladders": V. A. C. Gatrell, *The Hanging Tree: Execution and the English People, 1770–1868* (Oxford, 1994), 51.

3. Gatrell, *Hanging Tree*, 45, vii.

4. WC to Lord Dartmouth, Aug. 19, 1775, *NDAR*, 1:1184.

5. HL to John Laurens, July 30, 1775, *PHL*, 10:258.

6. HL to James Laurens, Feb. 5, Apr. 13, 1774, *PHL*, 9:266, 407.

CHAPTER I
"Slavery may truly be said to be the peculiar curse of this land"

1. "Charleston, S.C., in 1774 as Described by an English Traveller," in *The Colonial South Carolina Scene: Contemporary Views, 1697–1774*, ed. H. Roy Merrens (Columbia, S.C., 1977), 281; Jonathan H. Poston, *The Buildings of Charleston: A Guide to the City's Architecture* (Columbia, S.C., 1997), 109–110, 184. In the study of colonial wealth in 1774 by Alice Hanson Jones, Charles Town District was by far the wealthiest of the counties in her sample, which included those containing Boston and Philadelphia. Nine of the ten highest-value individual probate inventories she examined were from Charles Town. Alice Hanson Jones, *Wealth of a Nation to Be: The American Colonies on the Eve of Revolution* (New York, 1980), esp. 376–378. On Charles Town's buildings and harbor, including

pilot directions, see P. C. Coker, III, *Charleston's Maritime Heritage, 1670–1987: An Illustrated History* (Charleston, 1987); *The English Pilot; The Fourth Book; Describing the West India Navigation, from Hudson's-Bay to the River Amazones* (London, 1773), 24–25; and *A Draught of South Carolina and Georgia by Andrew Hughes*, map (with pilot directions), Map Collection, Harvard University Library.

2. Mark Antony De Wolfe Howe, ed., "Journal of Josiah Quincy, Jr., 1773," *Proceedings of the Massachusetts Historical Society* 49 (1915–1916): 441; Kenneth Severens, *Charleston: Antebellum Architecture and Civic Destiny* (Knoxville, Tenn., 1988), 8–13; Poston, *Buildings of Charleston*, 184–185; *SCG*, Mar. 7, 1774; Peter Timothy to Benjamin Franklin, Sept. 3, 1768, *Papers of Benjamin Franklin*, ed. Leonard W. Labaree et al., 37 vols. to date (New Haven, 1959–), 15:201–202.

3. The *South-Carolina Gazette* from 1762 to 1767 included advertisements or mentions of 110 men and 15 women in forty-six specialized crafts. It also included 232 retail establishments, 9 run by women. There is a considerable overlap between these groups of artisans and merchants. There were also many retail partnerships, so the 232 establishments included perhaps 300 principals. Not all of these would have been in business for all five years. Data summarized from Jeanne A. Calhoun, Martha A. Zierden, and Elizabeth A. Paysinger, "The Geographic Spread of Charleston's Mercantile Community, 1732–1767," *SCHM* 86 (1985): 207–211, 218–220.

4. "Col. Miles Brewton," *SCH and GM* 2 (1901): 44–47; Kinlock Bull, Jr., *The Oligarchs in Colonial and Revolutionary Charleston: Lieutenant Governor William Bull II and His Family* (Columbia, S.C., 1991); Frances Leigh Williams, *A Founding Family: The Pinckneys of South Carolina* (New York, 1978); Langdon Cheves, Esq., "Izard of South Carolina," *SCH and GM* 2 (1901): 205–240. On the founding of the colony and the growth of its gentry, see Peter H. Wood, *Black Majority: Negroes in South Carolina from 1670 through the Stono Rebellion* (New York, 1974), chap. 1; Richard Waterhouse, *A New World Gentry: The Making of a Merchant and Planter Class in South Carolina, 1670–1770*, 2nd ed. (Charleston, 2005); S. Max Edelson, *Plantation Enterprise in Colonial South Carolina* (Cambridge, Mass., 2006). Manigault quoted in Cara Anzilotti, *In the Affairs of the World: Women, Patriarchy, and Power in Colonial South Carolina* (Westport, Conn., 2002), 20; see also Maurice A. Crouse, "The Manigault Family of South Carolina, 1685–1783" (Ph.D. diss., Northwestern University, 1964).

5. HL to Martha Laurens, Aug. 18, 1771, *PHL*, 7:556; HL to George Appleby, Sept. 26, 1769, *PHL*, 7:150; HL to Martha Laurens, May 18, 1774, *PHL*, 9:458. See also Joanna Bowen Gillespie, *The Life and Times of Martha Laurens Ramsay, 1759–1811* (Columbia, S.C., 2001); Anzilotti, *In the Affairs of the World*; Lorri Glover, *All Our Relations: Blood Ties and Emotional Bonds among the Early South Carolina Gentry* (Baltimore, 2000); Elizabeth M. Pruden, "Investing Widows: Autonomy in a Nascent Capitalist Society," in *Money, Trade, and Power: The Evolution of Colonial South Carolina's Plantation Society*, ed. Jack P. Greene, Rosemary Brana-Shute, and Randy J. Sparks (Columbia, S.C., 2001), 344–362.

6. Elise Pinckney, ed., *The Letterbook of Eliza Lucas Pinckney, 1739–1762* (Chapel Hill, N.C., 1972); Darcy R. Fryer, "The Mind of Eliza Pinckney: An Eighteenth-

Century Woman's Construction of Herself," *SCHM* 99 (1998): 215–237; Harriott Horry Ravenel, *Eliza Pinckney* (New York, 1896); Harriott Pinckney to "My Dear Becky" [Rebecca Izard], Dec. 10, 1766, Harriott Pinckney Letterbook, 1763–1767, folder 11/332/8, Pinckney-Lowndes Papers, South Carolina Historical Society.

7. Glover, *All Our Relations*, 48, 96.

8. Sylvia Frey and Betty Wood, *Come Shouting to Zion: African American Protestantism in the American South and the British Caribbean to 1830* (Chapel Hill, N.C., 1998), 77; Howe, ed., "Josiah Quincy, Jr.," quotations on 450, 443, 448, 450, 451, 441–442. Quincy had come to Charles Town in 1773 in part for his health (he was suffering from tuberculosis), but more so as an informal ambassador of the Committee of Correspondence in Boston. On Charles Town's music and its patronage by the gentry, see Nicholas Michael Butler, *Votaries of Apollo: The St. Cecilia Society and the Patronage of Concert Music in Charleston, South Carolina, 1766–1820* (Columbia, S.C., 2007).

9. Howe, ed., "Josiah Quincy, Jr.," 444–446. Thanks to Kurk Dorsey for identifying the "pretty bird" at the dinner as, in all likelihood, a painted bunting.

10. Carolyn Wyche Dixon, "The Miles Brewton House: Ezra Waite's Architectural Books and Other Possible Design Sources" *SCHM* 82 (1981): 118–142; John Bivens and J. Thomas Savage, "The Miles Brewton House, Charleston, South Carolina," *Antiques* 143 (1993): 294–307; Bivens calls the main hall "certainly one of the finest rooms in America with regard to scale and detail" (298). On refinement and self-presentation, see Richard L. Bushman, *The Refinement of America: Persons, Houses, Cities* (New York, 1996); Edward Pearson, "'Planters Full of Money': The Self-Fashioning of the Eighteenth-Century South Carolina Elite," in *Money, Trade, and Power*, ed. Greene, Brana-Shute, and Sparks, 299–321.

11. Bernard Herman, "The Charleston Single House," in Poston, *Buildings of Charleston*, 37–41; Martha Zierden and Bernard Herman, "Charleston Townhouses: Archaeology, Architecture, and the Urban Landscape, 1750–1850," in *Landscape Archaeology: Reading and Interpreting the American Historical Landscape*, ed. Rebecca Yamin and Karen Bescherer Metheny (Knoxville, Tenn., 1996), 193–227; Bernard L. Herman, *Town House: Architecture and Material Life in the Early American City, 1780–1830* (Chapel Hill, N.C., 2005).

12. HL to Isaac King, Sept. 6, 1764, *PHL*, 4:399; *SCG*, Nov. 28, 1771, reprinted in *PHL*, 8:61–62; HL to Benjamin Addison, May 26, 1768, *PHL*, 5:702 (size); *Ramsay's History*, 2:128 (garden); Edelson, *Plantation Enterprise*, 220–227. See also George C. Rogers, Jr., "Gardens and Landscapes in Eighteenth-Century South Carolina," in *British and American Gardens in the Eighteenth Century: Eighteen Illustrated Essays on Garden History*, ed. Robert P. Maccubbin and Peter Martin (Williamsburg, Va., 1984), 148–158.

13. John Drayton, *A View of Carolina as Respects Her Natural and Civil Concerns* (Charleston, 1802; reprint, Spartanburg, S.C., 1972), 217; Poston, *Buildings of Charleston*, 184–185; Hennig Cohen, *The South Carolina Gazette, 1732–1775* (Columbia, S.C., 1953), 70 (Watson); Maurice A. Crouse, ed., "The Letterbook of Peter Manigault, 1763–1773," *SCHM* 70 (1969): 92, 188–189. The inventory is printed in Alice Hanson Jones, *American Colonial Wealth: Documents and Methods*, 3 vols. (New York, 1977), 3:1543–1557. The inven-

tory includes the property on two other plantations with few such amenities. Inventory values were expressed in local currency and have been converted to sterling at the standard rate of seven to one. In 1771, British customs officials reported that upholstered furniture shipped to Charles Town that year was worth £2,175, a number that should be multiplied three to five times estimating actual imports: M. Allison Carrill, "An Assessment of English Furniture Imports into Charleston, 1760–1800," *Journal of Early Southern Decorative Arts* 11, no. 2 (1985): 1–18. For an excellent brief discussion, see J. Thomas Savage and Robert A. Leath, "Buying British: Merchants, Taste, and Charleston Consumerism," in Maurie D. McInnis, in collaboration with Angela D. Mack, *In Pursuit of Refinement: Charlestonians Abroad, 1740–1860* (Columbia, S.C., 1999), 55–63.

14. Edelson, *Plantation Enterprise,* 137 ("pleasantest"); Cohen, *South Carolina Gazette,* 37, 118–120; Richard J. Hooker, ed., *A Colonial Plantation Cookbook: The Receipt Book of Harriott Pinckney Horry, 1770* (Columbia, S.C., 1984.) Hooker's introduction notes that several of the recipes come from midcentury English cookbooks. The arrival for a full season of David Douglas's American Company, in 1773, had raised the bar considerably for the theater, with Charles Town's first performances of Shakespeare, though the most frequently performed plays were the comedies of David Garrick.

15. See esp. McInnis, *In Pursuit of Refinement;* the Izards' portrait is discussed on 116–119. On Theus, see Margaret Simons Middleton, *Jeremiah Theus: Colonial Artist of Charles Town* (Columbia, S.C., 1953).

16. Cohen, *South Carolina Gazette,* 37, 90, and 25–39 passim; A. S. Salley, ed., "Diary of William Dillwyn during a Visit to Charles Town in 1772," *SCH and GM* 36 (July 1935): 73.

17. "Charleston, S.C., in 1774," 286; *SCG,* Oct. 29, 1772; Carl Bridenbaugh, *Cities in Revolt: Urban Life in America, 1743–1776* (New York, 1964), 31; *SCG,* Feb. 7, 1771, May 9, 1768; Alexander Hewatt, *An Historical Account of the Rise and Progress of the Colonies of South Carolina and Georgia,* 2 vols. (London, 1779; reprint, Spartanburg, S.C., 1962), 1:88. On slave housing in general and the Brewton household in particular, see Bernard Herman, "Slave and Servant Housing in Charleston, 1770–1820," *Historical Archaeology* 33, no. 3 (1999): 88–101; Martha Zierden, Elizabeth Reitz, and Karl J. Reinhard, "Archaeology at the Miles Brewton House 27 King Street, Charleston, S.C.," *Archaeological Contributions* 29 (Charleston, 2001). The highest death rates in South Carolina came from August through November: H. Roy Merrens and George T. Terry, "Dying in Paradise: Malaria, Mortality and the Perceptual Environment in Colonial South Carolina," *Journal of Southern History* 50 (1984): 533–550 ("paradise" quotation on 549). The connection between mosquitoes and malaria was not known at the time.

18. *SCG,* June 1, 8, 1769.

19. Joseph I. Waring, "Alexander Garden, M.D., and the Royal Society of Arts," *SCHM* 64 (1963): 16–17; HL to William Cowles and Co., Oct. 31, 1769, *PHL,* 7:184.

20. "The Economics of a Plantation Venture, 1755," in *Colonial South Carolina Scene,* ed. Merrens, 160–162. For slavery and rice in South Carolina, see esp. Philip D. Morgan, *Slave Counterpoint: Black Culture in the Eighteenth-Century Chesapeake and Lowcountry* (Chapel Hill, N.C., 1998); Daniel C. Littlefield, *Rice and Slaves: Ethnicity and the Slave*

Trade in Colonial South Carolina (Baton Rouge, La., 1981); Judith A. Carney, *Black Rice: The African Origins of Rice Cultivation in the Americas* (Cambridge, Mass., 2001). For the total (forced) immigration of Africans in the eighteenth century, see Morgan, *Slave Counterpoint,* 59. Morgan estimates that the slave population of South Carolina began to grow naturally (though very slowly) by about 1750 (84). The peak years for slave imports into South Carolina before the Revolution were 1772, with 7,201, and 1773, with 7,839: Walter Minchinton, "A Comment on 'The Slave Trade to Colonial South Carolina: A Profile,'" *SCHM* 95 (1994): 52. Minchinton's numbers do not always agree with those listed in David Eltis et al., eds., *The Trans-Atlantic Slave Trade: A Database on CD-ROM* (Cambridge, 1999), but these sources agree that 1773 was the peak year before the American Revolution.

21. Elkanah Watson, *Men and Times of the Revolution; or, Memoirs of Elkanah Watson . . .* (New York, 1856), 161; McInnis, *In Pursuit of Refinement,* 116–119; Linda Baumgarten, *What Clothes Reveal: The Language of Clothing in Colonial and Federal America* (New Haven, 2002), 56–60.

22. *PHL,* 1:3 and app.; Daniel J. McDonogh, *Christopher Gadsden and Henry Laurens: The Parallel Lives of Two American Patriots* (Sellinsgrove, Pa., 2000); *PHL,* 4:295–296; Warner Oland Moore, "Henry Laurens: A Charleston Merchant in the Eighteenth Century, 1747–1771" (Ph.D. diss., University of Alabama, 1974).

23. H. Roy Merrens, ed., "A View of Coastal Carolina in 1778: The Journal of Ebenezer Hazard," *SCHM* 73 (1972): 186; Howe, ed., "Josiah Quincy, Jr.," 455; John Adams to Abigail Adams, Aug. 17, 19, 1777, in *Adams Family Correspondence,* Vol. 2: *June 1776–March 1778,* ed. L. H. Butterfield et al. (Cambridge, Mass., 1963), 317–318, 320.

24. *Ramsay's History,* 2:260. On Laurens's religion, see chap. 2, below.

25. *Ramsay's History,* 2:260; HL to Ross and Mill, Oct. 8, 1767, *PHL,* 5:337; HL to Henry Byrne, May 7, 1763, *PHL,* 3:441; HL to Willing, Morris, and Co., Nov. 27, 1762, *PHL,* 3:177; HL to Lachlan McIntosh, Feb. 8, 1768, *PHL,* 5:588. On suits, see *PHL,* 7:94n4. With one exception, Laurens appeared in local courts only as a party in routine cases of debt recovery, usually long after debts had become due.

26. HL to Thomas Rose, Apr. 12, 1764, *PHL,* 4:241 (emphasis in original); *Ramsay's History,* 2:261.

27. HL to George Austin, Dec. 17, 1748, *PHL,* 1:182–183; HL to Foster Cunliffe, Jan. 20, 1749, *PHL,* 1:202; *Ramsay's History,* 2:260. On Charles Town's merchants and the operation of the Atlantic trade, including the slave trade, see the essays by R. C. Nash: "The Organization of Trade and Finance in the Atlantic Economy," in *Money, Trade, and Power,* ed. Greene, Brana-Shute, and Sparks, 74–107; and "South Carolina and the Atlantic Economy in the Late Seventeenth and Eighteenth Centuries," *Economic History Review* 45 (1992): 3–29. For a general summary of Laurens's slave-trading operations, see Moore, "Henry Laurens," 154–198.

28. HL to Devonshire, Reeve, and Lloyd, Dec. 22, 1755, *PHL,* 2:247–248; HL to Wells, Wharton, and Doran, May 27, 1755, *PHL,* 1:257. HL to Corsley Rogers and Son, Aug. 1, 1755, *PHL,* 1:307.

29. HL to Peter Furnell, June 12, 1755, *PHL,* 1:262; HL to Wells, Wharton, and

Doran, July 12, 1755, *PHL,* 1:267; HL to Devonsheir, Reeve, and Lloyd, June 24, 1755, *PHL,* 1:293.

30. HL to Smith and Clifton, May 26, 1755, *PHL,* 1:255; HL to John Knight, June 26, 1755, *PHL,* 1:255, 269. Details on these voyages were checked also in Eltis et al., eds., *Trans-Atlantic Slave Trade.*

31. HL to Knight, June 26, 1755 *PHL,* 1:269–272; HL to Devonsheir, Reeve, and Lloyd, July 4, 1755, *PHL,* 1:285–286 ("can't be remedied," "very unlucky"); HL to Wells, Wharton, and Dunn, May 27, 1755, *PHL,* 1:257–259.

32. HL to Smith and Clifton, July 21, 1755, *PHL,* 1:294; HL to Gidney Clarke, Nov. 20, 1756, *PHL,* 2:356–357; HL to Henry Weare and Co., July 2, Aug. 30, 1755, *PHL,* 1:282, 326; HL to Peter Furnell, Sept. 6, 1755, *PHL,* 1:331. On the slave trade, see James A. Rawley, *The Transatlantic Slave Trade: A History,* rev. ed. (Lincoln, Nebr., 2005); and for the best discussion of life and death on slave ships, see Marcus Rediker, *The Slave Ship: A Human History* (New York, 2007), 263–307. The dimensions of the *Emperor* are a rough estimate, based on its reported tonnage and using the standard formula of the era. Tonnage was a measure of volume, not carrying weight, calculated by the formula: ((keel length) × (beam [maximum breadth]) × (1/2 beam)) / 94).

33. A collection of documents, with commentary, on the Stono Rebellion is Mark M. Smith, ed., *Stono: Documenting and Interpreting a Southern Slave Revolt* (Columbia, S.C., 2005), quotations on 7, 4, 14, 12, 8.

34. "An Act for the Better Ordering of Negroes," *Statutes at Large,* 8:397–419; "Report of the Committee Appointed to Enquire into the Causes of the Disappointment of Success in the Late Expedition against St. Augustine," in Smith, ed., *Stono,* 29 ("shocked"), 28 ("Liberty and Life"); "Governor William Bull's Representation of the Colony, 1770," in *Colonial South Carolina Scene,* ed. Merrens, 260; "Johann Martin Bolzius Answers a Questionnaire on Carolina and Georgia," trans. and ed. Klaus G. Loewald et al., *William and Mary Quarterly,* 3rd ser., 14 (1957): 234; William Bull to the Earl of Hillsborough, *DAR,* 2:100.

35. "Diary of Timothy Ford, 1785–1786," *SCH and GM* 13 (July 1912): 142–143. He added, "They surround the table like a cohort of black guards & here it appears there is a superfluity; for no sooner is a call made than there is a considerable delay either from all rushing at once; or all waiting for one another to do the business"; Ravenel, *Eliza Pinckney,* 245; Hooker, ed., *Colonial Plantation Cookbook,* 81 (biscuits), 94 (soap), 124 (to wash silk stockings).

36. Numbers are based on the twenty-five Charleston probate records of artisans printed in Jones, ed., *American Colonial Wealth,* 3:2165–2167. Compare the crafts listed in Calhoun, Zierden, and Paysinger, "Geographic Spread of Charleston's Mercantile Community," with those of slaves in Philip D. Morgan, "Black Life in Eighteenth Century Charleston," *Perspectives in American History* 1 (1984): 199, table 4; entries in Jones, ed., *American Colonial Wealth,* vol. 3; Mabel L. Webber, "The Thomas Elfe Account Book, 1765–1775," *SCH and GM* 35 (January 1934): 14 (the account book entries continue through vol. 42, January 1942); "Diary of Timothy Ford," quotation on 142.

37. The eleven widows whose estates were inventoried at death in 1774 owned an

average of fifteen slaves and a median of ten. Only one widow owned no slaves. (Propertyless widows were less likely to be inventoried at all, so the numbers would be lower for all widows.) Jones, ed., *Documents and Methods*, 3:2165–2167. Quotation from "The Stranger," *SCG*, Sept. 24, 1772. For a discussion of the relationship of urban spaces, slavery, and the coming of the Revolution in Charles Town, see Benjamin L. Carp, *Rebels Rising: Cities and the American Revolution* (Oxford, 2007), 143–171.

38. *SCG*, Oct. 25, 1770; Morgan, "Black Life in Charleston," 195 (quoting *SCG and CJ*, Feb. 4, 1772); Robert Olwell, "'Loose, Idle and Disorderly': Slave Women in the Eighteenth-Century Charleston Marketplace,'" in *More Than Chattel: Black Women and Slavery in the Americas*, ed. David Barry Gaspar and Darlene Clark Hine (Bloomington, Ind., 1996), 98; *Statutes at Large*, 7:407–408; "The Stranger," *SCG*, Sept. 24, 1772.

39. "The Stranger," *SCG*, Sept. 24, 1772; *SCG*, Jan. 25, 1768, Jan. 25, 1770, Apr. 18, 1771, Sept. 10, 1772, Mar. 29, May 17, 1773. See also Morgan, "Black Life in Charleston," 202–203; and Betty Wood, *Women's Work, Men's Work: The Informal Slave Economies of Lowcountry Georgia* (Athens, Ga., 1995), chap. 4.

40. Now known as the Heyward-Washington House, it is open to the public as a museum. See also Herman, "Slave and Servant Housing"; and Zierden, Reitz, and Reinhard, "Archaeology at the Miles Brewton House." On slavery in Charles Town, see esp. Morgan, "Black Life in Charleston."

41. *SCG*, Feb. 7, 1771, Feb. 25, 1770; Leila Sellers, *Charleston Business on the Eve of the American Revolution* (Chapel Hill, N.C., 1934; reprint, New York, 1970), 20; Bridenbaugh, *Cities in Revolt*, 31.

42. Martha Zierden, "Object Lessons: The Journey of Miles Brewton's Bottle," *Common-Place* I (July 2001), at http://common-place.org; "The Stranger," *SCG*, Sept. 17, 1772.

43. *SCG*, Feb. 7, 1771, Nov. 2, 1767, June 2, 1766; Sharon V. Salinger, *Taverns and Drinking in Early America* (Baltimore, 2002), 198 (map showing location of liquor licenses); Poston, *Buildings of Charleston*, 65–66. Chalmers Alley is now Chalmers Street, which is farther from the water owing to harbor fill.

44. American Loyalist Claims, 47: 117–120 (quotation on 120); HL to John Laurens, Aug. 20, 1775, *PHL*, 10:322. On the Van Neck family, see, e.g., Jacob M. Price, "Buchanan and Simson, 1759–1763: A Different Kind of Glasgow Firm Trading to the Chesapeake," *William and Mary Quarterly*, 3rd ser., 40 (1983): 26.

45. "The Stranger," *SCG*, Sept. 24, 1772.

46. "Governor William Bull's Representation of the Colony, 1770," in *Colonial South Carolina Scene*, ed. Merrens, 262; *SCG*, May 24, 1773, Jan. 25, 1772, Nov. 2, 1767, Oct. 2, 1772. On slave patrols in the colony, see Sally E. Hadden, *Slave Patrols: Law and Violence in Virginia and the Carolinas* (Cambridge, Mass., 2001).

47. *SCG*, June 2, 1766, Nov. 2, 1767, Jan. 25, 1772, Feb. 22, 1773, Apr. 18, 1771. This behavior formed a pattern that anthropologists John and Jean Comaroff, in another context, have called the "gestures of tacit refusal and iconoclasm, gestures that sullenly and silently contest the forms of an existing hegemony: Jean Comaroff and John L. Comaroff, *Of Revelation and Revolution*, Vol. 1: *Christianity, Colonialism, and Consciousness in South Africa* (Chicago, 1991), 31.

48. "Governor James Glen's Valuation, 1751," in *Colonial South Carolina Scene,* ed. Merrens, 183; Hewatt, *Historical Account,* 2:97.

49. "The Stranger," *SCG,* Aug. 27, Sept. 17, 1772.

50. "The Stranger," *SCG,* Sept. 17, 1772.

51. Howe, ed., "Josiah Quincy, Jr.," 456–457.

CHAPTER 2

"Those natural and inherent rights that we all feel, and know, as men"

1. *The Rules and By-laws of the Charlestown Library Society: Together with the act of the General Assembly of South-Carolina for Incorporating the Society, confirmed by His Majesty: and a brief historical introduction* (Charlestown, 1762).

2. *SCG,* Apr. 23, 30, 1763; Jonathan H. Poston, *The Buildings of Charleston: A Guide to the City's Architecture* (Columbia, S.C., 1997), 87–88. For details of Campbell's career, see chap. 5, below.

3. Francis Hutcheson, *A System of Moral Philosophy,* 2 vols. (Glasgow, 1755), 1:34 ("impulse to society"); Hutcheson, *An Inquiry into the Origins of Our Ideas of Beauty and Virtue in Two Treatises,* 2nd ed. (Glasgow, 1772), 218–219. On the relationships between these ideas and slavery, see esp. David Brion Davis, *The Problem of Slavery in Western Culture* (Ithaca, N.Y., 1966), 374–378; Joyce E. Chaplin, "Slavery and the Principle of Humanity: A Modern Idea in the Early Lower South," *Journal of Social History* 24 (1991): 299–315. The Charles Town Library Society owned both of these books, although in different editions from those quoted here: *A Catalogue of Books, Belonging to the Incorporated Charlestown Library Society, with the Date of the Editions* (Charlestown, 1770), 13, 24.

4. *Ramsay's History,* 2:251, 261; Samuel C. Smith, "Henry Laurens: Christian Pietist," *SCHM* 100 (1999): 154; HL to James Habersham, Oct. 1, 1770, *PHL,* 7:375; HL to Henry Laurens, Jr., Nov. 7, 1774, *PHL,* 9:639.

5. Dr. Edmund Gibson, "Pastoral Letter to the Masters and Mistresses of Families in the English Plantations Abroad," in Frederick Dalcho, *An Historical Account of the Protestant Episcopal Church in South Carolina, from the First Settlement of the Province, to the War of the Revolution* (Charleston, 1820), 104–112, quotations on 109–110.

6. Boyd Stanley Schlenther, "Whitefield, George," *ODNB;* George Whitefield, "To the Inhabitants of *Maryland, Virginia, North* and *South Carolina,* concerning their Negroes," in *Three Letters from the Reverend Mr. G. Whitefield* (Philadelphia, 1740), 14. For more on Whitefield's influence, see chap. 3, below.

7. HL to John Ettwein, Nov. 10, 1763, *PHL,* 4:39–43; Ettwein to HL, *PHL,* 3:355–357, Apr. 3, 1763 ("very uneasy"); HL to Ettwein, Mar. 19, 1763, *PHL,* 3:373–374 ("Your observations"). On the Moravians and slavery, see Jon F. Sensbach, *A Separate Canaan: The Making of an Afro-Moravian World in North Carolina, 1763–1840* (Chapel Hill, N.C., 1998).

8. S. Max Edelson, *Plantation Enterprise in Colonial South Carolina* (Cambridge, Mass., 2006), 200–244; HL, Account Book, app. B, *PHL,* 6:609–613. A map showing the location of these plantations is in Edelson, *Plantation Enterprise,* 205. The practice of

investing profits in slave plantations was typical of large Charles Town merchants: R. C. Nash, "The Organization of Trade and Finance in the Atlantic Economy: Britain and South Carolina, 1670–1775," in *Money, Trade, and Power: The Evolution of Colonial South Carolina's Plantation Society*, ed. Jack P. Greene, Rosemary Brana-Shute, and Randy J. Sparks (Columbia, S.C., 2001), 74–107.

9. HL to Mr. Creamer, June 26, 1764, *PHL*, 4:319; HL to Joseph Brown, June 28, 1765, *PHL*, 4:645–646.

10. HL to James Lawrence, Jan. 1, 1763, *PHL*, 3:203; HL to Richard Clarke, Aug. 25, 1770, *PHL*, 4:149n; HL to John Smith, May 9, 1766, Aug. 1, 1765, *PHL*, 5:125, 4:661; HL to William Yate, Feb. 5, 1766, *PHL*, 5:70; HL to Peter Horlbeck, Mar. 7, 1765, *PHL*, 4:587–588; HL to Smith, Mar. 31, 1766, *PHL*, 5:94; HL to Benjamin Addison, May 26, 1768, *PHL*, 5:702.

11. HL to Abraham Schad, Aug. 23, 1765, *PHL*, 4:665–666; HL to Elias Ball, Apr. 1, 1765, *PHL*, 4:595–596.

12. HL to Richard Oswald, Dec. 2, 1773, *PHL*, 9:187; HL to Schad, Apr. 30, 1764, *PHL*, 4:616; HL to Smith, May 9, 1766, *PHL*, 5:125; HL to Lawrence, Jan. 1, 1763, *PHL*, 3:203; HL to Horlbeck, Apr. 6, 1765, *PHL*, 4:602. Francis Hutcheson, the moral philosopher, himself agreed that in certain circumstances, a form of slavery might be justified, albeit a much more limited form than existed in America: Davis, *Problem of Slavery*, 376; M. J. Rozbicki, "'To Save Them from Themselves': Proposals to Enslave the British Poor," *Slavery and Abolition* 22 (2001): 29–50.

13. HL to George Dick, June [n.d.], 1764, *PHL*, 4:299; HL to Smith, June 4, Aug. 15, Sept. 5, Oct. 1, 1765, *PHL*, 4:633, 661, 5:2–3, 11; HL to Yate, Feb. 5, 1766, *PHL*, 5:70.

14. HL to Dick, June [n.d.], 1764, *PHL*, 4:299. In fact, Laurens did not sell Abraham at this time. He appears in several letters in the next two years and then disappears from the surviving correspondence. Perhaps Laurens could not get his minimum price for such a valuable slave.

15. HL to Oswald, Apr. 27, 1768, *PHL*, 5:668. My interpretation is influenced especially by Chaplin, "Slavery and the Principle of Humanity"; Joyce E. Chaplin, *An Anxious Pursuit: Agricultural Innovation and Modernity in the Lower South, 1730–1815* (Chapel Hill, N.C., 1993), esp. 55–58, 122–125; and Philip D. Morgan, "Three Planters and Their Slaves: Perspectives on Slavery in Virginia, South Carolina, and Jamaica, 1750–1790," in *Race and Family in the Colonial South*, ed. Winthrop D. Jordan and Sheila L. Skemp (Jackson, Miss., 1987), 54–68.

16. HL to Lawrence, Jan. 1, 1763, *PHL*, 3:203; HL to Smith, May 30, 1765, *PHL*, 4:633. Philip D. Morgan estimates that Laurens had about thirty runaways on his plantations before 1777: Morgan, "Three Planters," 64; HL to Schad, Aug. 23, 1765, *PHL*, 4:665–666. See also Peter H. Wood, "Slave Labor Camps in Early America: Overcoming Denial and Discovering the Gulag," in *Inequality in Early America*, ed. Carla Gardina Pestana and Sharon V. Salinger (Hanover, N.H., 1999), 222–238; Edelson, *Plantation Enterprise*, 164–165, 210–218.

17. HL to William Fisher, Nov. 11, 1768, *PHL*, 6:149; HL to John Lewis Gervais, Dec. 31, 1772, Feb. 5, 1774, *PHL*, 8:517–518, 9:264.

18. HL to John Knight, June 12, 1764, *PHL,* 4:310; HL to Oswald, Feb. 15, 1763, *PHL,* 3:260; on the "Negro Contract," HL to Gervais, Feb. 28, 1772, *PHL,* 8:194; HL to Smith and Baillies, Feb. 9, 1764, *PHL,* 4:167–168.

19. Egerton Leigh, *The Man Unmasked, or, the World Undeceived, PHL,* 6:528 (citing Rev. 18:13); Henry Laurens, *Appendix to the Extracts* (Charlestown, 1769), *PHL,* 7:99–100. For a fuller discussion of this controversy and the resulting publications, see below, pp. 58–60.

20. HL to Smith and Baillies, Feb. 9, 1764, Jan. 1, Oct. 17, 1768, *PHL,* 4:167–168, 5:547, 6:137; HL to Henry Bright (Bristol), Oct. 31, 1769, *PHL,* 7:192; HL to John Holman (Island of Delos, Africa), Sept. 8, 1770, *PHL,* 7:345.

21. HL and William Hopton to John Hopton, Apr. 8, 1771, *PHL,* 7:488–489; HL to Gervais, Feb. 5, 1774, *PHL,* 9:263–264.

22. HL to Ettwein, Mar. 19, 1763, *PHL,* 3:373–374.

23. S. Max Edelson calculated these values from Laurens's Account Book: Edelson, *Plantation Enterprise,* 240–244. In 2009 dollars, £15,000 would be roughly equivalent to $3 million.

24. HL to John Laurens, Dec. 12, 1774, *PHL,* 10:2–3; John Laurens to HL, Feb. 18, 1775, *PHL,* 10:74.

25. Mark Antony De Wolfe Howe, ed., "Journal of Josiah Quincy, Jr., 1773," *Proceedings of the Massachusetts Historical Society* 49 (1915–1916): 434.

26. Information on the Commons House is summarized from Richard Waterhouse, *A New World Gentry: The Making of a Merchant and Planter Class in South Carolina, 1670–1770,* 2nd ed. (Charleston, S.C., 2005), esp. chap. 6; and Robert M. Weir, "'Liberty, Property, and No Stamps': South Carolina and the Stamp Act Crisis" (Ph.D. diss., Western Reserve University, 1967), 34–57. Seven pounds in local currency traded for about £1 sterling.

27. HL to George Appleby, Oct. 18, 1764, *PHL,* 4:467; Waterhouse, *New World Gentry,* 103–108; Jack P. Greene, *Quest for Power: The Lower Houses of Assembly in the Southern Royal Colonies, 1689–1776* (Chapel Hill, N.C., 1963); Jonathan Mercantini, *Who Shall Rule at Home? The Evolution of South Carolina Political Culture, 1748–1776* (Columbia, S.C., 2007). Charles Town did not have its own local government until 1783 (when its name was changed to Charleston): Walter J. Fraser, Jr., *Charleston! Charleston! The History of a Southern City* (Columbia, S.C., 1989), esp. 169–170. Laurens, for example, served on commissions for Charles Town's streets, for harbor pilots, and for building the new Exchange Building, among others.

28. Howe, ed., "Josiah Quincy, Jr.," 454; Eola Willis, *The Charleston Stage in the XVIII Century* (Columbia, S.C., 1924), 30, 33; Fredric M. Litto, "Addison's Cato in the Colonies," *William and Mary Quarterly,* 3rd ser., 23 (July 1966): 431–449; *SCG,* May 23, Sept. 19, 1774. Litto gives the first date as 1735, but this is based on a misreading of Willis, his source.

29. *Ramsay's History,* 2:253; E. Stanly Godbold, Jr., and Robert H. Woody, *Christopher Gadsden and the American Revolution* (Knoxville, Tenn., 1982), 3–21; Daniel J. McDonough, *Christopher Gadsden and Henry Laurens: The Parallel Lives of Two American Patriots* (Sellinsgrove, Pa., 2000).

30. *SCG,* Mar. 7, 1774 (quotation); Godbold and Woody, *Christopher Gadsden,* 3–21, 22–49 (quotations on 25, 43), 72–74; Mercantini, *Who Shall Rule at Home?* 120–186.

31. Richard Walsh, ed., *The Writings of Christopher Gadsden, 1746–1805* (Columbia, S.C., 1966), 18–19, 23, 30. Gadsden claimed further that Parliament could *not* be the Americans' "collective body" because no Americans could vote for Parliament. On the controversy, see also Jack P. Greene, "The Gadsden Election Controversy and the Revolutionary Movement in South Carolina," *Mississippi Valley Historical Review* 46 (1959): 469–492.

32. Christopher Gadsden to William Samuel Johnson and Charles Garth, Dec. 2, 1765, in Walsh, ed., *Writings of Christopher Gadsden,* 67; Commons House quoted in Robert M. Weir, *"A Most Important Epocha": The Coming of the Revolution in South Carolina* (Columbia, S.C., 1970), 19. For a detailed account of the passage of these and subsequent laws, see P. D. G. Thomas, *British Politics and the Stamp Act Crisis: The First Phase of the American Revolution, 1763–1767* (Oxford, 1975); for South Carolina's response, see Weir, " 'Liberty, Property, and No Stamps.' "

33. Richard Walsh, *Charleston's Sons of Liberty: A Study of the Artisans, 1763–1789* (Columbia, S.C., 1959), chap. 2; Weir, " 'Liberty, Property, and No Stamps' "; Weir, *Most Important Epocha,* 16 ("conduit pipe"); Godbold and Woody, *Christopher Gadsden,* 68–69. See also Pauline Maier, "The Charleston Mob and the Evolution of Popular Politics in Revolutionary South Carolina, 1765–1784," *Perspectives in American History* 4 (1970): 173–196.

34. Rosemary Niner Estes, "Charles Town's Sons of Liberty: A Closer Look" (Ph.D. diss., University of North Carolina, Chapel Hill, 2005), 252–276; "Cannon, Daniel," in *Biographical Dictionary of the South Carolina House of Representatives,* Vol. 2: *The Commons House of Assembly, 1692–1775,* ed. Walter B. Edgar and H. Louise Bailey (Columbia, S.C., 1977), 124–126; David Chesnutt, " 'Greedy Party Work': The South Carolina Election of 1768," in *Party and Political Opposition in Revolutionary America,* ed. Patricia Bonomi (Tarrytown, N.Y., 1980), 70–96; *SCG,* Oct. 3, 1768, reprinted in *PHL,* 6:122–123.

35. These statements occurred in a series of exchanges in the *SCG* in the summer and fall of 1769, which have been edited by Robert M. Weir in *The Letters of Freeman, etc.: Essays on the Nonimportation Movement in South Carolina* (Columbia, S.C., 1977), quotations on 29, 49, 85. The boycott worked reasonably well, cutting imports by half. When Parliament repealed all the duties except the one on tea, the colonies gradually abandoned their boycotts, with South Carolina being one of the last to concede, in December 1770: Weir, *Most Important Epocha,* 32–38.

36. Howe, ed., "Josiah Quincy, Jr.," 452. On the controversy, see Jack P. Greene, "Bridge to Revolution: The Wilkes Fund Controversy in South Carolina, 1760–75," *Journal of Southern History* 29 (1963): 19–52; Jack P. Greene, ed., *The Nature of Colony Constitutions* (Columbia, S.C., 1970); Mercantini, *Who Shall Rule at Home?* 237–241.

37. HL to Brown, Nov. 11, 1765, *PHL,* 5:23–24; McDonough, *Gadsden and Laurens,* 70–71; HL to James Grant, Oct. 1, Dec. 22, 1768, *PHL,* 6:119 and n., 231; Chesnutt, " 'Greedy Party Work.' " Robert M. Weir believes that this attitude was shared by most merchants: Weir, " 'Liberty, Property, and No Stamps,' " 194. On Laurens's politics, see Laura P. Frech, "The Republicanism of Henry Laurens," *SCHM* 76 (1975): 68–79.

38. McDonough, *Gadsden and Laurens,* 80–98.

39. Many documents relating to the conflicts between Moore and Charles Town merchants were published at Laurens's urging in a pamphlet, *A Representation of Facts, Relative to the Conduct of Daniel Moore, Esquire . . .* (Charles Town, 1767). Laurens's *Extracts from the Proceedings of the Court of Vice-Admiralty . . . [with] some General Observations on American Customs-House Officers, and Courts of Vice-Admiralty* appeared in Philadelphia at the end of 1768; the second, longer and with more biting comments, in Charles Town in February 1769. These, along with Leigh's *Man Unmasked* and Laurens's *Appendix,* are reprinted in *PHL,* 5:393–464, 6:184–216, 287–384, 450–566, and 7:2–114. Quotations from *PHL,* 6:296, 295.

40. Laurens, *Extracts* (Charles Town), *PHL,* 6:373; HL to Ralph Izard, Sept. 9, 1774, *PHL,* 9:566; HL to John Petrie, Sept. 7, 1774, *PHL,* 9:533; *Extracts* (Charles Town), *PHL,* 6:295; *Appendix, PHL,* 7:8.

41. Olaudah Equiano, *The Interesting Narrative of the Life of Olaudah Equiano Written by Himself,* ed. Robert J. Allison, 2nd ed. (New York, 2007). This is based on the first edition, published in London in 1789. For Vassa's name, I have followed Vincent Carretta, who shows that Equiano, as he is usually known today, at this time used a name given to him as a child by his owner: *Equiano the African: Biography of a Self-Made Man* (Athens, Ga., 2005), xv–xvi, 292–294.

42. Equiano, *Interesting Narrative,* 126–127.

43. William Bull to Lords Commissioners for Trade and Plantations, Dec. 17, 1765, CO 5/378, BPRO Transcripts, GR 23, 30–31; HL to Gervais, Jan. 29, 1766, *PHL,* 5:53 ("crying out '*Liberty*'" [emphasis in original], "gave vast trouble," "bitter weather," "soldiers in arms"); Journals of the Council and Upper House of Assembly, Dec. 17, Dec. 25, 1765, 32:680–681 ("design of Negroes"), 682–683, SCDAH.

44. Journals of the Commons House of Assembly, Jan. 14, Feb. 28, 1766, 37:pt. 1:34–35 (107 in Colleton County, "large numbers"), 76–77, SCDAH. See also Weir, "'Liberty, Property, and No Stamps,'" 277–279; *SCG,* Oct. 17, 1774.

45. "Governor William Bull's Representation of the Colony, 1770," in *The Colonial South Carolina Scene: Contemporary Views, 1697–1774,* ed. H. Roy Merrens (Columbia, S.C., 1977), 260; HL to Oswald, Apr. 27, 1768, *PHL,* 5:668; Bull to Earl of Hillsborough, June 7, 1770, *DAR,* 2:100.

CHAPTER 3
"God will deliver his own People from Slavery"

1. Jack P. Greene, "Empire and Identity from the Glorious Revolution to the American Revolution," in *The Oxford History of the British Empire,* Vol. 2: *The Eighteenth Century,* ed. P. J. Marshall (New York, 1998), 208–209. On the limited meaning of "liberty" in this era, see Michal Jan Rozbicki, "Between Private and Public Spheres: Liberty as Cultural Property in Eighteenth-Century British America," in *Cultures and Identities in Colonial British America,* ed. Robert Olwell and Alan Tully (Baltimore, 2006), 293–318; John Phillip Reid, *The Concept of Liberty in the Age of the American Revolution* (Chicago,

1988), esp. chap. 6. Although colonists like Christopher Gadsden wrote of "Turkey," they more properly should have referred to the Ottoman Empire.

2. John Trenchard and Thomas Gordon, *Cato's Letters* (London, 1748). "Destructive spirit" and "encroaching power" are quoted from letters numbered 19 and 115. This paragraph summarizes a large literature, the key text of which is Bernard Bailyn, *The Ideological Origins of the American Revolution* (Cambridge, Mass., 1967). On South Carolina, see, e.g., *SCG,* issues in July and August 1748; and Walter B. Edgar, "Some Popular Books in Colonial South Carolina," *SCHM* 72 (1971): 176. Robert M. Weir points out that a conservative version of this idea, associated especially with Henry St. John, Viscount Bolingbroke, was also quite popular: Weir, ed., *The Letters of Freeman, etc.: Essays on the Nonimportation Movement in South Carolina* (Columbia, S.C., 1977), xxiii–xxiv.

3. Trenchard and Gordon, *Cato's Letters.*

4. Bailyn, *Ideological Origins,* 232; *SCG,* June 22, 1769, reprinted in Richard Walsh, *The Writings of Christopher Gadsden, 1746–1805* (Columbia, S.C., 1966), 77–78.

5. Jan Lewis, "The Problem of Slavery in Southern Political Discourse," in *Devising Liberty: Preserving and Creating Freedom in the New American Republic,* ed. David Thomas Konig (Stanford, Calif., 1995), 268, quoting Richard Henry Lee, *Memoir of the Life of Richard Henry Lee and His Correspondence,* 2 vols. (Philadelphia, 1825).

6. James Otis, *The Rights of the British Colonists Asserted and Proved* (Boston, 1764), 43–44.

7. David Brion Davis, *The Problem of Slavery in the Age of Emancipation* (Ithaca, N.Y., 1975), 213–342; Alexander Hewatt, *An Historical Account of the Rise and Progress of the Colonies of South Carolina and Georgia* (London, 1779; reprint, Spartanburg, S.C., 1962), 94–95, 102, 95; Secretary of State, Miscellaneous Records, book SS, 49–50, SCDAH.

8. HL to William Gambell, Mar. 15, 1773, *PHL,* 8:621; HL to Lachlan McIntosh, Mar. 13, 1773, *PHL,* 8:621, 616–618; HL to Felix Warley, Dec. 5, 1771, *PHL,* 8:73; HL to James Laurens, Dec. 5, 1771, *PHL,* 8:67. In the case of Sam, Laurens told Warley that if Sam was properly humbled by a week's confinement, Warley should not carry out the threats to have him whipped.

9. HL to John Laurens, Feb. 21, 1774, *PHL,* 9:303, 304; HL to James Habersham, Nov. 23, 1773, *PHL,* 9:160; HL to John Laurens, Jan. 14, 1774, *PHL,* 9:224–225.

10. HL to Thomas Savage, Dec. 5, 1771, *PHL,* 8:77–78; HL to Alexander Garden, May 24, 1772, *PHL,* 8:327; Arthur Lee, *Answer to Considerations on Certain Political Transactions of the Province of South Carolina* (London, 1774), reprinted in *The Nature of Colony Constitutions,* ed. Jack P. Greene (Columbia, S.C., 1970), quotation on 46. Arthur Lee was the brother of Richard Henry Lee, quoted above. On the meetings with Campbell, see chap. 5, below.

11. HL to George Appleby, May 4, Feb. 15, 1774, *PHL,* 9:428, 278. A mass meeting in Charles Town had resolved that "the tea ought not to be landed, received, or vended, in this Colony," and Lieutenant Governor Bull stored the tea in the Exchange before it could be destroyed.

12. HL to James Laurens, Mar. 16, Apr. 13, 1774, *PHL,* 9:354, 407; Petition to House

of Lords, May 11, 1774, *PHL,* 9:447, 448; HL to Ralph Izard, Sept. 20, 1774, *PHL,* 9:566. Another "Intolerable Act" gave Catholics political rights in the former French colony of Quebec. On Ralph Izard, Jr., see *PHL,* 9:377n.

13. These events are summarized in Robert M. Weir, *"A Most Important Epocha": The Coming of the Revolution in South Carolina* (Columbia, S.C., 1970), 51–61, and are traced in detail in Edward McCrady, *The History of South Carolina under the Royal Government, 1719–1776* (New York, 1901), 724–789. HL to Habersham, Nov. 23, 1773, *PHL,* 9:160 ("Torrent").

14. HL to Izard, Sept. 20, 1774, *PHL,* 9:566.

15. Reid, *Concept of Liberty* (Chicago, 1988), esp. chap. 6; Samuel Johnson, *Taxation No Tyranny; an Answer to the Resolutions and Address of the American Congress,* 4th ed. (London, 1775), 89; Christopher Leslie Brown, *Moral Capital: Foundations of British Abolitionism* (Chapel Hill, N.C., 2006), 119–122.

16. Granville Sharp, *Declaration of the People's Natural Rights to a Share in the Legislature* (Boston, 1774), 19n25. Other editions appeared in New York and Philadelphia. Granville Sharp did not, in 1776, support full independence for America.

17. HL to William Cowles, Dec. 30, 1771, *PHL,* 8:143. There was more than one adaptation of the novel and it is uncertain which one Laurens saw. On rising antislavery sentiments, see Brown, *Moral Capital,* chap. 1.

18. James Oldham, "New Light on Mansfield and Slavery," *Journal of British Studies* 27 (1988): 45–68; Mark S. Wiener, "New Biographical Evidence on Somerset's Case," *Slavery and Abolition* 23 (April 2002): 121–136; Mark S. Weiner, *Black Trials: Citizenship from the Beginnings of Slavery to the End of Caste* (New York, 2004), 70–88. The most comprehensive account is Steven M. Wise, *Though the Heavens May Fall: The Landmark Trial That Led to the End of Human Slavery* (Cambridge, Mass., 2005).

19. [William Henry Drayton], *A Letter from Freeman of South Carolina, to the Deputies of North America . . . at Philadelphia* (Charles Town, 1774), 37, 41; *Some Thoughts on a Letter Signed Freeman Addressed to the Deputies Assembled at the High Court of Congress in Philadelphia. By a Back Settler* (Charles Town, 1774), 25.

20. HL to John Lewis Gervais, May 29, 1772, *PHL,* 8:353; HL to Garden, Aug. 20, 1772, ibid., 435–6. There is no record of further comment from Laurens to these or other correspondents.

21. HL to Joseph Clay, Sept. 22, 1772, *PHL,* 8:464, 466, 468; HL to James Laurens, Nov. 10, 1771, *PHL,* 8:4; HL to Gervais, May 29, 1772, *PHL,* 8:353; HL to Appleby, Mar. 10, 1774, *PHL,* 9:347; HL to John Laurens, Dec. 12, 1774, *PHL,* 10:2–3. The fate of Robert, who was faced with possible transportation back to the colonies if convicted, is not known.

22. HL to John Laurens, Dec. 12, 1774, *PHL,* 10:1, 4.

23. HL to John Laurens, July 2, 1775, *PHL,* 10:204; William Edwin Hemphill, ed., *Extracts from the Journals of the Provincial Congresses of South Carolina, 1775–1776* (Columbia, S.C., 1960), 6–8. Information on individual members and their relationships are from Walter B. Edgar and H. Louise Bailey, eds., *Biographical Dictionary of the South Carolina House of Representatives: The Commons House of Assembly, 1692–1775,* 2 vols. (Columbia, S.C., 1977).

24. The decisions of the Provincial Congress are summarized in Drayton, *Memoirs*, 1:166–180.

25. Eliza Pinckney to Harriott Pinckney Horry, Feb. 17, 20, 1775, Pinckney Papers, LC; HL to John Laurens, Feb. 18, 1775, *PHL*, 10:72; C. P. Seabrook Wilkinson, ed., "A Declaration of Dependence: Robert Smith's 1775 Humiliation Sermon," *SCHM* 100 (1999): 221–240, quotations on 228, 229, 230.

26. For the *Mermaid*'s arrival, see *SCG*, Jan. 2, 1775.

27. Harvey H. Jackson, "Hugh Bryan and the Evangelical Movement in Colonial South Carolina," *William and Mary Quarterly*, 3rd ser., 43 (1986): 595–614.

28. *SCG*, Jan. 1–7 (the letter is dated Nov. 20, 1740), Mar. 20–27, 1741; Eliza Lucas Pinckney, Memo on "long letter to my father," in Elise Pinckney, ed., *The Letterbook of Eliza Lucas Pinckney, 1739–1762* (Columbia, S.C., 1997), 30; Eliza Lucas Pinckney to Miss Bartlett, March 1742, in ibid., 29; "Extract of a Letter from South Carolina, March 22, 1742," *Boston Weekly Post-Boy*, May 3, 1742, quoted in Jackson, "Hugh Bryan and the Evangelical Movement," 33.

29. Whitefield quoted in Alan Gallay, *The Formation of a Planter Elite: Jonathan Bryan and the Southern Colonial Frontier* (Athens, Ga., 1989), 50–51; Hugh Bryan to William Bull, Jr., May 1, 1742, *The Journal of the Commons House of Assembly*, Vol. 3: *May 18, 1741–July 10, 1742*, ed. J. H. Easterby (Columbia, S.C., 1951–), 461–462; Jackson, "Hugh Bryan," 610–614.

30. William Henry Lyttleton to My Lords, Sept. 1, 1759, CO5/376, in BPRO Transcripts, 28:108. See also Robert Olwell, *Masters, Slaves, and Subjects: The Culture of Power in the South Carolina Low Country, 1740–1790* (Ithaca, N.Y., 1998), 136–137. Some sources refer to Johns as "Philip John" or "Philip Jones."

31. Olwell, *Masters, Slaves, and Subjects*, 136–137; Journal of the Governor's Council, June 9, 20, 1759, 28:105–106, 110–111, SCDAH ("God Almighty," "written paper," "killing all the Buckraas"); *SCG*, Aug. 18, 1759 ("communicating his Design").

32. Olwell, *Masters, Slaves, and Subjects*, 118; Annette Laing, "'Heathens and Infidels'? African Christianization in the South Carolina Low Country, 1700–1750," *Religion and American Culture* 12 (Summer 2002): 187–228; Boyd Stanley Schlenther, "Hastings, Selina, Countess of Huntingdon," *ODNB*; Edwin Welch, *Spiritual Pilgrim: A Reassessment of the Life of the Countess of Huntingdon* (Cardiff, 1995), 135–136. Hastings later broke with the Wesleys because of her strict adherence to the doctrine of predestination.

33. David Margrett to the Countess of Huntingdon, n.d., but probably c. 1770, no. F1–1221, CHAP; Piercy to Huntingdon, Nov. 28, 1774, in A 4/1 19, CHAP. Other historians have called him "David Margate," as he appears in some of the Huntingdon papers, but I have used "Margrett" because that is the spelling in the one letter in his own hand. See, e.g., Sylvia R. Frey and Betty Wood, *Come Shouting to Zion: African American Protestantism in the American South and the British Caribbean to 1830* (Chapel Hill, N.C., 1998), 112–134.

34. See the invoices for "Mr. Margate" and "Mr Margreet" in A2/8, nos. 21, 22, 24, 30, 34, CHAP; HL to Robert and John Thompson and Co., Apr. 12, 1757, *PHL*, 2:523–524.

35. John Edwards to William Piercy, Jan. 11, 1775, A 3/6 9; Richard Piercy to Hunt-

ingdon, June 16, 1775, A 1/13 10 ("outward condition"); Edwards to William Piercy, Jan. 16, 1775, A 3/6 10, all in CHAP. Hinds owned property west of King Street and north of Beaufain: "Hind Street," http://www.scottishritecalifornia.org/charleston—street%27s .htm. Records relating to Hinds's career are in the files of the Museum of Early Southern Decorative Arts, Winston-Salem; see also *PHL,* 2:523–524n. When Hinds died in 1798, he left slaves to his children and property to the Baptist Church.

36. Edwards to William Piercy, Jan. 16, 1775, A 3/6 10, CHAP; *SCG,* Mar. 27, 1775.

37. HL to John Laurens, Jan. 22, 1775, *PHL,* 10:45.

CHAPTER 4
"A plan, for instigating the slaves to insurrection"

1. *SC and AGG,* May 5, 1775; Drayton, *Memoirs,* 1:182–187, 221–226. The notice did not mention the name of the ship, but the *Lloyd,* Joseph Smith master, was the only ship to leave Charles Town for Philadelphia that day.

2. Drayton, *Memoirs,* 1:231; *PHL,* 10:113–114n5. Lee's pamphlet was sparked by the Wilkes controversy, discussed in chap. 2, above. Ralph Izard and Laurens together had paid for Lee's pamphlet, *Answer to Considerations on certain Political Transactions of the Province of South Carolina* (London, 1774).

3. William Lee to Robert Carter Nicholas, Mar. 6, 1775, in Lee, *The Letters of William Lee, Sheriff and Alderman of London; Commercial Agent of the Continental Congress in France; and Minister to the Courts of Vienna and Berlin, 1766–1783,* ed. Worthington Chauncy Ford (Brooklyn, N.Y., 1891), 143. (Lee added, "These might not be his [Dunmore's] precise words, but the meaning is the same.") Drayton, *Memoirs,* 1:231. Arthur Lee had earlier written to his brother Richard Henry Lee that "Sir Willm Draper has publishd a proposal for emancipating your Negroes by royal Proclamation & arming them against you. The proposal met with approbation from ministerial People." Arthur Lee to Richard Henry Lee, Dec. 6, 1774, *NDAR,* 1:378.

4. For Dunmore's actual letters, see Dunmore to Earl of Dartmouth, Dec. 23, 1774, May 1, 1775, *DAR,* 8:252–270, 9:109.

5. William Piercy to Countess of Huntingdon, May 7–8, 1775, A 4/2 16, CHAP. This letter is a leaf misfiled as part of a different letter in CHAP; the sheet can be accurately dated from internal evidence, as a note from the archivist indicates.

6. William Piercy to Huntingdon, Jan. 24, 1775, A 4/2 13; James Habersham to Huntingdon, Apr. 19, 1775, A 3/6 15; Richard Piercy to Huntingdon, June 16, 1775, A 1/13 10, all in CHAP.

7. William Piercy to Huntingdon, May 7–8, 1775, A 4/2 16 (sent from Charles Town); Richard Piercy to Huntingdon, June 16, 1775, A 1/13 10; Habersham to Robert Keen, May 11, 1775, in *The Letters of Hon. James Habersham, 1756–1775,* Collections of the Georgia Historical Society, 6 (1904), 243–44 (*Georgia Planter*).

8. *SC and AGG,* May 12, 1777. The original appeared in the *Essex Gazette* (Salem, Mass.), Apr. 25, 1775.

9. *PHL,* 10:45, 118; Drayton, *Memoirs,* 1:221, 231; "South Carolina [Association],"

Broadside, Early American Imprints. In addition to Bee, the members of the Special Committee were Thomas Lynch, Jr., Barnard Elliott, George Gabriel Powell, William Tennant, and John Huger, William Henry Drayton, Arthur Middleton, Charles C. Pinckney, William Gibbes, and Edward Weyman. The last five of these were the members of the "Secret Committee" previously authorized by the Provincial Congress. The broadside with the Association was filmed from a copy in the Henry Laurens Papers in the New York Public Library and is annotated, in his hand, "In General Committee Thursday, 11th May 1775. . . . unanimously approved of to be recommended in Provincial Congress as proposals to be signed by the Inhabitants of this Province."

    10. Evangeline Walker Andrews and Charles McLean Andrews, eds., *Journal of a Lady of Quality* . . . (New Haven, 1921), 199; James Wright to Dartmouth, May 25, 1775, *DAR*, 9:144; John Stuart to Dartmouth, July 21, 1775, *DAR*, 11:53–54 (this had occurred at "about" the time of Stuart's previous letter of May 20); L. H. Butterfield, ed., *Diary and Autobiography of John Adams*, Vol. 2: *Diary, 1771–1781* (Cambridge, Mass., 1961), 182–183 (Sept. 24, 1775). On the North Carolina scare, see Jeffrey Crow, "Slave Rebelliousness and Social Conflict in North Carolina, 1775–1802," *William and Mary Quarterly*, 3rd ser., 37 (1980): 32–36.

    11. "New York, April 27; Extract of a letter from London, Feb. 10, 1775," and letter from Caroliniensis, *SCG*, May 29, 1775; WC to Dartmouth, Aug. 31, 1775, *DAR*, 11:94.

    12. HL to James Laurens, June 7, 1775, *PHL*, 10:162–163; Josiah Smith to James Poyas, May 18, 1775, Josiah Smith Letterbook, Southern Historical Collection, University of North Carolina.

    13. William Edwin Hemphill, ed., *Extracts from the Journals of the Provincial Congresses of South Carolina, 1775–1776* (Columbia, S.C., 1960), 51.

    14. Hemphill, ed., *Extracts*, 36. Before adopting the Association statement, the congress also banned corn exports from the colony. Those leading resistance to the British in Charles Town had begun to call themselves "Patriots" as early as mid-1774. James Laurens to HL, July 22, 1774, *PHL*, 9:524.

    15. Hemphill, ed., *Extracts*, 36–43; HL to John Laurens, June 8, 1775, *PHL*, 10:164–167. On Bee, see Robert E. Rector, "Thomas Bee and the Revolution in South Carolina" (M.A. thesis, University of South Carolina, 1971).

    16. HL to John Laurens, June 8, 1775, *PHL*, 10:164–167, 174–179.

    17. Drayton, *Memoirs*, 1:300–302 (Hubart's petition); HL to John Laurens, June 8, 1775, *PHL*, 10:167 ("threatned vengeance"). On the reported arms shipment, see *SCG*, May 29, 1775.

    18. *SCG and CJ*, June 13, 1775; *SC and AGG*, June 9, 1775; Alexander Innes to Dartmouth, June 10, 1775, in B. D. Barger, "Charles Town Loyalism in 1775: The Secret Reports of Alexander Innes," *SCHM* 63 (1962): 132; HL to John Laurens, June 8, 1775, *PHL*, 10:171. On the origins of tar and feathering, see Alfred F. Young, "Tar and Feathers and the Ghost of Oliver Cromwell: English Plebeian Culture and American Radicalism," in Young, *Liberty Tree: Ordinary People and the American Revolution* (New York, 2006), 144–179.

    19. HL to John Laurens, June 18, 1775, *PHL*, 10:184.

20. Philip D. Morgan, "Black Life in Eighteenth Century Charleston," *Perspectives in American History* 1 (1984): 196–200; Laurens's boats and crews (as of 1766) listed in extracts from his account book in *PHL*, 6:610–612. The *SCG*, Jan. 18, 1770, included an advertisement for a cypress canoe twenty-eight feet long, more than four feet wide, and able to accommodate ten passengers; *SCG*, Oct. 25, 1770. On African Americans in the maritime world generally, see W. Jeffrey Bolster, *Black Jacks: African American Seamen in the Age of Sail* (Cambridge, Mass., 1997); and David Cecelski, *The Waterman's Song: Slavery and Freedom in Maritime North Carolina* (Chapel Hill, N.C., 2001).

21. "An Act for the Better Ordering and Governing Negroes and other Slaves in this Province," *Statutes at Large*, 7:398; Robert A. Olwell, "Becoming Free: Manumission and the Genesis of a Free Black Community in South Carolina, 1740–90," *Slavery and Abolition* 1 (1996): 1–18. A summary tax return for the colony in 1768 noted the presence of just 77 "free negroes," including 25 in Charles Town, compared with almost 80,000 slaves (6,336 in Charles Town), but this included only those subject to a head tax, so it does not include every free black. Extrapolating from what is known of the rate of manumission between 1770 and 1790, perhaps 500 or so free blacks lived in South Carolina in 1775, and about 200 in Charles Town. Whatever the total, it was a tiny percentage of the total African and African-American population. "A 1768 Tax Account," in *The Colonial South Carolina Scene: Contemporary Views, 1697–1774*, ed. H. Roy Merrens (Columbia, S.C., 1977), 248–252. On Scipio Handley, a free fisherman, see American Loyalist Claims, 47:117–120.

22. William Falconer, *An Universal Dictionary of the Marine* (London, 1769), s.v. "Banks," "Coasting," "Coasting-Pilot," "Navigation," "Pilot"; "An Act for Settling and Regulating the Pilotage of This Province," *Statutes at Large*, 3:225–228. The act was updated in 1734 and 1777.

23. *SCG*, Feb. 13, 1755, May 7, 1756; WC to Dartmouth, Aug. 31, 1775, *DAR*, 11:94–95.

24. P. C. Coker III, *Charleston's Maritime Heritage, 1670–1987: An Illustrated History* (Charleston, 1987), 35–36; *Statutes at Large*, 3:225–228; "Pilots of Charleston Bar Petition to the Commons House of Assembly," 1755, Charleston Library Society; Rusty Fleetwood, *Tidecraft: The Boats of Lower South Carolina and Georgia* (Savannah, Ga., 1982), 56–60.

25. *SCG*, June 20, 1768; Fleetwood, *Tidecraft*, 179–181; Carl Bridenbaugh, *Cities in Revolt: Urban Life in America, 1743–1776* (New York, 1964), 279–280.

26. Secretary of State Miscellaneous Records, book OO, 624, SCDAH.

27. *SCG*, Sept. 10, Sept. 24, 1772. Anchors were advertised at a cost of £12 local currency, per hundred pounds: *SC and AGG*, May 5, 1775. *Ramsay's History*, 1:66 ("poor man's country"). Estimates of Jeremiah's wealth are from WC to Dartmouth, Aug. 31, 1775, *DAR*, 11:95; and "Narrative by George Millegen of his Experiences in South Carolina," Sept. 15, 1775, *DAR*, 11:111. The wealthiest free black family in the colony was probably that of James Pendarvis, son of white planter Joseph Pendarvis, who left land, including a plantation on Charleston Neck, to his seven children by his African mistress, Parthena. He also left them slaves to work the land. James Pendarvis accumulated more than 155 slaves before he died in 1798: Larry Koger, *Black Slaveowners: Free Black Slave Masters in South Carolina, 1790–1860* (Columbia, S.C., 1995), 109. Paul Cuffe of Massachusetts

(born 1759) and James Forten of Philadelphia (born 1766) made larger fortunes in the maritime trade and related businesses, but not until after the American Revolution.

28. Copies of these statements were enclosed in letter from WC to Dartmouth, Aug. 31, 1775, BPRO Transcripts, 25:191–216. That the Fish Market was located at the base of Prioleau's Wharf is shown on a map by Edmund Petrie, "Ichonography of Charleston . . . Taken from Actual Survey, 2nd August 1788," in the South Carolina Historical Society.

29. See "The Stranger," *SCG,* Sept. 17, 1772; "Act for the Better Ordering of Negroes," *Statutes at Large,* 7:397–417.

30. Drayton, *Memoirs,* 2:24n; *Statues at Large,* 7:402; Walter J. Fraser, Jr., *Charleston! Charleston! The History of a Southern City* (Columbia, S.C., 1989), 70–71; Gabriele Gottlieb, "Theater of Death: Capital Punishment in Early America, 1750–1800" (Ph.D. diss., University of Pittsburgh, 1998), 30.

31. HL to John Laurens, June 18, 23, 1775, *PHL,* 10:185, 191. It is unclear whether there was a formal trial of Thomas Jeremiah at this time or whether his later trial in August was the first.

32. HL to John Laurens, Aug. 20, June 23, 1775, *PHL,* 10:321–322, 191. On Abraham, see chap. 2, above.

CHAPTER 5
"The Young King was about to alter the World, & set the Negroes Free"

1. HL to John Laurens, June 18, 1775, *PHL,* 10:183–184.

2. Inventory in "Memorial of Lord William Campbell," 1768, T1/542, fols. 395–410, NAUK. The inventory has been reprinted in an appendix to Graham Hood, *The Governor's Palace in Williamsburg: A Cultural Study* (Williamsburg, Va., 1991), 507–513. The Hone portraits are discussed in Maurie D. McInnis, in collaboration with Angela D. Mack, *In Pursuit of Refinement: Charlestonians Abroad, 1740–1860* (Columbia, S.C., 1999), 108–111.

3. Inventory in "Memorial of Lord William Campbell." The house is still standing at 34 Meeting Street: Jonathan H. Poston, *The Buildings of Charleston: A Guide to the City's Architecture* (Columbia, S.C., 1997), 256–257; Alice R. Huger Smith and D. E. Huger Smith, *The Dwelling Houses of Charleston* (Philadelphia, 1917; reprint, Charleston, 2007), 40–42. The mantle was listed in the inventory as still in its box.

4. Inventory, "Memorial of Lord William Campbell."

5. James Raven, *London Booksellers and American Customers: Transatlantic Literary Community and the Charleston Library Society, 1748–1811* (Columbia, S.C., 2002).

6. R. A. Houston and W. W. J. Knox, eds., *The New Penguin History of Scotland: From the Earliest Times to the Present Day* (London, 2001), chaps. 4 and 5; entries related to the Campbells and Argyll in George Way, *Collins Scottish Clan and Family Encyclopedia* (Glasgow, 1994); John Stuart Shaw, *The Political History of Eighteenth-Century Scotland* (Basingstoke, 1999), 1–83.

7. Patricia Dickson, *Red John of the Battles: John, 2nd Duke of Argyll and 1st Duke of Greenwich, 1680–1743* (London, 1973), Pope quoted on 232; Neil Grant, *The Campbells of*

Argyll (London, 1975); Daniel Szechi, *1715: The Great Jacobite Rebellion* (New Haven, 2006).

8. James Fergusson, *Argyll in the Forty-Five* (London, 1951); Journal of Lt. Col. John Campbell, Ms no. 3736, in Letters of John Campbell (4th Duke of Argyll), National Library of Scotland.

9. Ruth M. Larson, "Campbell [née Bellenden], Mary, of Mamore," *ODNB;* Ian Gordon Lindsay and Mary Cosh, *Inveraray and the Dukes of Argyll* (Edinburgh, 1973), 31; WC to Earl of Dartmouth, Feb. 13, 1773, CO 217/49, NAUK ("younger brother"). In reference sources Campbell's birth date has been given as "c. 1730," but his lieutenant's passing certificate shows that he was born in 1736: ADM 107/5, 310, NAUK.

10. See N. A. M. Rodger, *The Wooden World: An Anatomy of the Georgian Navy,* 2nd ed. (New York, 1996), 252–273.

11. Campbell's naval service can be traced through his lieutenant's passing certificate and the pay books of the *Penzance, Tyger,* and *Yarmouth:* ADM 107/5, 310; ADM 33/417, SBN 359; ADM 32/271, SBN 584; ADM 33/598, SBN 738. My thanks to Bob O'Hara of searchers-na.uk for the research in these records. Campbell also summarized his wartime service twice during petitions to his government, once in 1771, asking for leave from his post in Nova Scotia, and once as part of his petition for reimbursement for property lost in South Carolina: WC to Lord Hillsborough, Apr. 13, 1771, in CO 217/48, NAUK, and "Memorial of Lord William Campbell," T1/542, fols. 395–410. (The latter list is not included with the inventory reprinted in Hood, *Governor's Palace.*) For accounts of these engagements, see Lawrence Henry Gipson, *The Great War for Empire: The Culmination, 1760–1763,* Vol. 8 of *The British Empire before the American Revolution* (New York, 1954), 106–136, 175–185; J. S. Corbett, *England in the Seven Years' War: A Study in Combined Strategy,* 2 vols. (London, 1907), 1:339ff.; and Edward Ives, *A Voyage from England to India in the Year 1754* (London, 1773). I have followed the place-name spellings in Gipson, rather than in Campbell's own hand.

12. Gipson, *Great War for Empire,* 8:178–185; "Captain's Logs of the Nightingale, 1763," ADM 51/4273, and "Master's Log of the Nightingale," ADM 52/1385, both in NAUK; entry for William Campbell in David Syrett and R. L. DiNardo, eds., *The Commissioned Sea Officers of the Royal Navy, 1660–1815* (Aldershot, 1994); *SCG,* Apr. 23, 1763; A. S. Salley, ed., *Register of St. Philip's Parish Charles Town or Charleston, South Carolina, 1754–1810* (Columbia, S.C., 1971), 171.

13. WC to Hillsborough, Apr. 13, 1771, CO 217/48, NAUK; Sir Lewis Namier and John Brooke, *The House of Commons, 1754–1790,* 3 vols. (London, 1964), 1:40, 470–471; 2:192; Francis A. Coghlan, "Campbell, Lord William," *Dictionary of Canadian Biography*; Clive Towse, "Conway, Henry Seymour (1719–1795)," *ODNB;* P. D. G. Thomas, *British Politics and the Stamp Act Crisis: The First Phase of the American Revolution, 1763–1767* (Oxford, 1975).

14. WC to Hillsborough, June 13, 1770, CO 217/47, 44, NAUK; WC to Hillsborough, Apr. 13, 1771, CO 217/48, NAUK (Campbell added that the wound to his eye had occurred when he was a schoolboy, not in battle); Coghlan, "Campbell"; Duke of Argyll to Dartmouth, Jan. 13, 1773, Royal Commission on Historical Manuscripts, *The Manuscripts*

of the Earl of Dartmouth, Vol. 2: *American Papers,* Fourteenth Report, app., pt. 10 (London, 1895), 130; WC to Hillsborough, Apr. 13, 1771, CO 217/48, NAUK.

15. Robert M. Weir, "'Liberty, Property, and No Stamps': South Carolina and the Stamp Act Crisis" (Ph.D. diss., Western Reserve University, 1967), 450; Robert M. Weir, "The Role of the Newspaper Press in the Southern Colonies on the Eve of the Revolution: An Interpretation" in *The Press and the American Revolution,* ed. Bernard Bailyn and John B. Hench (Boston, 1980), 122–124, 141–142.

16. Langdon Cheves, Esq., "Izard of South Carolina," *SCH and GM* 2 (July 1901): 205–240. Carolinians pronounce his first name as "Rafe." Other Izards married Blakes, Middletons, Manigaults, and Brewtons.

17. Will of Ralph Izard, 1761, WPA Will Transcripts, 9:64–66, SCDAH; Inventory and Appraisement of the Estate of Ralph Izard, dec'd, Inventory Book T, 1758–1761, 507–522, SCDAH; *SCG,* Apr. 23, 1763.

18. William Campbell marriage settlement for Sarah Izard marriage, Miscellaneous Records, book MM, 24–26, April 1763, SCDAH. Sarah was given the right to pass about one-third of the estate to anyone she wished; the remainder would go to their children.

19. The "Additional Instruction" had been provoked by the decision of the Commons House, back in 1769, to donate funds to the Society for the Bill of Rights in London, an organization created to support John Wilkes; for this dispute, see chap. 2, above; WC to Dartmouth, Apr. 2[?], 1774, CO5/405. The "Additional Instruction" was reprinted in Leonard Woods Labaree, ed., *Royal Instructions to British Colonial Governors, 1670–1776,* 2 vols. (New York, 1935), 2:208–209.

20. HL to James Laurens, Mar. 11, 1773, *PHL,* 8:610; HL to John Laurens, Mar. 8, 1774, *PHL,* 9:345; HL to Henry Louis Gervais, Apr. 9, 1774, *PHL,* 9:398–399.

21. WC to Dartmouth, Apr. 2[?], 1774, CO5/405.

22. HL to Thomas Smith, July 21, 1774, *PHL,* 9:521–522; Lawrence S. Rowland, "'Alone on the River': The Rise and Fall of the Savannah River Rice Plantations," *SCHM* 89 (1987): 127–128; Inventory, "Memorial of Lord William Campbell."

23. William Bull II to Dartmouth, Mar. 28, May 1, 1775, *DAR,* 9:88–89, 111.

24. George C. Rogers, Jr., *Charleston in the Age of the Pinckneys* (Norman, Okla., 1969), xi–xiii; *SC and AGG,* June 23, 1775; HL to John Laurens, June 18, 1775, *PHL,* 10:183–184; Drayton, *Memoirs,* 1:257.

25. Alexander Innes to Dartmouth, May 1, 1775, *DAR,* 9:113–115; Drayton, *Memoirs,* 1:258; Smith and Smith, *Dwelling Houses of Charleston,* 40–43. Mary Izard Brewton and Elizabeth Izard Blake were sisters.

26. William H. Drayton to William Drayton, July 4, 1775, *DAR,* 11:36.

27. William Edwin Hemphill, ed., *Extracts from the Journals of the Provincial Congresses of South Carolina, 1775–1776* (Columbia, S.C., 1960), 59–60; Drayton, *Memoirs,* 1:259.

28. Hemphill, ed., *Extracts,* 65; WC to Dartmouth, July 2, 1775, *DAR,* 11:33–35.

29. WC to General Thomas Gage, July 1, 1775, *NDAR,* 1:800–801; WC to Dartmouth, July 2, 1775, *DAR,* 11:33–35; HL to John Laurens, June 23, 1775 (but written June 24), *PHL,* 10:194–195.

30. Drayton, *Memoirs,* 2:5–15, quotations on 5, 6, 7, 9, 10.

31. HL to John Laurens, June 23, 1775 (but written June 24), *PHL,* 10:186–187, 191; HL to James Laurens, July 2, 1775, *PHL,* 10:202; Gabriel Manigault to Gay [Gabriel Manigault II], July 8, 1775, in Maurice A. Crouse, ed., "The Papers of Gabriel Manigault, 1771–1784," *SCHM* 64 (1963): 2; William Henry Drayton to South Carolina Delegation, July 4, 1775, in *Documentary History of the American Revolution: Consisting of Letters and Papers Relating to the Contest for Liberty, Chiefly in South Carolina, from Originals in Possession of the Editor, and Other Sources,* ed. R. W. Gibbes (New York, 1855; reprint, New York, 1971), 117–118.

32. Thomas Hutchinson to Council of Safety, July 5, 1775, *PHL,* 10:206–208; Josiah Smith, Jr., to George Austin, Jan. 31, 1774, Josiah Smith Letterbook, Southern Historical Collection, University of North Carolina. Hutchinson's letter was written from "Chehaw." The Chehaw River is a small stream that empties into the Combahee River upstream from St. Helena Sound. In 1790, 82 percent of St. Bartholomew's population was enslaved: Philip D. Morgan, "Black Society in the Lowcountry, 1760–1810," in *Slavery and Freedom in the Age of the American Revolution,* ed. Ira Berlin and Ronald Hoffman (Charlottesville, Va., 1983), 94.

33. Hutchinson to Council of Safety, July 5, 1775, *PHL,* 10:206–208.

34. For more on these events, see chap. 3, above.

35. George II died on October 25, 1760. On David Margrett, see chap. 3, above.

36. Council of Safety to St. Bartholomew Committee, July 18, 1775, *PHL,* 10:231; Hutchinson to Council of Safety, July 5, 1775, *PHL,* 10:206. Burnet, in fact, worked on Henry Laurens's plantation in Georgia: HL to Christopher Zahn, June 20, 1777, *PHL,* 11:374–375.

37. *PHL,* 10:199n1; HL to John Laurens, July 14, 1775, *PHL,* 10:220; WC to Dartmouth, July 19, 20, 1775, *DAR,* 11:51.

CHAPTER 6
"Dark, Hellish plots"

1. HL to John Laurens, July 2, July 14, 1775, *PHL,* 10:204–205, 222.

2. The suspected insurrectionists had been "committed to the workhouse where there is a prison for them": George Millegen, "Narrative by George Millegen of his Experiences in South Carolina," Sept. 15, 1775, *DAR,* 11:110. On the Charles Town Work House, see J. H. Easterby, "Public Poor Relief in Colonial Charleston: A Report to the Commons House of Assembly about the Year 1767," *SCH and GM* 42 (April 1941): 83–87; Walter J. Fraser, Jr., *Charleston! Charleston! The History of a Southern City* (Columbia, S.C., 1989), 57, 117–118, 122, 128.

3. *SCG,* Sept. 7, 1775. An advertisement in this issue listed slaves brought in earlier and still being held; included are dates when the slave arrived—in these cases, June 6 and 15. *SC and AGG,* Aug. 11, 1775.

4. HL to John Laurens, July 14, 18, 1775, *PHL,* 10:220n9, 230n4; HL to Clement Lempriere, July 27, 1775, *PHL,* 10:248–249; Drayton, *Memoirs,* 1:268–273, 304–308.

5. Rachel N. Klein, *Unification of a Slave State: The Rise of the Planter Class in the South Carolina Backcountry, 1760–1808* (Chapel Hill, N.C., 1990), 9–20.

6. Klein, *Unification of a Slave State*, esp. 47–77; Woodmason quoted on 81. There was, of course, no single country of "Germany" at this time, but Carolinians referred to German speakers as either "Germans" or "Dutch" (after "deutsch").

7. *PHL*, 10:242n9; Drayton, *Memoirs*, 1:311–312, 321–323; Klein, *Unification of a Slave State*, 84–89; William Edmund Hemphill, ed., *Extracts from the Journals of the Provincial Congresses of South Carolina, 1775–1776* (Columbia, S.C., 1960), 47. This ammunition consisted of 250 pounds of powder and 500 pounds of lead that had been taken from Fort Charlotte on the Savannah River by patriot Major James Mayson: Drayton, *Memoirs*, 1:317–318.

8. HL (as president of the Council of Safety) to Thomas Fletchall, July 14, 1775, *PHL*, 10:214–218.

9. Fletchall to president of Council of Safety, July 24, 1775, *PHL*, 10:244–248; enclosure with William Thomson to HL, July 29, 1775, *PHL*, 10:255.

10. Drayton, *Memoirs*, 1:278, 325, 326–329; William Henry Drayton and William Tennant to Council of Safety, Aug. 7, 1775, *PHL*, 10:278; Klein, *Unification of a Slave State*, 89 (Hart quotation). As Klein shows, most of the leading Regulators, who usually owned substantial property, ultimately sided with the patriots during the Revolution. See also Keith Krawczynski, *William Henry Drayton: South Carolina Revolutionary Patriot* (Baton Rouge, La., 2001), 153–195.

11. Drayton, *Memoirs*, 2:4–15; WC to Earl of Dartmouth, July 19–20, 23, 1775, *DAR*, 11:49–53 (quotations on 50, 51), 55 ("more irksome"). The battle had in fact occurred at Breed's Hill, but the mistaken identification was already current.

12. WC to Thomas Gage, July 1, 1775, in *NDAR*, 1:800–801; WC to Dartmouth, July 19–20, 1775, *DAR*, 11:50–51.

13. Drayton and Tennant to Council of Safety, Aug. 7, 1775, *PHL*, 10:284; American Loyalist Claims, 57:127; Council of Safety to Thomson, Aug. 11, 1775, *PHL*, 10:290–291; Council of Safety to Drayton, Sept. 15, 1775, *PHL*, 10:386.

14. Drayton, *Memoirs*, 1:318–320; HL to John Laurens, July 30, 1775, *PHL*, 10:256, 258. Other radicals on the council included Arthur Middleton, Charles Pinckney, and Thomas Ferguson.

15. Drayton, *Memoirs*, 1:290 (Stuart on Indians); HL to John Laurens, July 30, 1775 (and postscript Aug. 19), *PHL*, 10:260 and n; Drayton, *Memoirs*, 1:338–349 ("drawing the sword," 345).

16. HL to John Laurens, July 30, 1775, *PHL*, 10:259.

17. Drayton, *Memoirs*, 1:314–315.

18. Millegen, "Narrative by George Millegen," 111–112; WC to Dartmouth, July 23, 1775, *DAR*, 11:54–55.

19. The trial was held on August 11 (see below), but Henry Laurens reported that it had been "above three Weeks on the Carpet." Enclosure dated Aug. 18, 1775, in HL to John Laurens, Aug. 20, 1775, *PHL*, 10:334.

20. *SCG*, June 8, 1769, reprinting resolutions passed in Boston on May 11, emphasis

in the original; Sir William Blackstone, *Commentaries on the Laws of England,* 4 vols. (Oxford, 1765–1769), bk. 6:342–343, bk. 3:379; *PHL,* 6:214. Blackstone then quoted the Latin version of the passage in the Magna Carta that had been translated into English by the Boston Town Meeting. On Blackstone's popularity in the colonies, see Daniel Coquillette, "The Legal Education of a Patriot: Josiah Quincy Jr.'s Law Commonplace (1763)," Boston College Law School Legal Studies Research Paper Series, Research Paper 114 (2006), 10n28. On the history of juries in South Carolina, see William S. McAninch, "Criminal Procedure and the South Carolina Jury Act of 1731," in *South Carolina Legal History,* ed. Herbert A. Johnson (Columbia, S.C., 1980), 179–198.

21. HL, *Extracts from the Proceedings of the Court of Vice-Admiralty, in Charles-Town, South Carolina . . .* (Philadelphia, 1768), in *PHL,* 6:213 (quoting Blackstone, *Commentaries,* bk. 3:379); Blackstone, *Commentaries,* bk. 4:343.

22. Blackstone, *Commentaries,* bk. 4:343–344.

23. Peter King, "Decision-Makers and Decision-Making in the English Criminal Law, 1750–1800," *Historical Journal* 27 (1984): 25–58; Douglas Hay, "Property, Authority and the Criminal Law," in Douglas Hay et al., *Albion's Fatal Tree: Crime and Society in Eighteenth-Century England* (New York, 1975), 46. In the colonies—e.g., Richmond County, Virginia—the great majority of those accused of noncapital crimes did not even ask for a trial before a jury but allowed the judge alone to decide their cases. Peter C. Hoffer, "Disorder and Deference: The Paradoxes of Criminal Justice in the Colonial Tidewater," in *Ambivalent Legacy: A Legal History of the South,* ed. David J. Bodenhamer and James W. Ely, Jr. (Jackson, Miss., 1984), 187–201. Hoffer found that in only six out of almost two hundred cases did the accused get jury trials (for noncapital cases). There is no equivalent study for South Carolina. A short survey of the development of trial by jury is Leonard W. Levy, *The Palladium of Justice: Origins of Trial by Jury* (Chicago, 1999).

24. King, "Decision-Makers and Decision-Making," 27 (middling group), 58 ("widely agreed criteria"); J. M. Beattie, *Crime and the Courts in England, 1600–1800* (Princeton, N.J., 1986), 90 (1760–1779 period), 440, 10. Of the other cases, about one-fifth were not indicted, another one-fifth were found not guilty, and more than a third were convicted of manslaughter rather than murder—meaning a brand on the hand and release. King's study, based on cases in Essex County, 1782–1787, found a similar result. About 30 percent of the accused were fully acquitted and another 12 percent acquitted of some, but not all, the charges: King, "Decision-Makers," 45n29. In Peter Linebaugh's study of criminal court cases in London in January 1715, twenty-five of fifty-seven indicted felons were acquitted; six of the thirty-two convicted were sentenced to hang. The jurors clearly at times assigned arbitrarily low values to goods stolen in order to reduce the degree of punishment. Peter Linebaugh, *The London Hanged: Crime and Civil Society in the Eighteenth Century,* 2nd ed. (London, 2003), 74–82. Linebaugh places a negative valuation on King's point about jurors: "Jurors were not, as we understand the term, 'peers' of the defendants. They were landowners—small landowners, to be sure, but landowners nonetheless" (78).

25. McAninch, "Criminal Procedure," esp. 179–180; *Statutes at Large,* 7:397.

26. *Statutes at Large,* 7:398–399, 402. In a 1751 statute, the colonial assembly passed revisions to the Negro Act of 1740, one of them raising the standard of evidence required

for a capital conviction for planning to steal or entice away slaves. Provisions for insurrection, however, were not changed. *Statutes at Large,* 7: 420–425.

27. William Simpson, *The Practical Justice of the Peace and Parish-Officer, of His Majesty's Province of South Carolina* (Charles Town, 1761), 189, 400–401. The act specified two justices and three to five freeholders, but usually only three nonjustices participated. For noncapital crimes the court included only one justice and two freeholders.

28. Both quoted in Coquillette, "Legal Education of a Patriot," 33–34. On copying law reports, see Mark Antony De Wolfe Howe, ed., "Journal of Josiah Quincy, Jr., 1773," *Proceedings of the Massachusetts Historical Society* 49 (1915–1916): 450–451. See also Richard D. Brown, "Quincy, Josiah Jr.," *Oxford Dictionary of American Biography Online.*

29. Emily Vanessa Blanck, "Revolutionizing Slavery: The Legal Culture of Slavery in Revolutionary Massachusetts and South Carolina" (Ph.D. diss., Emory University, 2003), 163 (quotation), 195–242 (Adams on 230).

30. Howe, ed., "Josiah Quincy, Jr.," 446, emphases in the original. "Mr. Pinckney" might have been either Charles Cotesworth Pinckney or Thomas Pinckney, both lawyers.

31. Simpson, *Practical Justice of the Peace,* 189. One exception is analyzed in Robert Olwell, *Masters, Slaves, and Subjects: The Culture of Power in the South Carolina Low Country, 1740–1790* (Ithaca, N.Y., 1998), 59–60, 83–88. Governor Campbell wrote later that for Jeremiah's trial there were five freeholders—allowed under the law but rarely used—but Henry Laurens, who was in a better position to know, wrote of three freeholders. WC to Dartmouth, 31 Aug. 31, 1777, *DAR,* 11:95; HL enclosure with HL to John Laurens, Aug. 20, 1775, *PHL,* 10:334. For an analysis of trials for a later period, in jurisdictions where records survived, see Michael Hindus, "Black Justice under White Law: Criminal Prosecution of Blacks in Antebellum South Carolina," *Journal of American History* 63 (1976): 576–599.

32. On Cannon, see chap. 2, above.

33. Third witness: HL to John Laurens, Aug. 20, 1775, *PHL,* 10:321; willing to pilot men-of-war: Drayton, *Memoirs,* 2:24n (quotation) and WC to Dartmouth, Aug. 31, 1775, *DAR,* 10:95; set fire: Drayton, *Memoirs,* 2:24n.

34. HL to John Laurens, Aug. 20, 1775, *PHL,* 10:321. For examples of free blacks buying the freedom of family members, see Robert Olwell, "Becoming Free: Manumission and the Genesis of a Free Black Community in South Carolina, 1740–90," *Slavery and Abolition* 1 (1996): 1–18.

35. Unanimity: HL note enclosed with HL to John Laurens, Aug. 20, 1775, *PHL,* 10:334.

36. *Statutes at Large,* 7:403 ("in their discretion," "executed for example"), 400 ("deter others").

CHAPTER 7
"Justice is Satisfied!"

1. "Memorial" and "Evidence" of George Walker, American Loyalist Claims, 46:53–56, 58–59; Drayton, *Memoirs,* 2:17 ("damning us all"); Peter Timothy [secretary, Council

of Safety] to William Henry Drayton, Aug. 13, 1775, *NDAR*, 1:1135; WC to Lord Dartmouth, Aug. 19, 1775, *NDAR*, 1:1185; Robert M. Weir, "'Liberty, Property, and No Stamps': South Carolina and the Stamp Act Crisis" (Ph.D. diss., Western Reserve University, 1967), 74–75 (bribing jockey).

2. George Millegen-Johnston, *A Short Description of the Province of South-Carolina, with an Account of the Air, Weather, and Diseases, at Charles-Town, Written in the Year 1763* (London, 1770); Millegen-Johnston, "Additions" to a pamphlet originally published in 1761 by James Glen, *A Description of South Carolina*, first published in 1761, and re-published in 1775 with "Additions" by Millegen-Johnston; both are reprinted in facsimile in Chapman J. Milling, ed., *Colonial South Carolina: Two Contemporary Descriptions* (Columbia, S.C., 1951), quotations on 107–108, 126. While in South Carolina, Millegen-Johnston used only "Millegen" as a last name.

3. "Loved and respected": WC to Dartmouth, Aug. 19, 1775, *NDAR*, 1:1185; Gentry description and Library advertisement, both in Millegen-Johnston, *Short Description*, 134–135, 148–149 (including handwritten marginal note that it was "written by the author of this pamphlet"); "Demon of Rebellion," Millegen-Johnston, "Additions," 109. At the end of the French and Indian War in 1764, Millegen retired from the British army on half pay, but he kept a commission as surgeon for any British forces who happened to be in the colony. Henry Laurens noted that it had rained every day for weeks in July and August: HL to John Laurens, Aug. 20, 1775, *PHL*, 10:326; the journal of the sloop *Commerce*, anchored at Port Royal just south of Charles Town, recorded repeated days of "Squally weather, with a great deal of rain": Journal of South Carolina sloop *Commerce*, Aug. 15, 16, 17, *NDAR*, 1:1156, 1162, 1169 (quotation on 1156).

4. George Millegen, "Narrative by George Millegen of his Experiences in South Carolina," *DAR*, 11:112–113; "Memorial" of George Walker; Timothy to Drayton, Aug. 13, 1775, *NDAR*, 1:1135 ("did not tremble"). According to Timothy, Walker was "discharged at Milligan's door": Timothy to Drayton, *NDAR*, 1:1135. Millegen does not mention this, and Walker's own testimony that he was held under pumped water, then tossed in the harbor, seems more credible, especially since pouring water on the victim was sometimes the practice of tar-and-feather crowds.

5. Manumission of Thomas Gullan, July 12, 1775, in Secretary of State Miscellaneous Records, book RR, 325–326, SCDAH; Arthur Middleton to Drayton, Aug. 22, 1775, *NDAR*, 1:1207–1208. Other members of the subcommittee were Charles Pinckney, Powell, Thomas Bee, and Thomas Heyward: Drayton, *Memoirs*, 1:221.

6. Drayton, *Memoirs*, 2:19–20.

7. Commons House of Assembly to WC, *PHL*, 10:306–307; Drayton, *Memoirs*, 2:21, 22. The official reply was shortened and sharpened in some respects as compared with Laurens's draft, but except for omission of the words "nor within the line of our Duty," the words quoted here from Laurens's draft are almost identical in the official reply, as printed in Drayton, *Memoirs*, 2:20–22. It was delivered to Campbell on August 18. The word "punishment," included in the official reply, was omitted in the draft. The reply was the last item ever entered in the Journal of the Commons House of Assembly.

8. HL to John Laurens, Aug. 20, 1775, *PHL*, 10:327 ("froth & folly").

9. *SCG*, Sept. 7, 1775 ("Sango"); HL to John Laurens, Aug. 20, 1775, *PHL*, 10:320, 330–331; WC to Dartmouth, Aug. 30, 1775, *DAR*, 11:96.

10. Frederick Dalcho, *An Historical Account of the Protestant Episcopal Church in South Carolina, from the First Settlement of the Province, to the War of the Revolution* (Charleston, 1820), 201–205 (quotations on 202–203). Bullman's sermon was preached on August 14, 1774; the congregation voted to dismiss him four days later. He left Charles Town the following March.

11. Dalcho, *Historical Account*, 219; C. P. Seabrook Wilkinson, "A Declaration of Dependence: Robert Smith's 1775 Humiliation Sermon," *SCHM* 100 (1999): 223; Eliza Pinckney to My dear Harriott, Feb. 17, 20, 1775, Charles C. Pinckney Papers, Library of Congress; Drayton, *Memoirs*, 2:11.

12. *SCG*, Aug. 1, 1769; WC to Dartmouth, Aug. 31, 1775, *DAR*, 11:96. On the strong pressure for confession, see Robert Olwell, *Masters, Slaves, and Subjects: The Culture of Power in the South Carolina Low Country, 1740–1790* (Ithaca, N.Y., 1998), 88–89.

13. WC to Dartmouth, Aug. 31, 1775, *DAR*, 11:96.

14. Campbell's account of these events is in WC to Dartmouth, Aug. 31, 1775, *DAR*, 11:95–96. Enclosures with this letter, referred to below, were not included in this printed collection, but they are included in the copies of the correspondence in the BPRO Transcripts, 35:207–214. The day of the meeting is provided in correspondence between Alexander Innes, Campbell's secretary, and Henry Laurens, and reprinted in *PHL*, 10:328–335: HL to Innes, Aug. 18, 1775, and Innes's reply the same day, *PHL*, 10:331–332.

15. WC to Dartmouth, Aug. 31, 1775, *DAR*, 11:96; HL to Innes, Aug. 18, 1775, *PHL*, 10:331 (quoting Coram and "greatly affected").

16. WC to Dartmouth, Aug. 31, 1775, *DAR*, 11:96. The opinions are in BPRO Transcripts, 35:207–214. Fewtrell later did provide an opinion in writing, agreeing with Coslett on the legality of the trial (214). In addition to Simpson, some of the justices may also have been visited by the tar-and-feather crowd. Sources cite "10 or 12" stops by the crowd but mention only seven individuals. Drayton, *Memoirs*, 2:17.

17. WC to Dartmouth, Aug. 31, 1775, *DAR*, 11:96; WC [to John Coram], HL note, *PHL*, 10:334.

18. WC to HL, Aug. 17, 1775, *PHL*, 10:328; HL to WC, Aug. 17, 1775, *PHL*, 10:329.

19. HL to John Laurens, Aug. 20, 1775, *PHL*, 10:321 ("good manners"); HL to WC, Aug. 17, 1775, *PHL*, 10:329.

20. HL to WC, Aug. 17, 1775 (sent at 10:30 p.m.), *PHL*, 10:329; HL to John Laurens, July 14, 1775, *PHL*, 10:220. In Laurens's papers is a cryptic comment on the copy of this letter: "I know the history but as it was communicated to me in confidence I dare not inflame the people by divulging it to them—but thought it necessary to let the Governor know—that I had some feeling for the Majesty of the People—as well as for the Representative of Majesty." I am not certain what "the history" refers to. *PHL*, 10:330.

21. The exchange is in *PHL*, 10:330–333. Jemmy's pardon, dated August 17, is recorded in Secretary of State Miscellaneous Records, book RR, 239, SCDAH.

22. *PHL*, 10:332.

23. WC to Dartmouth, Aug. 31, 1775, *DAR*, 11:96–97. Jemmy's pardon includes the time at which he and Jeremiah had been sentenced to hang (see n. 21, above).

24. HL to Innes, Aug. 18, 1775, *PHL*, 10:333–334.

25. HL to John Laurens, Aug. 20, 1775, *PHL*, 10:321.

26. Frances Reece Kepner, ed., "A British View of the Siege of Charleston, 1776," *Journal of Southern History* 11 (1945): 95; Millegen, "Narrative of George Millegen," 110–111.

27. For a discussion of how historians have interpreted Thomas Jeremiah's trial and hanging, see the Afterword, below. On Margrett, see chap. 3, above; on George, see chap. 5, above.

28. WC to Dartmouth, Aug. 31, 1775, *DAR*, 11:95.

29. HL to John Laurens, Aug. 20, 1775, *PHL*, 10:321–322.

30. Millegen, "Narrative of George Millegen," 111.

31. Douglas Hay, "Property, Authority and the Criminal Law," in Douglas Hay et al., *Albion's Fatal Tree: Crime and Society in Eighteenth-Century England* (New York, 1975), 32–33.

32. *Statutes at Large,* 7:402; the opinion is in BPRO Transcripts, 35:208–210.

33. BPRO Transcripts, 35:213. Coslett was referring to section 53 of the Negro Act, *Statutes at Large,* 7:415.

34. J. M. Beattie, *Crime and the Courts in England, 1600–1800* (Princeton, N.J., 1986), 377; Blackstone, *Commentaries,* bk. 4:344: "When therefore a prisoner on his arraignment has pleaded not guilty, and for his trial hath put himself upon the country, which country the jury are."

35. Peter King, "Decision-Makers and Decision-Making in the English Criminal Law, 1750–1800," *Historical Journal* 27 (1984): 37; Olwell, *Masters, Slaves, and Subjects,* 67–68.

36. HL to George Appleby, Feb. 28, 1774, *PHL,* 9:317.

EPILOGUE

1. John Laurens to HL, Oct. 4, 1775, *PHL,* 10:450; R. C. Simmons and P. D. G. Thomas, eds., *Proceedings and Debates of the British Parliament Respecting North America, 1754–1768,* 6 vols. (Millwood, N.Y., 1982), 6:365, 369; *Public Advertiser* (London), Dec. 16, 1775; [John Lind and Jeremy Bentham], *An Answer to the Declaration of the American Congress,* 2nd ed. (London, 1776), 99–100. The case also came up in conversations among supporters of the administration in London: Thomas Hutchinson, *Diary and Letters of His Excellency Thomas Hutchinson, Esq.,* ed. Peter Orlando Hutchinson (London, 1883), 1:543. Information in Hutchinson's diary and in Lind and Bentham's pamphlet clearly was taken directly from William Campbell's letter to Lord Dartmouth, Aug. 31, 1775, *DAR,* 11:93–98.

2. David Ramsay, *The History of the Revolution of South-Carolina, from the British Province to an Independent State* (Trenton, N.J., 1785); William Moultrie, *Memoirs of the American Revolution: So Far as It Relates to the States of North and South Carolina, and Georgia* (New York, 1802); John Drayton, *Memoirs of the American Revolution as Relating to the State of South Carolina,* 2 vols. (Charleston, 1821; reprint, New York, 1969), 2:24; Joseph Johnson, *Traditions and Reminiscences Chiefly of the American Revolution in the*

South (Charleston, 1851), 226. Johnson places "Jerry's" execution in 1779, allegedly for piloting a British force to an encampment on the Stono River south of Charleston. The Jeremiah case was covered in John Donald Duncan, "Servitude and Slavery in Colonial South Carolina, 1670–1776" (Ph.D. diss., Emory University, 1971), 837–843, but the historian mainly responsible for bringing attention to the case is Peter H. Wood, especially in "'Taking Care of Business' in Revolutionary South Carolina: Republicanism and the Slave Society," in *The Southern Experience in the American Revolution*, ed. Jeffrey J. Crow and Larry E. Tise (Chapel Hill, N.C., 1978), 268–293. See also the Afterword, below.

3. Drayton, *Memoirs*, 2:163–164; Council of Safety to Captain Edward Thornborough [master of the *Tamar*], Dec. 18, 1775, *NDAR*, 3:164. One historian has cited a "family legend" according to which Miles Brewton warned Campbell that he was about to be seized by the patriots, but Brewton had left Charles Town with his family weeks earlier, so the importance of such a specific warning seems doubtful. See Kinlock Bull, Jr., *The Oligarchs in Colonial and Revolutionary Charleston: Lieutenant Governor William Bull II and His Family* (Columba, S.C., 1991), 241; *SC and AGG*, Aug. 25, 1775.

4. Memorial of Lord William Campbell, July 2, 1778, Treasury T1/542, NAUK.

5. Memorial of Lord William Campbell; Drayton, *Memoirs*, 2:159–161. Claim of Scipio Handley, American Loyalist Claims, 47:117–118; "Memorial" and "Evidence" of Scipio Handley, American Loyalist Claims, 47:117–120. Handley later participated in the capture of Savannah, where he was wounded. For reports on the seizure of a canoe "clandestinely attempting" to reach the *Cherokee* with slaves, provisions, and letters, see Minutes of the South Carolina Council of Safety, Dec. 16, 1775, *NDAR*, 3:133.

6. Josiah Smith, Jr., to James Poyas, 10 Jan. 10, 1776, *NDAR*, 3:724–725; HL to Committee at Beaufort, Jan. 19, 1776, *NDAR*, 3:896; Graham Hodges, ed., *The Black Loyalist Directory: Africans in Exile* (New York, 1996), 33; Drayton, *Memoirs*, 2:293–305; Commodore Sir Peter Parker to Philip Stephens, July 9, 1776, *NDAR*, 5:997–1002 (quotation about Campbell on 1001); John Charnock, *Biographia Navalis; or, Impartial Memoirs of the Lives and Characters of Officers of the Navy of Great Britain, from the Year 1660 to the Present Time*, vol. 6 (London, 1798), 53–54 ("Parker, Peter"), 506–507 ("Campbell, Lord William"); Walter J. Fraser, Jr., *Charleston! Charleston! The History of a Southern City* (Columbia, S.C., 1989), 149–150; Master's Log, *Cherokee*, Feb. 19, 1777, *NDAR*, 7:1236.

7. Langdon Cheves, Esq., "Izard of South Carolina," *SCH and GM* 2 (July 1901): 235n3, quoting "Mrs. Daniel Blake's letter, 5 Jan. 1779" ("lingering consumption"); *General Evening Post* (London), Sept. 8, 1778; *Public Advertiser* (London), Sept. 10, 1778 (St. Anne's). "Mrs. Daniel Blake's" letter, to "Mrs. Horry," must have been written by Elizabeth Izard Blake, cousin of Sarah Izard Campbell, to Harriott Pinckney Horry, but the letter is not otherwise identified, nor is it available in any archive, as far as I know. Sarah Izard Campbell's life after 1778 can be traced through the letters of Horace Walpole, who was a friend of the Conways. See, e.g., Walpole to Henry Seymour Conway, Oct. 5, 1777, in Horace Walpole, *Correspondence*, ed. J. S. Lewis, 48 vols. (New Haven, 1937–1983), 39:295; Walpole to Lady Ossory, Sept. 16, 1778, Walpole, *Correspondence*, 33:50–51; Walpole to George Selwyn, July 20, 1779, Walpole, *Correspondence*, 30:270; Walpole to Sir Horace Mann, Sept. 7, 1781, Walpole, *Correspondence*, 25:184; Walpole to Mann, Oct. 30,

1785, Walpole, *Correspondence,* 25:613. Campbell's son William, after serving in the Royal Navy, did return to South Carolina, where he lived on one of the Izard plantations: Maurie D. McInnis, in collaboration with Angela Mack, *In Pursuit of Refinement: Charlestonians Abroad, 1740–1860* (Columbia, S.C., 1999), 108. He died without heirs.

8. HL to John Laurens, Feb. 22, 1776, *PHL,* 11:114, 115; Thomas Paine, *Common Sense* (Philadelphia, 1776), 47.

9. HL to John Laurens, Aug. 14, 1776, *PHL,* 11:228. Miles Brewton, though a member of the Council of Safety and reelected to the Second Provincial Congress in early August 1775, left the province later that month on the brig *Polly,* with his wife and children. He was headed to Philadelphia, and from there, or so Henry Laurens believed, to England. He never made it; the *Polly* foundered in a storm off Cape May, with all on board lost: *SC and AGG,* Aug. 25, 1775; HL to James Laurens, Oct. 20, 1775, *PHL,* 11:478.

10. For Laurens's period in the Congress, see Daniel J. McDonough, *Christopher Gadsden and Henry Laurens: The Parallel Lives of Two American Patriots* (Cranbury, N.J., 2000), 202–236.

11. McDonough, *Gadsden and Laurens,* 249–260. The language of his petitions, in which he rehearsed his history of moderation and proclaimed his support of the king's government until very late in the conflict, came in for considerable criticism in the Continental Congress when they were made public.

12. HL to James Bourdieu, May 6, 1785, *PHL,* 16:558; HL to Baron Von Steuben, Jan. 5, 1786, *PHL,* 16:625; Will of Henry Laurens, appendix, *PHL,* 16:801.

13. HL to John Laurens, Aug. 14, 1776, *PHL,* 11:228. The Declaration arrived on August 2; the procession and reading took place on August 5.

14. HL to John Laurens, Aug. 14, 1776, *PHL,* 11:224–225.

15. Gregory D. Massey, *John Laurens and the American Revolution* (Columbia, S.C., 2000), 62–63; John Laurens to HL, Oct. 26, 1776, *PHL,* 11:276–277. See also Gregory D. Massey, "The Limits of Antislavery Thought in the Revolutionary Lower South: John Laurens and Henry Laurens," *Journal of Southern History* 63 (1997): 495–530.

16. John Laurens to HL, Jan. 14, 1778, *PHL,* 11:305. The essential source for John Laurens's plans and his efforts to put them into effect is Massey, *John Laurens.*

17. HL to Bourdieu, May 6, 1785, *PHL,* 16:559; HL to William Drayton, Feb. 23, 1783, *PHL,* 16:155–156.

18. HL to Alexander Hamilton, Apr. 19, 1785, *PHL,* 16:554. In the same letter Laurens claimed that "some of my Negroes to whom I have offered freedom have declined the Bounty." There is no way to corroborate this claim. On Frederic, see, in addition to the letter to Hamilton cited here, HL to Jacob Read, July 16, Sept. 15, 1785, *PHL,* 16:579–580 and 580n2, 596–597. On freeing George at his death, see HL to David Ramsay, July 7, 1790, *PHL,* 16:762. The 1790 Census credited him with 298 slaves: *PHL,* 16:545n.

19. Massey, *John Laurens,* 130–137, 141–144, 207–209; Christopher Gadsden to Samuel Adams, July 6, 1779, in Richard Walsh, *The Writings of Christopher Gadsden, 1746–1805* (Columbia, S.C., 1966), 166.

20. These numbers do not include a larger number—about seven thousand—who left as slaves with their loyalist owners. Nor does it include runaways who did not join the

British, some of whom died, some of whom escaped to freedom, and some of whom were reenslaved. See Cassandra Pybus, "Jefferson's Faulty Math: The Question of Slave Defections in the American Revolution," *William and Mary Quarterly*, 3rd ser., 62 (2005): esp. 30, 35. Pybus's estimates are lower than found in many other sources but are based on the most thorough examination of the documentation to date. For the story of what happened to those freed by the war and evacuated, see Cassandra Pybus, *Epic Journeys of Freedom: Runaway Slaves of the American Revolution and Their Global Quest for Liberty* (Boston, 2006); and Simon Schama, *Rough Crossings: Britain, the Slaves, and the American Revolution* (New York, 2006). For the fuller story of the southern colonies and slavery during the era of the Revolution, see Sylvia R. Frey, *Water from the Rock: Black Resistance in a Revolutionary Age* (Princeton, N.J., 1992). For Laurens runaways, see Samuel Massey to HL, June 12, 1780, *PHL*, 16:304–307.

21. McDonough, *Gadsden and Laurens*, 263; L. H. Butterfield, ed., *The Diary and Autobiography of John Adams*, Vol. 3: *Diary, 1782–1804; Autobiography Part One to October 1776* (Boston, 1961), 82–33 (Nov. 30, 1782). The text of the treaty, included the clerk's note about the insertion of the phrase on page 8, is available online at the Yale Avalon Project, http://avalon.law.yale.edu/18th—century/prel1782.asp.

AFTERWORD

1. John Donald Duncan, "Servitude and Slavery in Colonial South Carolina, 1670–1776" (Ph.D. diss., Emory University, 1971), 837–843; Peter H. Wood, " 'Taking Care of Business' in Revolutionary South Carolina: Republicanism and the Slave Society," first published in *South Atlantic Urban Studies* 1 (1978), but more widely available in *The Southern Experience in the American Revolution*, ed. Jeffrey J. Crow and Larry E. Tise (Chapel Hill, N.C., 1978), 268–293. As Wood noted, he drew on the excellent thesis of a Harvard undergraduate, David Zornow, "A Troublesome Community: Blacks in Revolutionary Charles Town, 1765–1775" (Harvard University, 1976). See also a later essay by Wood, " 'Liberty Is Sweet': African American Freedom Struggles in the Years before White Independence," in *Beyond the American Revolution: Explorations in the History of American Radicalism*, ed. Alfred F. Young (DeKalb, Ill., 1993), 149–184.

2. Robert M. Weir, *Colonial South Carolina: A History* (Millwood, N.Y., 1983), 200–202; Walter J. Fraser, Jr., *Charleston! Charleston! The History of a Southern City* (Columbia, S.C., 1989), 144–147; Philip D. Morgan, "Black Life in Eighteenth Century Charleston," *Perspectives in American History* 1 (1984): 213; Morgan, "Conspiracy Scares," *William and Mary Quarterly*, 3rd ser., 59 (2002): 159–166; Morgan, "Jeremiah, Thomas," in *Oxford Dictionary of American Biography Online;* Robert Olwell, *Masters, Slaves, and Subjects: The Culture of Power in the South Carolina Low Country, 1740–1790* (Ithaca, N.Y., 1998), 234–238; Olwell, " 'Domestick Enemies': Slavery and Political Independence in South Carolina, May 1775–March 1776," *Journal of Southern History* 55 (1989): 21–48; William R. Ryan, "The Worlds of Thomas Jeremiah: Charles Town on the Eve of the American Revolution" (Ph.D. diss., Duke University, 2006), 8–11, 71–97; Ryan, " 'Under the Color of Law': The Ordeal of Thomas Jeremiah, a Free Black Man, and the Struggle

for Power in Revolutionary South Carolina," in *George Washington's South*, ed. Tamara Harvey and Greg O'Brien (Gainesville, Fla., 2004), 223–256; Emily Vanessa Blanck, "Revolutionizing Slavery: The Legal Culture of Slavery in Revolutionary Massachusetts and South Carolina" (Ph.D. diss., Emory University, 2003), 105–110; Gabrielle Gottlieb, "Theater of Death: Capital Punishment in Early America, 1750–1800" (Ph.D. diss., University of Pittsburgh, 2005), 31, 171–176.

3. Sylvia R. Frey, *Water from the Rock: Black Resistance in a Revolutionary Age* (Princeton, N.J., 1992), 55–58; Gary B. Nash, *The Unknown American Revolution: The Unruly Birth of Democracy and the Struggle to Create America* (New York, 2005), 161; Ray Raphael, *A People's History of the American Revolution: How Common People Shaped the Fight for Independence* (New York, 2001), 252–253; Marcus Rediker and Peter Linebaugh, *The Many-Headed Hydra: Sailors, Slaves, Commoners, and the Hidden History of the Revolutionary Atlantic* (Boston, 2000), 226.

4. Cassandra Pybus, *Epic Journeys of Freedom: Runaway Slaves of the American Revolution and Their Global Quest for Liberty* (Boston, 2006), 3; Simon Schama, *Rough Crossings: Britain, the Slaves, and the American Revolution* (New York, 2006), 59–65.

5. Frey, Nash, and Rediker and Linebaugh do not mention Jeremiah's ownership of slaves. Those who do, including Raphael and historians focusing on South Carolina, have been much more skeptical about whether Jeremiah in fact had anything to do with overt resistance by slaves.

6. Schama does not mention Campbell's ownership of a slave plantation.

A Note on Sources

This study has been based on the available primary sources. With few exceptions, these same sources have been used by other scholars of Charleston's history in the era of the American Revolution, and, in particular, by those who have written about Thomas Jeremiah. (See the Afterword for a discussion of Jeremiah.)

Primary Sources

Many of the most important primary sources related to Thomas Jeremiah have appeared in print. The papers of Henry Laurens provide the essential sources for Laurens's life and thought and include several crucial documents about Jeremiah. The most important of these documents appear in an outstanding collection, *The Papers of Henry Laurens,* ed. David R. Chesnutt and others, 16 vols. (Columbia, S.C., 1985–2003). There are extensive collections of papers left by several of the great families of early South Carolina, especially at the South Carolina Historical Society and the South Caroliniana Library at the University of South Carolina, but aside from the Laurens papers, these contain relatively little material from the years before the Revolution. The Papers of Ralph Izard and the Papers of Charles Pinckney, both at the Library of Congress, have a few items of interest. The Letterbook of Josiah Smith, Jr., at the Southern Historical Collection, University of North Carolina, Chapel Hill, includes observations of, and commentary on, events in 1775. The extant papers of Christopher Gadsden are collected in Richard Walsh, ed., *The Writings of Christopher Gadsden, 1746–1805* (Columbia, S.C., 1966). The fascinating early letters of an influential gentry woman are printed in Elise Pinckney, ed. *The Letterbook of Eliza Lucas Pinckney, 1739–1762*

(Chapel Hill, N.C., 1972; reprint, Columbia, S.C., 1997). A letterbook of Pinckney's daughter, Harriott, is in the collections of the South Carolina Historical Society. Useful letters of the Manigault family have been reprinted in the *South Carolina Historical Magazine,* whose early volumes (under the title *South Carolina Historical and Genealogical Magazine*) include many genealogies of major figures.

The correspondence between the royal governors, especially Lord William Campbell, and their superiors in London have been a major source for this study. Most of the originals are in the Records of the Colonial Office, in the National Archives of the United Kingdom, in Kew, which incorporates what was formerly known as the British Public Record Office. Those relating to South Carolina were transcribed and deposited in the South Carolina Department of Archives and History (SCDAH), where they are now available on microfilm. A calendar of these records and complete transcripts of many important ones appear in K. G. Davies, ed. *Documents of the American Revolution, 1770–1783 (Colonial Office Series)* (Shannon, Ireland, 1972–). Other important documents are included in William Bell Clark, William James Morgan, and Michael J. Crawford, eds., *Naval Documents of the American Revolution* (Washington, D.C., 1968–), a series far more expansive than its title might suggest. In most cases, I have examined both the printed and the original documents; citations in the notes are to the most widely available source: to *Documents of the American Revolution;* if not there, to *Naval Documents of the American Revolution;* if not there, to the Transcripts of Records in the British Public Record Office, SCDAH; if not there, to the National Archives of the United Kingdom (NAUK). Also at the NAUK are the records of the Admiralty, including ship logs, lieutenants' passing certificates, and other material related to the naval career of William Campbell. Many loyalists told their stories to British authorities in an effort to recover property lost or confiscated during the Revolution. I consulted the microfilm edition of these records, published as *American Loyalist Claims; Series I and Series II* (London, 1972). The Papers of the Duke of Argyll, unfortunately, are not open to researchers, nor is the calendar of those papers at the National Archives of Scotland, in Edinburgh. A few items of Lord William's brother, John, are in the National Library of Scotland in Edinburgh.

Many of South Carolina's early government records, such as census and tax records for the colonial period, have not survived. The journals of the Commons House of Assembly and His Majesty's Council are exceptions; they are in the SCDAH, which has published several volumes of the Commons House journals. The journals of the Provincial Congress, published by Peter Timothy in 1775 and 1776, have been reprinted in William Edwin Hemphill, ed., *Extracts from the Journals of the Provincial Congresses of South Carolina, 1775–1776* (Columbia, S.C., 1960). The journal of the Council of Safety was published in South Carolina Historical Society *Collections,* vol. 2 (1858). The SCDAH also holds wills, inventories, and other items of interest, such as the manumissions recorded in the Secretary of State Miscellaneous Records Books.

Newspapers, especially the *South-Carolina Gazette,* but also the *South-Carolina Gazette: And Country Journal* and the *South-Carolina and American General Gazette,* are a valuable source of opinion, local news, and advertisements. Modern editions of pamphlets include Robert M. Weir, ed., *The Letters of Freeman, etc.: Essays on the Nonimportation Movement in South Carolina* (Columbia, S.C., 1977); and Henry Laurens's publications on the Admiralty Courts, reprinted in the *Papers of Henry Laurens.* Originals of these and other pamphlets are available from Eighteenth Century Collections Online, which I accessed through Dimond Library at the University of New Hampshire.

Many contemporary documents, including some whose originals are no longer available, were reprinted in early accounts of the Revolution in South Carolina, especially in John Drayton, *Memoirs of the American Revolution as Relating to the State of South Carolina,* 2 vols. (Charleston, 1821; reprint, New York, 1969); and R. W. Gibbes, *Documentary History of the American Revolution: Consisting of Letters and Papers Relating to the Contest for Liberty, Chiefly in South Carolina, from Originals in Possession of the Editor, and Other Sources* (New York, 1855; reprint, New York, 1971). Useful early histories of South Carolina include David Ramsay, *The History of the Revolution of South-Carolina, from the British Province to an Independent State* (Trenton, N.J., 1785); David Ramsay, *Ramsay's History of South Carolina from Its First Settlement in 1670 to the Year 1808,* 2 vols. (Charleston, 1809; reprinted from an 1858 edition, Spartanburg, S.C., 1959); and Alexander Hewatt, *An Historical Account of the Rise and Progress of the Colonies of South Carolina and Georgia,* 2 vols. (London, 1779; reprint, Spartanburg, S.C., 1962). Ramsay's history is heavily derivative of Hewatt's, but Ramsay, who married Henry Laurens's daughter Martha, includes additional material on the Revolution and on Laurens in particular.

Some of the most informative primary sources on the colony, including travel accounts, are collected in H. Roy Merrens, ed., *The Colonial South*

Carolina Scene: Contemporary Views, 1697–1774 (Columbia, S.C., 1977). Two others are in Chapman J. Milling, ed., *Colonial South Carolina: Two Contemporary Descriptions* (Columbia, S.C., 1951), which includes the published works of George Millegen. An exceptionally interesting traveler's account for the years just before the Revolution is Mark Antony De Wolfe Howe, ed., "Journal of Josiah Quincy, Jr., 1773," *Proceedings of the Massachusetts Historical Society* 49 (1915–1916): 424–481.

South Carolina's colonial laws were collected in Thomas Cooper and David J. McCord, eds., *The Statutes at Large of South Carolina*, 10 vols. (Columbia, S.C., 1836–1841), though some statutes are missing from this compilation. The laws relating to slaves were included, with occasional commentary, in William Simpson, *The Practical Justice of the Peace and Parish Officers of His Majesty's Province of South Carolina* (Charles Town, 1761). Other published primary sources with valuable insights are Richard J. Hooker, ed., *A Colonial Plantation Cookbook: The Receipt Book of Harriott Pinckney Horry, 1770* (Columbia, S.C., 1984); Alice Hanson Jones, *American Colonial Wealth: Documents and Methods*, 3 vols. (New York, 1977), which includes transcripts of every surviving probate inventory from Charles Town County in 1774; and Mark M. Smith, ed., *Stono: Documenting and Interpreting a Southern Slave Revolt* (Columbia, S.C., 2005). Joseph F. W. Des Barres, *The Atlantic Neptune* (1777, but with many reprints), includes Charles Town among its harbor maps, along with information for pilots. William Falconer, *An Universal Dictionary of the Marine* (London, 1769), and *The English Pilot; The Fourth Book; Describing the West India Navigation, from Hudson's-Bay to the River Amazones* (London, 1773), provide context for understanding the work of harbor pilots.

David Eltis et al., eds., *The Trans-Atlantic Slave Trade: A Database on CD-ROM* (Cambridge, 1999), provides a comprehensive database on the slave trade, including all the shipments to Charles Town known as of the date of its publication.

Secondary Sources
RACE, SLAVERY, AND THE AMERICAN FOUNDING

Three modern classics provide essential background to questions about race and slavery in the colonial and revolutionary United States: Winthrop D. Jordan, *White Over Black: American Attitudes toward the Negro, 1550–1812* (Chapel Hill, N.C., 1968); David Brion Davis, *The Problem of Slavery in the*

Age of Emancipation (Ithaca, N.Y., 1975); and Edmund S. Morgan, *American Slavery, American Freedom: The Ordeal of Colonial Virginia* (New York, 1975). Bernard Bailyn, *The Ideological Origins of the American Revolution* (Cambridge, Mass., 1967), is the starting point for exploring the motivating ideologies of Americans in the Revolution. Recent studies of the connection between slavery and freedom in the era of the Revolution, and in the lives and work of the leading American patriots, have usually focused on Virginia and Virginians. These include Woody Holton, *Forced Founders: Indians, Debtors, Slaves, and the Making of the Revolution in Virginia* (Chapel Hill, N.C., 1999); Rhys Isaac, *Landon Carter's Uneasy Kingdom: Revolution and Rebellion on a Virginia Plantation* (New York, 2004); Henry Wiencek, *An Imperfect God: George Washington, His Slaves, and the Creation of America* (New York, 2003); Annette Gordon-Reed, *The Hemingses of Monticello: An American Family* (New York, 2008); and several of the essays in Peter S. Onuf, ed., *Jeffersonian Legacies* (Charlottesville, Va., 1993). David Waldstreicher, *Runaway America: Benjamin Franklin, Slavery, and the American Revolution* (New York, 2004), extends the question to a figure seldom included in such examinations. For South Carolina, an eloquent exploration of the issues is Edward Ball, *Slaves in the Family* (New York, 1998), in which Ball approaches the questions through an account of his own family's history.

Two important examinations of the impact of the American Revolution on slaves, and vice versa, are Sylvia R. Frey, *Water from the Rock: Black Resistance in a Revolutionary Age* (Princeton, N.J., 1992); and Sylvia R. Frey and Betty Wood, *Come Shouting to Zion: African American Protestantism in the American South and the British Caribbean to 1830* (Chapel Hill, N.C., 1998). Two recent studies focus on the slaves who were liberated by British forces during the Revolution: Cassandra Pybus, *Epic Journeys of Freedom: Runaway Slaves of the American Revolution and Their Global Quest for Liberty* (Boston, 2006); and Simon Schama, *Rough Crossings: Britain, the Slaves, and the American Revolution* (New York, 2006). Gary B. Nash, *The Unknown American Revolution: The Unruly Birth of Democracy and the Struggle to Create America* (New York, 2005), synthesizes recent scholarship on slaves and slavery in the Revolution. Douglas R. Egerton, *Death or Liberty: African Americans and Revolutionary America* (New York, 2009), appeared too late to inform this study.

Two studies help to place African Americans within the Atlantic maritime world: W. Jeffrey Bolster, *Black Jacks: African American Seamen in the Age of Sail* (Cambridge, Mass., 1997); and David S. Cecelski, *The Waterman's*

Song: Slavery and Freedom in Maritime North Carolina (Chapel Hill, N.C., 2001). A good survey of the Transatlantic slave trade is James A. Rawley, *The Transatlantic Slave Trade: A History* (Lincoln, Nebr., 2005). Marcus Rediker, *The Slave Ship: A Human History* (New York, 2007), gives a human face to the experience of the middle passage. Not related to the slave trade, but offering an analysis of Britain's navy that helps to place William Campbell's career in context, is N. A. M. Rodger, *The Wooden World: An Anatomy of the Georgian Navy* (London, 1986; reprint, New York, 1996).

SOUTH CAROLINA: POLITICS AND POLITICAL CULTURE

Walter Edgar, *South Carolina: A History* (Columbia, S.C., 1998), is the standard survey of the subject. For the colonial period, Robert M. Weir, *Colonial South Carolina: A History* (Millwood, N.Y., 1983) is essential, though for some purposes, the highly detailed older accounts by Edward McGrady remain useful: *The History of South Carolina under the Royal Government, 1719–1776* (New York, 1899), and *The History of South Carolina in the Revolution, 1775–1780* (New York, 1902). The political history of the colony's first century is covered in M. Eugene Sirmans, *Colonial South Carolina: A Political History, 1663–1763* (Chapel Hill, N.C., 1966). Studies of South Carolina politics that focus on political culture and the coming of the Revolution include work by Jack P. Greene, especially *Quest for Power: The Lower Houses of Assembly in the Southern Royal Colonies, 1689–1776* (Chapel Hill, N.C., 1963), and several of the essays collected in his *Negotiated Authorities: Essays in Colonial Political and Constitutional History* (Charlottesville, Va., 1994). Robert M. Weir has also written important studies of this subject, including "'Liberty, Property, and No Stamps': South Carolina and the Stamp Act Crisis" (Ph.D. diss., Western Reserve University, 1967), and several of the essays collected in his book *"The Last of the American Freemen": Studies in the Political Culture of the Colonial and Revolutionary South* (Macon, Ga., 1986). Robert Olwell, *Masters, Slaves, and Subjects: The Culture of Power in the South Carolina Low Country, 1740–1790* (Ithaca, N.Y., 1998), analyzes the relation between slavery and South Carolina's political culture in the Revolutionary era. A recent account of political disputes in the colony is Jonathan Mercantini, *Who Shall Rule at Home? The Evolution of South Carolina Political Culture, 1748–1776* (Columbia, S.C., 2007).

Studies of people and topics relevant to the understanding of South Carolina in the Revolution include E. Stanly Godbold and Robert H. Woody,

Christopher Gadsden and the American Revolution (Knoxville, Tenn., 1982); Keith Krawczynski, *William Henry Drayton: South Carolina Revolutionary Patriot* (Baton Rouge, La., 2001); Kinloch Bull, Jr., *The Oligarchs in Colonial and Revolutionary Charleston: Lieutenant Governor William Bull II and His Family* (Columbia, S.C., 1991); Pauline Maier, "The Charleston Mob and the Evolution of Popular Politics in Revolutionary South Carolina, 1765–1784," *Perspectives in American History* 4 (1970): 173–196; and Richard Walsh, *Charleston's Sons of Liberty: A Study of the Artisans, 1763–1789* (Columbia, S.C., 1959). A study of the place of black South Carolinians in the events leading to Revolution is William Randolph Ryan, "The Worlds of Thomas Jeremiah: Charles Town on the Eve of the American Revolution" (Ph.D. diss., Duke University, 2006). It includes a chapter on Jeremiah's case that has appeared as William R. Ryan, "'Under the Color of Law': The Ordeal of Thomas Jeremiah, a Free Black Man, and the Struggle for Power in Revolutionary South Carolina," in *George Washington's South*, ed. Tamara Harvey and Greg O'Brien (Gainesville, Fla., 2004), 223–256. Jim Piecuch, *Three Peoples, One King: Loyalists, Indians, and Slaves in the Revolutionary South* (Columbia, S.C., 2008), appeared too late to influence this study.

SOUTH CAROLINA: SOCIAL AND ECONOMIC HISTORY

For slavery, the essential works on South Carolina are Philip D. Morgan, *Slave Counterpoint: Black Culture in the Eighteenth-Century Chesapeake and Lowcountry* (Chapel Hill, N.C., 1998), and, for the early decades, Peter H. Wood, *Black Majority: Negroes in Colonial South Carolina from 1670 through the Stono Rebellion* (New York, 1974). Useful specialized and comparative studies include Betty Wood, *Slavery in Colonial Georgia, 1730–1775* (Athens, Ga., 1984); Daniel C. Littlefield, *Rice and Slaves: Ethnicity and the Slave Trade in Colonial South Carolina* (Baton Rouge, La., 1981); Judith Ann Carney, *Black Rice: The African Origins of Rice Cultivation in the Americas* (Cambridge, Mass., 2001); and Sally E. Hadden, *Slave Patrols: Law and Violence in Virginia and the Carolinas* (Cambridge, Mass., 2001). Connections between slavery and the law in South Carolina are illuminated by Michael Stephen Hindus, *Prison and Plantation: Crime, Justice, and Authority in Massachusetts and South Carolina, 1767–1878* (Chapel Hill, N.C., 1980); Emily Vanessa Blanck, "Revolutionizing Slavery: The Legal Culture of Slavery in Revolutionary Massachusetts and South Carolina" (Ph.D. diss., Emory University, 2003); and Gabrielle Gottlieb, "Theater of Death: Capital Punishment in Early

America, 1750–1800" (Ph.D. diss., University of Pittsburgh, 2005). A. Leon Higginbotham, Jr., *In the Matter of Color: Race and the American Legal Process,* Vol. 1: *The Colonial Period* (New York, 1978), is a comprehensive summary.

Especially important for understanding the economic foundations of the colony are Peter A. Coclanis, *The Shadow of a Dream: Economic Life and Death in the South Carolina Low Country* (New York, 1989); S. Max Edelson, *Plantation Enterprise in Colonial South Carolina* (Cambridge, Mass., 2006); and Joyce E. Chaplin, *An Anxious Pursuit: Agricultural Innovation and Modernity in the Lower South, 1730–1815* (Chapel Hill, N.C., 1993). Many of the essays in Jack P. Greene, Rosemary Brana-Shute, and Randy J. Sparks, eds., *Money, Trade, and Power: The Evolution of Colonial South Carolina's Plantation Society* (Columbia, S.C., 2001), are also valuable for this subject.

Important analyses of the ruling gentry are Richard Waterhouse, *A New World Gentry: The Making of a Merchant and Planter Class in South Carolina, 1670–1770,* 2nd ed. (Charleston, 2005); Alan Gallay, *The Formation of a Planter Elite: Jonathan Bryan and the Southern Colonial Frontier* (Athens, Ga., 1989); and Jeffrey Robert Young, *Domesticating Slavery: The Master Class in Georgia and South Carolina, 1670–1837* (Chapel Hill, N.C., 1999). On gentry families, and the place of women in them, see Cara Anzilotti, *In the Affairs of the World: Women, Patriarchy, and Power in Colonial South Carolina* (Westport, Conn., 2002); and Lorri Glover, *All Our Relations: Blood Ties and Emotional Bonds among the Early South Carolina Gentry* (Baltimore, 2000). Rachel Klein, *Unification of a Slave State: The Rise of the Planter Class in the South Carolina Backcountry, 1760–1808* (Chapel Hill, N.C., 1990), is the best analysis of the backcountry settlers in this period.

SOUTH CAROLINA: CHARLES TOWN

Walter J. Fraser, Jr., *Charleston! Charleston! The History of a Southern City* (Columbia, S.C., 1989) is an excellent comprehensive history. (Before 1783, the city's name was Charles Town, sometimes also spelled Charles-Town or Charlestown.) George C. Rogers, Jr., *Charleston in the Age of the Pinckneys* (Norman, Okla., 1969), offers valuable insights into the culture of the city and its rulers in this period. Philip D. Morgan, "Black Life in Eighteenth Century Charleston," *Perspectives in American History* 1 (1984): 187–232, is essential for slavery in Charles Town. The early chapters of Cynthia M. Kennedy, *Braided Relations, Entwined Lives: The Women of Charleston's Urban Slave Society* (Bloomington, Ind., 2006), offers insights into the lives of both free and enslaved women in the city. Benjamin L. Carp, *Rebels Rising: Cities and the American Revolution* (New York, 2007), includes a chapter on the urban landscape of Charles Town in these years. Stanley Kenneth Deaton, "Revolutionary Charleston, 1765–1800" (Ph.D. diss., University of Florida, 1997), focuses on the class divisions exposed in the city during the Revolution.

Among the many studies of the material culture of Charleston in the eighteenth century, the most valuable for this study have been Jonathan H. Poston, *The Buildings of Charleston: A Guide to the City's Architecture* (Columbia, S.C., 1997); Maurie D. McInnis, in collaboration with Angela D. Mack, *In Pursuit of Refinement: Charlestonians Abroad, 1740–1860* (Columbia, S.C., 1999); Bernard Herman, "Slave and Servant Housing in Charleston, 1770–1820," *Historical Archaeology* 33, no. 3 (1999): 88–101; and the work of Martha Zierden, archaeologist at the Museum of Charleston, and her colleagues. Among their many studies are Zierden, with contributions by Elizabeth Reitz and Karl J. Reinhard, "Archeology at the Miles Brewton House, 27 King Street, Charleston, SC" (Charleston, 2001). Maurie D. McInnis, *The Politics of Taste in Antebellum Charleston* (Chapel Hill, N.C., 2005), though focusing on a later period, includes much of interest for anyone interested in the material culture of the revolutionary era. A comprehensive account of Charleston's maritime history is P. C. Coker III, *Charleston's Maritime Heritage, 1670–1987: An Illustrated History* (Charleston, 1987); also helpful is Rusty Fleetwood, *Tidecraft: The Boats of Lower South Carolina and Georgia* (Savannah, Ga., 1982).

HENRY LAURENS

The only full biography of Henry Laurens is David Duncan Wallace, *The Life of Henry Laurens, with a Sketch of the Life of Lieutenant-Colonel John Laurens* (New York, 1915). It is still valuable, but the author's views on race, typical for a white southerner of his time, distort his interpretations, and a new biography of this important figure is needed. A number of studies help to fill the gap until one appears, including Daniel J. McDonough, *Christopher Gadsden and Henry Laurens: The Parallel Lives of Two American Patriots* (Sellingsgrove, Pa., 2000); Joanna Bowen Gillespie, *The Life and Times of Martha Laurens Ramsay, 1759–1811* (Columbia, S.C., 2001); Gregory D. Massey, *John Laurens and the American Revolution* (Columbia, S.C., 2000). Valuable analyses of particular aspects of Laurens's life and work are in the work of S. Max Edelson, noted above, and in Gregory D. Massey, "The Limits of Antislavery Thought in the Revolutionary Lower South: John Laurens and Henry Laurens," *Journal of Southern History* 63 (1997): 495–530; Philip D. Morgan, "Three Planters and Their Slaves: Perspectives on Slavery in Virginia, South Carolina, and Jamaica, 1750–1790," in *Race and Family in the Colonial South,* ed. Winthrop Jordan and Sheila Skemp (Jackson, Miss, 1987), 54–68; and Robert Olwell, "'A Reckoning of Accounts': Patriarchy, Market Relations, and Control on Henry Laurens's Lowcountry Plantations, 1762–1785," in *Working toward Freedom: Slave Society and Domestic Economy in the American South,* ed. Larry E. Hudson, Jr. (Rochester, N.Y., 1994), 33–52.

Acknowledgments

Works of scholarship have the names of individuals on the title page, but they are always collective projects. It is a pleasure to acknowledge the many people who have contributed to this one.

My first thanks must go to the historians of Charleston, and of South Carolina, upon whose work I have built. Many of their specific studies are discussed in the Note on Sources, and others, mentioned below, were more helpful than I had a right to expect. Like all historians, I have been dependent on the labors of archivists and librarians who collect the basic sources and make them known and accessible. These include the staffs of the Dimond Library at the University of New Hampshire (especially the interlibrary loan staff); Widener Library, Houghton Library, and the Map Collection at Harvard University; the Library of Congress; the Museum of Early Southern Decorative Arts; the Southern Historical Collection at the University of North Carolina; the South Carolina Department of Archives and History; the South Caroliniana Library at the University of South Carolina; the South Carolina Historical Society; the Special Collections division of the library at the University of Charleston; the National Archives of the United Kingdom; the Cheshunt Institute at Westminster College, in Cambridge, England; the Greenwich Maritime Museum; the National Library of Scotland; and the National Archives of Scotland. Special thanks go to those who provided service beyond the ordinary: Margaret Thompson at the Cheshunt Institute; Martha Rowe at the Museum of Early Southern Decorative Arts; Duncan Graham at the South Caroliniana Library; Mike Coker at the South Carolina Historical Society; and Tessa Spencer at the National Archives of Scotland. In a different category is Bob O'Hara of searcher-na.co.uk, who dug up valuable records on Lord William Campbell's naval career. Andrea Mack of the Gibbes Museum in Charleston and Philip Mould in London helped me track down the descendants of William and Sarah Campbell, and particular thanks go to the Campbell-Johnston family for their encouragement, and for permission to reproduce portraits of their ancestors. Thanks to Sarah Beighton at the Greenwich Maritime Museum, Jennifer Bean Bower and Gary Albert at the Museum of Early Southern Decorative Arts, Joyce Baker at the Gibbes Museum, and Lizanne Garrett at the National Portrait Gallery for assistance with illustrations; thanks to Bill Nelson (once again) for expertly preparing the maps.

Travel and other research expenses were covered, in part, with funds from the Carpenter Professorship, the Signal Fund of the History Department, and the College of Liberal Arts at the University of New Hampshire. The college also provided a sabbatical semester, and the university a Faculty Scholars' Award, which in combination provided a full year's release from teaching while I completed a draft of the book. Travel was made more enjoyable by the hospitality of Ellen and Mark Richardson, Don Doyle and Marjorie Wheeler, and Larry Klein.

Colleagues and students at UNH have helped me in many ways. Ross Cleveland, an undergraduate, provided research assistance on the slave trade. The Lindberg Award gave me the opportunity to try out some of my ideas, at an early stage, in the form of a lecture. The History Faculty Seminar, where I presented a draft of one chapter, produced the sort of lively and constructive exchange that I have learned to expect from it, and Cathy Frierson, Janet Polasky, Jeffry Diefendorf, Alison Mann, and Mary Fuhrer followed up that seminar with more detailed comments and suggestions. Lucy Salyer read two chapters and shared her expertise on several of the legal issues raised by the Jeremiah case.

Beyond UNH, I presented an early draft of one chapter at a meeting of Southern Historians in New England, and the discussion that followed was both encouraging and helpful. An exchange with Philip D. Morgan early on in the project helped me more than he probably thought. Martha A. Zierden and Maurie D. McInnis, who know the material culture of early Charleston as well as anyone, both gave me valuable comments on a draft of chapter 1.

Several people read and commented on drafts of the entire manuscript. Charles Lesser, David Moltke-Hansen, and Vernon Burton offered important suggestions and pointed out—politely—numerous errors related to the history of Charleston and South Carolina. I have been fortunate to share a department with two superb historians of the revolutionary era, Jeffrey Bolster and Eliga Gould. Both read the manuscript with great care and provided guidance on small details as well as large matters of interpretation. Terry

Rockefeller once again brought her filmmaker's eye and sharp pencil to a reading of my work. An anonymous reader for Yale University Press made several helpful suggestions. Collectively, these readers saved me from countless sins of commission and omission, suggested new sources, and smoothed ragged prose. I followed the advice of every one of them, in part, but since I also rejected advice from all of them, the errors that remain must be attributed to me alone.

My agent, Geri Thoma, contacted me out of the blue, listened over breakfast while I outlined an idea for book, and encouraged and spurred me as the idea grew into an actual manuscript. I have appreciated her reader's sensibility as much as her keen business sense. For the fourth time, I have worked on a big project with Jeannette Hopkins. As before, her questions often made me wince, her cocktails eased the sting, and her red pen made this a much better book. At Yale, Chris Rogers's enthusiasm for the project was immensely helpful, as was his editorial advice at a crucial moment. Laura Davulis eased my way through the production process, and Laura Jones Dooley's meticulous copyediting improved almost every page.

This book is dedicated to the memory of my wife's sister, Laura Rockefeller. Laura was an actress and singer, living in New York City, and like many actors and singers living in New York City, she took short-term jobs to help pay the rent and keep food on the table. It was one of those short-term jobs— assisting in the organization of a conference for financial professionals—that placed her at the top of the North Tower of the World Trade Center on September 11, 2001. She was one of the nearly three thousand who was murdered by religious fanatics that day. It was a crushing loss to her parents, her sister, to our children, Hannah and Logan, whom she adored, and to me.

I don't know what Laura would have thought of this book, though I am pretty sure that if she didn't like it, she would have pretended otherwise. I am certain, however, that she would have been horrified had she known about some of the political uses to which her death, and the deaths of so many others, were later put, and appalled at the way those deaths became an excuse for gross miscarriages of justice. Benjamin Franklin wrote, in 1759, "They that can give up essential liberty to obtain a little temporary safety deserve neither liberty nor safety." This judgment, true as it was and is, elides the harsher truth that, too often, Americans have tried to protect their own sense of safety by sacrificing, not their own liberties, but the liberties of others deemed unworthy of freedom's bounties. If this book serves as a reminder that the roots of that tendency go back to the moment of America's founding, I will be well satisfied. I'm sorry that Laura is not still here to read it.

Index